JEFFERSON'S
MONTICELLO

WITH PRINCIPAL PHOTOGRAPHY BY LANGDON CLAY

JEFFERSON'S MONTICELLO

By William Howard Adams   Abbeville Press · New York

Dedicated to the Trustees and Staff

of the Thomas Jefferson Memorial Foundation

Editor: Walton Rawls

Designer: Janet Odgis

Library of Congress Cataloging in Publication Data

Adams, William Howard.
  Jefferson's Monticello.

  Bibliography: p. 269
  Includes index.
  1. Monticello (Va.) 2. Jefferson, Thomas, 1743–1826
—Homes—Virginia—Albemarle County. I. Title.
E332.74.A3 1983 973.4'6'0924 83-6330
ISBN 0-89659-950-7

First paperback edition

15 14 13 12 11 10 9

I am as happy nowhere else, and in no other society, and all my wishes end, where I hope my days will, at Monticello. Too many scenes of happiness mingle themselves with all the recollections of my native woods and fields to suffer them to be supplanted in my affections by any other.

Th: Jefferson

CONTENTS

PREFACE

SINCE IT WAS THE COUNTRY'S fortune to have been defined and shaped by an extraordinarily talented Virginian, it is natural that hundreds of thousands of Americans should make a pilgrimage to his estate each year to experience a brief historic whiff of Thomas Jefferson's remarkable personality. Few are disappointed, even though his illusive historical shadow sometimes makes the pursuit difficult and even frustrating in spite of the enormous preserved record. From the swell of the dome on Monticello's west front to the silver coffee urn in the tea room, the place actually embodies more than a whiff of Jefferson's potent intelligence. The house—its furnishings, its art works and library, the gardens, and even the "lofty prospects" from the mountain he selected for its site—presents an unsurpassed autobiographical legacy.

No man ever lived in more civilized elegance than Jefferson. Taking his clues and inspirations wherever he could find them in history or in contemporary experience, he strove to build a house harmonious with human dignity, the same ideal he followed in formulating the philosophy of the government. The definition for the new nation that Jefferson spelled out in 1776 was rooted in his native region and tradition, from which he also drew his first architectural and building ideas. Yet the seeming gap between those political aspirations enunciated in Philadelphia

and the rarefied environment of Monticello impresses the visitor with how little one really knows about the man and how little one understands of the complex social texture out of which Jefferson and the country grew.

My own pursuit of but one facet of Jefferson's historic personage, centering on his interest in the broad field of the arts and architecture, began in earnest during three years of work on "The Eye of Thomas Jefferson," the exhibition mounted at the National Gallery of Art in celebration of America's Bicentennial. It required a certain temerity to undertake a book-length study of Monticello, but such a book at least had the promise of bridging a gap in the growing library of Jeffersonian studies.

Without the existence of this library, the present work could not have been completed. Of first importance, and well known to every student of Jefferson, are the volumes of his correspondence regularly issued by Princeton University Press and the magisterial six-volume biography by Dumas Malone. For Jefferson's architectural background, we must go to Fiske Kimball's folio edition of the drawings, along with indispensable notes, essays, and a reconstruction of Jefferson's architectural library. Long out of print, this volume was reissued under the editorial supervision of Frederick Doveton Nichols, who has continued to advance the study of Jefferson's work through scholarship, friendly encouragement, and enthusiasm. As both know well, Dumas Malone and Fred Nichols have been inspirations to me.

Although the work on the present volume was a fairly solitary affair, I was keenly aware that I labored in the company of all the scholars who contributed so much to the catalog and the exhibition at the National Gallery in 1976, and my scholarly debts to these former colleagues are foremost in my acknowledgments. Besides those already mentioned, I must thank James A. Bear, Jr., Director of the Thomas Jefferson Memorial Foundation, and the members of his staff who have again made available to me the entire massive files and collections that have been assembled at Monticello. This archive addresses every conceivable subject related to Monticello, including the building, the garden, and the life that Jefferson created there for himself and his family. In the *Guide to Sources* at the back of this book I have provided a select bibliography for each chapter.

Without the cooperation of the Massachusetts Historical Society and the Alderman Library of the University of Virginia, keepers of the greater trove of Jefferson's drawings and documents, the present work could not have been begun. Many other institutions and individuals have generously made available photographs for inclusion, for which I am deeply grateful, and these were assembled with consummate skill and good humor by Christopher Sweet. For the new photography identified elsewhere, it was my great fortune to be introduced to the work of Langdon Clay, who undertook the assignment with all of the commitment and integrity of a true artist.

With the warm support of my family, the first draft was completed in the luxurious isolation of the apartment of my dear friend Saville Ryan, whose periodic travels abroad had inspired the loan of the apartment, a gift par excellence for a writer. Her generosity was equaled only by the hospitality of Betty and Mario di Valmarana, whose house near Monticello was always open to me during the many trips I made to Charlottesville over the past two years. Edgar Shannon, Jr., scholar and fellow trustee at Monticello, took time out of a busy schedule to give me the benefit of his thoughtful reading of the manuscript.

My gratitude to my publisher Robert Abrams and my friends Mark Magowan and Walton Rawls at Abbeville Press is not just the perfunctory nod authors sometimes make on these occasions. I shall be forever grateful for their support, constructive criticism, and unfailing willingness to carry out their part of the enterprise.

W.H.A.

HAZELFIELD

JUNE 4, 1983

JEFFERSON'S
MONTICELLO

THE
ARCHITECT

1   Thomas Jefferson's drawing equipment. In the beginning, young Jefferson studied architecture and design through illustrated books, and his own plans and drawings depended upon them for their chief inspiration.

Let me begin with Monticello's creator, since it is impossible to separate the life of the house from that of its architect and builder Thomas Jefferson. Certainly, the artist Jefferson cannot be separated or divorced from his major work, even as the visionary statesman cannot be isolated from the nation he helped to create.

As the work of a romantic, even radical idealist, Jefferson's architecture, particularly in his most personal creation, Monticello, can best be understood within the framework of those social and political ambitions that shaped Jefferson's hopes and dreams for the new nation. Often doctrinaire in private as well as public concerns, in Monticello Jefferson manages to embody, nevertheless, both his worldly ideology and those native pragmatic qualities that were combined in his complex personality. In its design, history, symbolism, and metaphor, Monticello is the quintessential example of the autobiographical house.

Rational, austere, experimental, Jefferson's architecture as it evolved during the last quarter of the eighteenth century and the first decades of the nineteenth was in many ways as radical as his political reforms. His predilection for Virginia's traditional red brick in contrast with white wood and plaster details continues to hide the visionary achievement beneath a conventional "colonial" mask. Neither the first Monticello or its surviving successor can be termed "colonial" in comparative, stylistic terms when one looks at any other American house of the period. The first Monticello, begun in 1769, is of course "colonial" in a chronological sense, but its anti-Georgian bias, its subtle affront to vernacular Virginia house plans and proportions, places it outside the popular label that persists in journalistic descriptions.

2 **Thomas Jefferson** *by John Trumbull, Paris, 1788. This painting was given to Maria Cosway by Jefferson to commemorate the friendship that had developed in Paris through Trumbull's introduction. It was later presented to the White House in 1976 to commemorate the Bicentennial.*

Even the expanded and remodeled second version, which had to give up some of the "noble simplicity" of the first house, remains a coherent, sensitive, personal expression of the designer's totally original genius, a monument to the humanistic idealism that Jefferson affirmed in every detail.

In 1760, the year the tall, gangly young squire from the western frontier in Albemarle County entered the College of William and Mary, the run of the mill domestic architecture of colonial Virginia, including its capitol at Williamsburg, could not have been less inspiring compared to British standards. As a profession, architecture in the American colonies was virtually a monopoly of carpenter craftsmen,

3 Monticello from the west. "*. . . they reached the foot of the isolated mountain, on the top of which was the dwelling of the sage of Monticello. But like the temple of Fame, in which he had secured himself a place, his mansion was of most difficult access. . . .*"

masons, and related building tradesmen. The builders who put up and decorated the great James River houses of the early part of the eighteenth century had brought with them to the new world the traditional construction skills and some understanding of English and European vernacular architecture, but little else. While it was once assumed that at least the more enlightened Virginia planters, armed with architectural treatises, designed their own mansions, recent research points in a more practical, less sophisticated direction. In the first place, stylish architectural design books were by no means common, either in Virginia Libraries or in the other colonies. However, there were notable exceptions, for example William Byrd's Library at Westover. Byrd was as fashion-conscious in his building as he was in his general style of living, learned firsthand in London. But few buildings actually were modeled on book sources. "Virginia," Fiske Kimball has observed, "especially was then wanting in men or buildings that might have imparted a formal knowledge of architecture as understood in Europe.

Few great houses with architectural pretensions had been built in Virginia before 1700. In fact those first tentative, preliminary plans Jefferson drew for Monticello, are the earliest working drawings for a Virginia house to have survived. This is not to suggest that working drawings and specifications for important colonial buildings in Virginia had not been made and used. Surviving records show that the assembly in Williamsburg specifically requested the royal Governor to provide a drawing of the Governor's Palace. Other plans of public buildings may also have been reviewed on occasion by government officials.

The study of architecture as a profession in the modern sense did not exist in the colonies when the ambitious heir of Peter Jefferson decided in 1760 that it was time he went to college. In the often-quoted letter to his guardian John Harvie requesting permission to enter the College of William and Mary, the seventeen-year-old student revealed an uncommon capacity for application as well as a maturity that undoubtedly made it possible during these formative years to begin to teach himself the rudiments of architecture from the most meager of resources. After complaining to Harvie of losing at least one fourth of his time at home to "so much company"—a condition he would surround himself with for the rest of his life—he said that he wanted to continue his classical studies, "learn something of mathemat-

4 Peyton Randolph House, Williamsburg, probably built before 1725. Such simple vernacular frame houses of colonial Virginia were dismissed by Jefferson as unsophisticated in design. He thought their chief virtue was their susceptibility to fire.

ics," and at the same time gain "a more universal acquaintance," which might be available in the provincial capital. The classics and mathematics were, of course, subjects that not only would advance Jefferson's studies ultimately in the law but would also stimulate the beginnings of his life-long search for a common, accessible architectural language.

Building craftsmen working in the vernacular traditions of the colonies had not yet been grounded in academic training. There was no accepted course of professional studies or even a system of higher apprenticeship such as existed in the law and other fields. For smart builders in the colonies who wished to put up either a private house or a public building, which in most cases was a church, they might be inclined to follow Francis Price's dictum in his *Builder's Dictionary*. "First, let no person, who intends to build a structure that shall be either useful or ornamental, begin it without the advice or assistance of a Surveyor or Master Workman, who understands the Theory of Building and is capable of drawing a Draught or Model according to the Rules of Art. In a Draught (which may serve indifferently well in small buildings) there ought to be an Ichonography of each

Floor, and also the Orthography of each face of the Building, viz, the Front, the Flanks and the Rear." It was probably such a Master Workman that Jefferson had in mind when he wrote on June 1, 1771, to Thomas Adams, a business correspondent in the Tidewater, saying, "I desired the favor of you to procure an architect. I must repeat the request earnestly, that you will send him as soon as you can."

5 Westover, Charles City County, built 1726–30. Jefferson knew this great house, built by William Byrd II, when he was a student at William and Mary. No doubt he was impressed with Byrd's cultivation and especially his library, which contained a number of books on architecture.

The first phase of the construction at Monticello had just gotten underway when he wrote to Adams, and the busy young lawyer/farmer needed the professional assistance of someone with at least the skills called for in Price's *Dictionary*.

Peter Harrison's claim to being America's first professional architect is founded on the number of documented buildings with which he is identified. Their formal, correct style, which surpassed the work of other colonial builders of his day, and his practical engineering skills in shipbuilding and fortification helps to support the professional label. But beyond that, he displayed some knowledge and appreciation of the higher art of architecture that was expected of a gentleman in the eighteenth century, especially since he was well read and had traveled abroad. The fact that Harrison was not paid for his work nor personally involved in the actual construction separates him from the role of the professional architect as we now understand the function.

It is in this tradition and background of the gentleman amateur that one must view Jefferson's own development and practical education, a private career centered primarily on the work that he carried out at Monticello. Over the decades—"They was forty years at work upon that house before Mr. Jefferson stopped building," his servant Issac Jefferson was to remark in his memoirs—Monticello was changed and reshaped not only for pragmatic reasons of family needs, but also to experiment with new architectural ideas and inspirations, since it was to serve as a laboratory where Jefferson could pursue his insatiable passion for building.

In eighteenth-century Virginia, recorded references to actual commissions for building designs are very few. Thomas Waterman discovered a reference in the records of Christ Church, Middlesex, where in July, 1707, it was noted that "the rafters . . . for the body of the church to be according to the architect." William Buckland, an immigrant who came to Virginia as an indentured servant in 1755 to work on Gunston Hall, was classified as a joiner when he arrived. It was not until later, after he had worked for some time in Maryland that he was actually recognized as a builder/architect.

With the building of the Governor's Palace in 1706 in Williamsburg, where Jefferson was to live as governor, the great era of Virginian colonial architecture begins. Tuckahoe, where Jefferson was to live as a child, probably was begun around 1712, Nomini Hall and Westover probably in 1730, Carter Hall between 1751 and 1753, and Stratford about 1725, to name only a few of the more famous plantation houses that followed the building of the Palace. Shirley is dated to 1769, Gunston Hall between 1755 and 1758, and Mount Airy and Mannsfield around 1760, which places these well known and surviving houses close to or within the decade of the 1760s when Jefferson began his studies in Williamsburg and started to dream of the house he would one day build on his own plantation.

These few celebrated names give some indication of the scale of building in Virginia that marked the era and the wealth that made it possible. No other English colony was to produce on the grand scale as many Georgian manor houses during the first half of the eighteenth century. The young Jefferson was, of course, well acquainted with most of the families who were involved in this extended architectural activity, which was centered in the Virginian Tide-

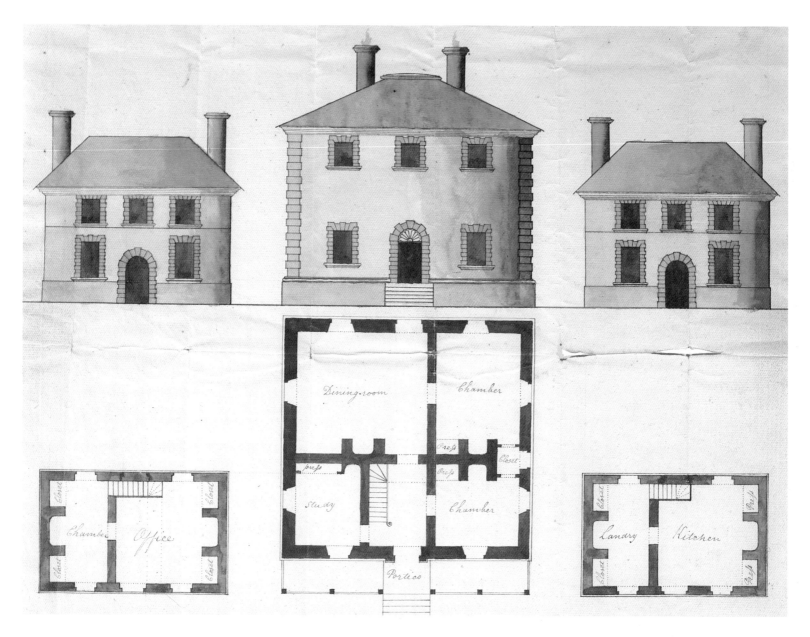

water and stretched along the banks of the James, the Potomac, and York rivers, where the landed and tobacco-rich planters were anxious to set themselves up in a style appropriate to their aristocratic (but

6 Menokin, a Virginia plantation house, 1769, elevation and plan. Small and rather provincial, Menokin was stuccoed and painted white in an attempt to interpret a grander English Palladian model, a style Jefferson rejected at the beginning of his architectural career.

7 John Page of Rosewell *by John Wollaston, 1768*. *Jefferson's boyhood friend John Page grew up at Rosewell, Gloucester County, one of the greatest private houses built in the American colonies before the Revolution.*

was very much a part of the family tradition and social world where he grew up.

Shadwell, the house Peter Jefferson built and in which Jefferson was born on April 13, 1743, was not in the Tidewater class or scale, based on what can be drawn from scattered references and imperfect archeology. In fact, no main house seems ever to have been built at Shadwell. Rather it was a collection of plantation buildings resembling a small settlement. Fronting on the Rivanna River and eventually extending some two hundred feet, it included a smoke house, dairy building, and other scattered out-buildings, as well as the rather simple frame building where the family lived and where Jefferson was born.

Jefferson has nothing to say about the architecture of Shadwell itself, and when it burned in 1770, shortly after he had begun the first building at Monticello, his chief complaint was over the loss of his papers and valuable books, which he related in a surviving letter to his close friend John Page of Rosewell. His silence regarding Shadwell can only be viewed as confirming its insignificant architectural qualities, apparently beneath the attention of someone with more ambitious taste and aspirations. On February 22, 1770, the *Virginian Gazette* merely reported that "the house of Thomas Jefferson, Esq. . . . was burnt to the ground, together with all of his furniture, books, papers, etc by which that Gentleman sustains a very great loss."

Among the manor houses of a better sort that Jefferson knew intimately as a child and young man was Tuckahoe, a Randolph house near Richmond, where his father Peter removed his family in 1745 to fulfill his promise to his late friend William Randolph

mostly newly established) positions. Through his mother Jane Randolph, Jefferson actually was related to many of these families, so that the idea of building a large house with an extensive domestic establishment of smaller service buildings grouped around it that he would act as guardian and manager of the plantation for the benefit of Randolph's children. A large, plain, "H" shaped house of frame and Flemish bond brick construction, it has few of the obvious

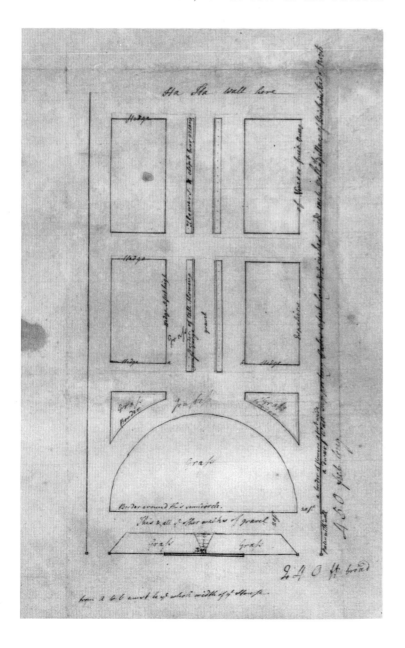

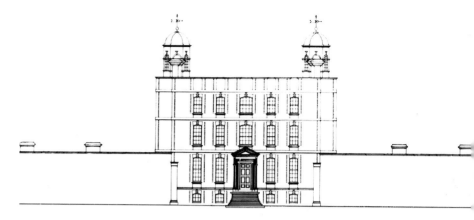

architectural qualities of a Carter's Grove or Rosewell, where William Randolph's wife was born. In its evolution, or by the design of its builder, Tuckahoe seems to conform to the recommendations that appeared in Blome's *The Gentleman's Recreation* published in London in 1709, where "the Capital Roman H" form was commended for architectural translation because the shape "makes it stand against the winds, and lets in both light and air and disposes every room nearer to one another." When one considers Jefferson's long preoccupation with light, air, and efficient interconnecting relationships between rooms at Monticello (and the effective solutions he achieved), the place of Tuckahoe in Jefferson's earliest architectural experience cannot be dismissed, although as with Shadwell Jefferson never spoke of it with admiration.

It was at Rosewell, however, the fabled seat of the Page family of Gloucester County built in 1726 by Thomas Page I, that Jefferson would have experi-

10 Ruins of Rosewell. *The thirty-room manor house was the center of an immense estate on the York River. Its central block was three stories above a high basement sixty feet square. After years of abuse, Rosewell was destroyed by fire in 1916.*

enced a great domestic establishment with architectural distinction and on a scale with the best contemporary English manor houses of the period.

With its thirty rooms it was in fact one of the greatest private houses built in the American colonies before the Revolution. Overlooking the York River, it was an impressive, even princely establishment by colonial standards, and its name still echoes with the sound of a lost grandeur long after its destruction in this century.

Because of his close friendship with John Page, Jefferson was a frequent visitor to Rosewell, where many "philosophical evenings" took place that he would recall later. On the great lead rooftop young Page and Jefferson would spend evenings absorbed in their favorite pursuit of astronomy. When Jefferson's own house at Shadwell burned, he wrote Page that he "cherished some treasonable thoughts of leaving these my native hills. Indeed I should be much happier were I near Rosewell. . . . However the gods I fancy were apprehensive that if we were placed together we should pull down the moon or play some such devilish pranks with their works."

Rosewell finally was reduced to ruins by fire in 1916 after a long history of abuse, but late-nineteenth-century photographs and surviving brick walls give some idea of its monumental appearance. The central block was three stories above a high basement measuring sixty by sixty feet. The facades on each side were five bays long. The windows on the first floor were of great height, and the pediments were finished with Portland stone imported from England. Two substantial dependencies were twenty-four by sixty feet each, and were balanced on either side of the central building. Connecting passageways between the main house and the dependencies were never built. For sheer craftsmanship in brick and woodwork nothing finer had been seen in all of North

11 Stratford, Westmoreland County, c. 1725. *The plan for Stratford may have been taken from a book of 1667 by Stephen Primatt. It was fairly common in the colonies for designer/builders to fish for inspiration in architectural design books of the period.*

America. While the designer/builder has not been identified, it is obvious that he was familiar with English architecture and architectural design books of the period. For example, the doorways at Rosewell were similar to the plans that appear in plates 23 and 27 of William Salmon's *Palladio Londonensis*, although it was not published in London until 1734, eight years after Rosewell was started. William Byrd's great house at Westover in Charles County, Virginia, that ranks in style if not in scale with Rosewell, exhibits a riverfront door, 1730–34, which is even closer to a plate in Salmon, confirming the fashionable interest Virginia grandees took in the latest London designs. Westover's doorway is all the more remarkable when one considers that the book appeared in London the very year Westover was completed. Historians have suggested that this was only coincidental, and that Byrd and his builder were merely successful in re-

membering London doorways they had known earlier. As an example of architecture reflecting fashionable tenets of the Burlington and the English Palladians, Rosewell was as good a model as the young Jefferson

12 Great Hall of Stratford. *Begun around 1725 by Thomas Lee, this is considered the most important early paneled room in Virginia. The small stairs, placed in a passage off the hall, are similar in arrangement to those at Monticello, but there is no evidence that Jefferson ever visited Stratford.*

was to encounter outside of the design books of the period before he finally traveled in England in 1786. His later critical rejection of the contemporary English building styles, along with their Virginian counterparts, leaves us with the conclusion that Rosewell had little or no influence on Jefferson's growing interest in architecture. We can assume, however, that the sensitive and curious young student who was already developing a perceptive and informed eye, was not completely indifferent to the scale and the variety of architectural experience Rosewell would have given even the most uninterested visitor.

Rosewell, like a number of the larger Virginian houses of the colonial period, was probably surrounded by landscaped gardens and grounds. Surviving among the Jefferson Papers in the Massachusetts Historical Society is the plan of a formal garden 240 feet wide and extending 450 feet from the facade of a house that is only indicated by a line. The far end of the garden is terminated by a ha-ha. The plan of this garden can be linked to Rosewell by relating the walks to known locations of the central door and the windows. With the axial symmetry of its central walk running from the door or portico of the house and reinforced with parallel hedges, it is a copybook example of the classic eighteenth-century formal garden. It is also a plan that could easily have been lifted from *The Theory and Practice of Gardening* by Dezallier d'Argentville and translated by John Jones in 1728, the first book on gardening that was to enter the young Jefferson's library when he was barely twenty-one. Dezallier d'Argentville's book was one of the most influential garden books of the eighteenth century and was widely circulated in Europe. It reduced to rules and plans—if not to music—the formal theories of garden design that had been brought to their apogee in André LeNotre's great classical French gardens in the seventeenth century. Until the romantic English garden revolution of the latter half of the century displaced the formal garden, d'Argentville's

13 Paneling detail, Marmion, around 1760, now in The Metropolitan Museum of Art. Marmion's marbleized woodwork with classical pilasters represents one of the most sumptuous surviving colonial interiors. Although interested in painted wall decorations, Jefferson did not use them at Monticello.

book and the practitioners who followed it dominated garden design in England and elsewhere, extending even to the river plantations of colonial Virginia. It is difficult to establish a priority for all of Jefferson's many "passions"—mathematics, architecture, the classics—but gardening was certainly high on his list. "No occupation is so delightful to me as the culture of the earth & no culture comparable to that of the garden," he confessed in a letter to Charles Willson Peale in 1811, and it had been an all consuming "occupation" throughout his life, beginning in his school years in Williamsburg and visits to the Page family at Rosewell.

On one of the earliest plans for Monticello, two rectangular flower beds are indicated that parallel the west facade, but as Jefferson continued to "consult the genius of the place," his gardening style quickly shifted away from stiff geometric patterns and toward the romantic picturesque, a style much more adaptable to his mountaintop "airy." The fact that he would have seen an impressive piece of architecture carefully placed in a seriously considered garden setting, as at Rosewell, would have been a significant if unconsciously noted part of his early esthetic education, eventually leading to the remarkable achievement at Monticello where architecture and landscape would be brought together in a harmonious composition.

In addition to Rosewell, Jefferson knew well the grounds of the Palace and the College of William and Mary in Williamsburg, stylishly formal and well ordered where the contemporary English fashion prevailed. An early engraved view of the College shows the courtyard foreground laid out with a fine topiary garden, accenting the severe Georgian build-

14 *Plaster ceiling decoration, Kenmore, Fredericksburg, 1752. The ceilings of Kenmore, built by Fielding Lewis, are superb examples of American plaster work. Jefferson abandoned any ideas of such florid decoration in favor of chaste classical detailing and plain surfaces.*

ings that surround it on three sides.

Mount Airy, the estate of Colonel John Tayloe in Richmond County, Virginia, was, along with Rosewell, another impressive Tidewater house with extensive formal grounds. Young Jefferson undoubtedly knew the "elegant seat" and its garden, for Alice Corbin Tayloe of Mount Airy was the stepmother of his close friend John Page at Rosewell, later a William and Mary classmate. Mount Airy had been built between 1758 and 1762 on a rising piece of ground overlooking the Rappahannock River. The house itself, with its superb setting, must be remembered as one of the finest surviving Palladian houses of the colonial period. Its connections, dependencies, and minor flanking outbuildings on either side of the rectangular main block show a clear relationship to plates in William Adam's *Vitruvius Scoticus* and James

Gibbs' *Book of Architecture*, those two great source books of English Palladian architectural design. John Ariss, a native Virginian who may have studied architecture in England, had advertised in the *Maryland Gazette* of May 22, 1751, that he could design houses "either in the Ancient or Modern Order of Gibbs' Architect." Mount Airy's arched, open loggia of rusticated masonry facing onto the garden side suggests direct inspiration from the work of Andrea Palladio that would have passed for the "ancient order," although Ariss himself is not connected to Mount Airy's design.

The house, built of a striking local brownstone in a spreading symmetrical plan, was approached through a deer park to a forecourt entrance. On the other side of the house, formal, patterned gardens were laid out on either side of the central walk. The assertive main axis of the house is carried through into the landscape and beyond, over the edge of the hill to the valley below. At one side, an orangerie, similar to the one at Mount Vernon, was built to house Colonel Tayloe's extensive collection of delicate plants and trees. Philip Vickers Fithian, who tutored Robert Carter's children at nearby Nomini Hall, was a frequent visitor to Mount Airy and described the estate in his journal in 1774: "Here is an elegant seat!—The House is about the size of Mr. Carters, built with Stone & finished curiously & ornamented with various & rich paintings. . . . He has also a large well formed Garden, as fine as in every respect as I have seen in Virginia. In it stands four large beautiful Marble Statues. From this house there is good prospect of the River Rappahannock."

In any attempt to determine how Jefferson formed an adequate idea of or an "eye" for architecture and

15   *Mount Airy, Richmond County, 1758, elevation of entrance facade.* Built by John Tayloe, Mount Airy is one of the finest Virginia houses of the period. Its design was inspired by several English Palladian sources, including James Gibbs' Book of Architecture.

the arts at an early age, these few familiar examples scattered in and around Williamsburg must be kept in mind, for certainly his own family home at Shadwell was no Mount Airy embellished with painting and sculpture. If his earliest recorded references to painting, sculpture, and architecture seem unsophisticated and amateurish, "the wonder," as Hyatt Mayor observed, "is not that his eye for [the arts] was uncertain but that he was able to develop any eye at all." The general cultural and esthetic poverty of Williamsburg in 1760, when Jefferson entered college, has been commented on by historians as well as by contemporaries. The town itself was a rutty, straggling affair strung out along a main street that was dusty in summer and muddy in winter, and punctuated at intervals with a few impressive Virginia dwellings. "The private dwellings," as Jefferson was to describe them in his *Notes on Virginia*, "are very rarely constructed of stone or brick, much the greatest portion

being of scanttling and boards, plastered with lime. It is impossible to devise things more ugly, uncomfortable, and, happily [is Jefferson recalling his own secret reaction to the burning of Shadwell?] more perishable. . . . The poorest people build huts of logs laid horizontally in pens, stopping the interstices with mud." Of architecture, as of political systems, Jefferson displayed well-developed critical faculties and an intelligence ready to propose reforms for both.

Robert Beverley, in *The History of the Present State of Virginia*, written in 1705, has left us one of the earliest contemporary descriptions of gentlemen's houses

16 Mount Airy, garden facade. *This was probably the first five-part Palladian villa in the colonies. Although Jefferson liked this method of breaking up the mass, its monumental central block with its Georgian formality was something that he tried to avoid.*

of the better sort in Williamsburg. They "built themselves large brick houses, of many rooms on a floor; but they don't covet to make them lofty," he observed, "having extent enough of ground to build upon; and now and then they are visited by winds which would incommode a towering fabric. They love to

15

have large rooms, that they be cool in summer. Of late, they have made their stories much higher than formerly, and their windows larger, and sasht with crystal glass; adorning their apartments with rich furniture. All their drugeries such as cookery, washing, dairies etc are performed in offices apart from the dwelling house, which by this means are kept more cool & sweet." In Beverly's description of the Virginian's love of light, spaciousness, elegant furnishings, and a desire to place at a distance both everyday activities and servants, one sees the elements of the aristocratic yet pragmatic building tradition out of which Jefferson's ideas for Monticello would evolve. It is an arrangement that prevailed in the plantation village of Tuckahoe and on a simple scale at Shadwell where each domestic function was given a special building.

However, that "the genius of architecture seems to have shed its maledictions over this land," his native Virginia, appeared quite evident to Jefferson. The college and hospital according to the same critic, who was also harboring skeptical views of the existing government structure itself, "are rude, misshapen piles which, but that have roofs, would be taken for brick-kilns." Jefferson was ready to "scrap" much of what he saw as outmoded native building traditions—represented by the "misshapen piles" of Williamsburg and even of Rosewell and Mount Airy—in order to pursue the fresh ideas inspired by a new rationality. His kinsman Edmund Randolph later wrote that Jefferson "panted" after the arts, including architecture, and was "not easily satisfied with such scanty means as existed in the colony" since his advanced tastes caused him "to run before the times in which he lived."

Jefferson's school, the College of William and Mary, named for the sovereigns who had chartered it under the auspices of the Church of England, was the second institution of higher learning to be founded on the North American continent, but it had never done very well. As one historian has written, "Its management was poor and its instruction worse," even though it followed, "the grand old fortifying classical curriculum" of Latin, Greek, mathematics, and moral philosophy. The fine arts were manifestly not a part of the college's formal curriculum. However, among the "more universal acquaintance" Jefferson had told his guardian John Harvie he hoped to make in Williamsburg were a few remarkable and cultivated individuals who undoubtedly had a profound effect on the susceptible student, newly arrived from the Piedmont. By the merest chance, an odd company of four "alien spirits," as Jefferson called his new circle of friends, came together in Williamsburg in 1760 and remained in close association over the next two years, meeting for dinner at least once a week in order to make as much as they could of the tedious life they found in the provincial capital. The youngest and most impressionable member of the group—the only real provincial—who would have everything to gain and little to contribute to the worldly experience of the much senior members, was later to record "that at these dinners I have heard more good sense, more rational and philosophical conversations, than in all my life besides."

Probably the most influential new companion from Jefferson's standpoint was Dr. William Small, a Scotsman and young professor of mathematics at William and Mary. As a man whose interests and scholarship extended over a number of disciplines, he must have

had a profound and immediate impact on Jefferson, for at one time or another, in addition to mathematics, Small had taught moral philosophy, rhetoric, and literature. He had also pursued an active interest in applied science. Later, when Small returned to England, he continued his intellectual career as professor in Birmingham and counted among his friends Erasmus Darwin, James Watt—with whom he helped to design the steam engine—Joseph Priestly, and Joshua Wedgwood. Small was immediately attracted to Jefferson, who responded with obvious appreciation and enthusiasm. As a member of the Scottish Enlightenment, that renaissance which was to have such an influence on the thinking of the men and leaders of the American Revolution, Small would have had an enlightened eighteenth-century gentleman's interest in the fine arts and in architectural

17 *College of William and Mary, Williamsburg. William and Mary was the only college in the Virginia colony when Jefferson matriculated. He studied philosophy, mathematics, and the classics, but architecture was not part of the curriculum. Later, as governor, he was instrumental in moving the capital from Williamsburg to Richmond, eschewing colonial architecture as outmoded for the new republic.*

theory and practice. At the age of seventy-seven, Jefferson would write in his autobiography a tribute to Small: "It was my great good fortune and what probably fixed the destinies of my life, that Dr. William Small of Scotland, was the Professor of Mathematics, a man profound in most of the useful branches of science, with a happy talent of communication, correct and gentlemanly manners, and an enlarged and liberal mind. He most happily for me, became soon attached to me and made me his daily compan-

17

18, 19 Governor's Palace, Williamsburg, begun 1706 (reconstructed), perspective drawing, c. 1740, from the Bodleian Library (above) and palace gardens (below). Jefferson lived in the palace as governor and planned to remodel it along classical lines, including a temple portico across the front. The formal gardens also did not appeal to Jefferson, who preferred the new and more irregular compositions just becoming fashionable in England and on the continent.

ion when not engaged in the school; and from his conversation I got my first view of the expansion of science, and the system of things in which we are placed."

It was through Small that the raw-boned, red-haired youth was introduced to the other two members, George Wythe and Francis Fauquier, who "formed a *partie quarrie*, and to the habitual conversations on these occasions I owed much instruction." Wythe, a jurist and teacher in his late thirties, would later become Jefferson's professor of law and lifelong friend. Fauquier, the British royal governor of the Virginia colony, a country gentleman from Hertford, and Fellow of the Royal Society, was nearly sixty. It is reasonable to assume that Wythe and Fauquier, like Small, had an interest both in art and architecture, although music was Fauquier's special passion, which he shared with Jefferson.

Jefferson's own natural interest in mathematics—he described its study as "peculiarly engaging and delightful"—was no doubt sharpened by Small's liberal application of the discipline to practical everyday problems, which may well have included building and construction calculation in the classroom. Fiske Kimball, in his study of Jefferson the architect, noted Jefferson's characteristic manner of working: ". . . he gave a preference to mathematical over graphical methods of deriving his designs. Otherwise stated, the inevitable mathematical processes, instead of coming last, came first. From Jefferson's habit of scientific observation and record it followed that these calculations were not hastily scribbled and thrown away, but were arranged with the precision and intelligibility of geometrical proofs and preserved for subsequent reference."

The most available body of materials for a student interested in architectural studies in the colonial world of Boston, New York, Philadelphia, or Williamsburg was, of course, illustrated books and prints, a source that Jefferson would collect and study throughout his life. It was to him the very backbone of his architectural education. In the early part of the eighteenth century, a revolution in English taste, primarily in architecture, was carried out by Lord

20 Wythe House Garden, Williamsburg. *Jefferson's mentor and teacher George Wythe lived in a town house, built about 1755, whose service buildings were laid out very much like a plantation street, with kitchens, smokehouses, and other domestic functions housed in separate buildings.*

Burlington and his followers, establishing the earlier work of Andrea Palladio and Inigo Jones as a foundation for reform. The victory of English Palladianism, resolutely rejected by Jefferson in his own architecture, was overwhelming, and by the middle of the century it had through illustrated books, prints, and treatises—but especially the superb folio volumes —conquered virtually every aspect of English archi-

*21 **Tuckahoe, the Randolph plantation house, c. 1712.** Jefferson lived at Tuckahoe as a child, and it solidly reflected the established values of the Randolph family, Jefferson's kinsmen on his mother's side. Its H shape plan evolved when a new extension was added after 1730.*

tectural design. Books, not only on architecture but in every field of learning, were virtually the only source for study and information for most educated men and women in the American colonies. Good and enlightened conversation helped to sustain the learned few at dinner tables and coffee houses of Philadelphia, Boston, and Williamsburg in season, but for the most part—and particularly in the isolated plantation houses in the South—it was the carefully assembled bookshelf passing for a library that kept the life of the mind alive and stimulated.

Jefferson discovered the paramount importance of books on every subject at an early stage. He was never to free himself from the addiction of book collecting, even under the most adverse economic circumstances in the latter part of his life. Having sold his major library collection to Congress in 1815 as a means of relieving his pressing indebtedness, he resolutely and recklessly (in view of his precarious financial condition) continued to spend heavily for books. Only a few weeks after the sale, in a letter to John Adams, he declared, "I cannot live without books," and promptly began to build a new library.

Architectural books were important to Jefferson from the beginning, even in his first library at Shadwell, and by the time he died he had in his successive libraries assembled the most important collection of books on architecture in America. Jefferson's library at Shadwell was destroyed by fire in 1770 and no book lists survive, but in 1771, at the request of his friend Robert Skipwith, he drew up a *List of Books for a Private Library* and it is fair to assume that it was based on his own collection. "Criticism of the Fine Arts" as well as "Fine Arts" are two of the captions and categories, but architecture and archeology are not included. This may have been due to Skipwith's request that the books be "suited to a common reader who understands little of the classics and who had

not leisure for any intricate or tedious study." He had also insisted that the cost of the entire library was not to exceed twenty-five pounds sterling.

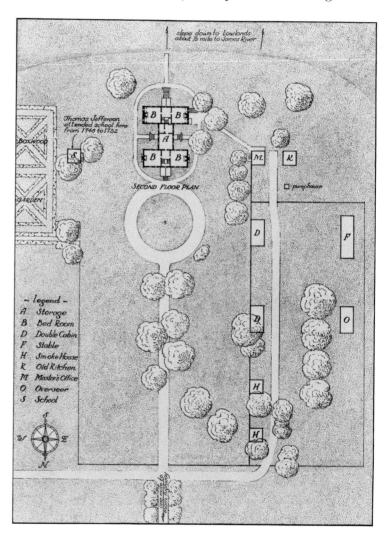

22 Tuckahoe, Goochland County, general layout. *The arrangement of buildings and grounds at Tuckahoe, Jefferson's childhood home, shows a well-organized plantation village centered on the main house, a plan similar to what would evolve at Monticello along Mulberry Row and in the service wings.*

Kimball, in his study of Jefferson's architecture, understood fully the importance of books to the development of Jefferson as an architect and his reliance upon books for the inspiration of his designs. Indeed, Jefferson's architectural specifications habitually recited a compendium of book references, indicating specific plates for orders, proportions, and other design details required by the builder/carpenter.

His earliest notebook entries make reference to his use of James Gibbs' *Rules for Drawing Orders*, a book that he owned before 1769. James Gibbs was an enormously popular architect who designed many great houses in England and Scotland. Campbell's *Vitruvius Britannicus* was also popular in the colonies, where his English Palladian ideas were quickly adapted to colonial conditions. Conservative and simple, his interpretation of Palladio appealed to English colonial taste, although not to young Jefferson. But, as Kimball noted, "since he scarcely accepted the current traditions for a moment," he promptly recalculated the Gibbsian details in Palladio's proportions "on the conviction," in Kimball's words, "that they were better." One of the earliest architectural studies for Monticello, probably dating from 1769, notes that "the pediments should be in height two ninths of their span," a rule of proportion that occurs only in Palladio's *The Four Books of Architecture* and would not have been familiar to the carpenters of the day, who understood and relied on the standard English builder's guides not approved by Jefferson. On almost every count, and for the rest of his life, Palladio would be given the benefit of the doubt, to the point that the sixteenth-century architect's influence on Jefferson almost became a religion. He called *The*

Four Books his "Bible" and urged it on others with the fervor of a missionary, for Jefferson the eighteenth-century Virginian planter was drawn spiritually as

23 Portrait of Andrea Palladio. *This 16th-century Italian architect was a major influence on Jefferson, and Palladio's descriptions of life at his Villa Emo were taken to heart by Jefferson at an early stage of his planning of the service wings of Monticello.*

well as intellectually to Palladio's system. In Palladio's villas, Jefferson found the Vicentine's ideas about domestic architecture thoroughly compatible and adaptable to the self-sufficient agrarian life of the Virginia plantation.

By the 1760s Jefferson was already developing thoroughly radical, anti-British political ideas when "the dull monotony of a colonial subservience" was broken by Patrick Henry's bold attack on the Stamp Act, which was passed by the British Parliament earlier in the spring of 1765. Jefferson was deeply stirred by Henry's revolutionary address, and it is possible to read a subtle political gesture in his rejection of Gibbs' proportions for pediments in the Palladian formula used in the first Monticello drawings at the very moment that the alarm bells of revolution were beginning to sound throughout the colonies. As William Pierson, Jr., has perceptively noted, "Although Jefferson might not have admitted it, his architectural judgment was clearly tinged by his political opinions." There is no doubt that his sentiments of independence prompted him to search for an architecture that represented as clear a break with the Anglo-Palladian style as the ultimate political break by the colonies with the mother country itself.

"Their architecture," Jefferson wrote of English Georgian buildings, "is in the most wretched style I ever saw, not meaning to except America where it is bad, nor here in Virginia, where it is worse than any other part of America that I have seen." In his rejection of the dominant English architectural style there was an unacknowledged effort to discover a building style expressive of the American experience itself, a search that distinguishes Jefferson's contribution to his country's architecture.

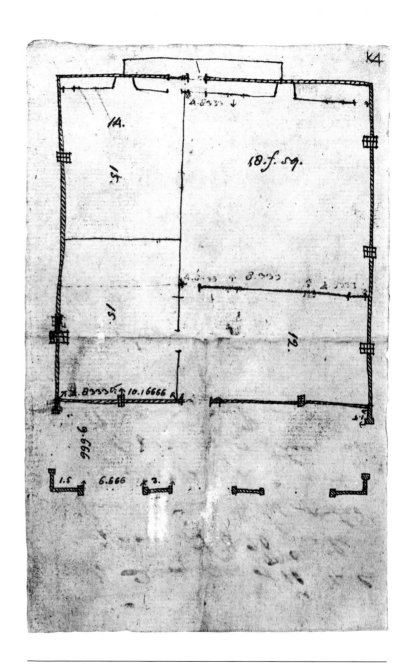

24 Jefferson's first study plans for Monticello. *Both Fiske Kimball and Frederick Nichols have called this amateur plan the first study for Monticello, and it was probably done in 1767. Of wood construction, its open, arcaded extension was to be projected the full width of the main block.*

Neoclassicism, in its efforts to push further and further into the past in order to discover the roots of positive, universal truth as it was understood by the ancients, invented the science of archeology in the eighteenth century. In the field of architecture, where "truth and beauty" could be savored in its purest, most abstract form, antique mathematical formulas —discovered by measuring Roman ruins, an activity that was to grow throughout the latter half of the eighteenth century—could easily be applied to modern buildings. In the case of Palladio's proportions for the pediment, Jefferson thought his measurements were closer to its antique source and therefore superior to Gibbs. To Jefferson the mathematician, and Jefferson the student, trained in the laws of nature and the laws of reason, the invigorating importance of the classical past as revealed in new books illustrating the latest archeological discoveries became important tools in the process of his education. Greco-Roman architecture offered the New World models of antiquity having "the approbation of thousands of years," a condition important to a parvenue government trying to establish its position with old, established nations. Architecture with such impeccable credentials, and free of any bankrupt cultural or political ties to outmoded contemporary British or European society, would later be all the more appealing to the Secretary of State and President, who would be looking for a condition of architecture that would match his ideals of the social and political state of the New Republic. By the last quarter of the eighteenth century, architectural students in Europe had turned to the fresh new evidence found at Spolato, Palmyra, Baalbeck, Paestum, and Agrigentium as a cleansing agent. a means to rub off the artificial icing of the Rococo and other inherited architectural fancies that barely hid the worn-out tradition beneath the decoration.

It is likely that Jefferson's first introduction to an enlarged study of the ancient world was in the classical works in the library of the College of William and Mary, although there were no books that actually illustrated the new archeological discoveries in Italy and Greece. But at William Byrd's Westover, not far from Williamsburg, its builder had assembled the largest private library in the colonies where there was a comparatively wide selection of books on architecture and archeology, numbering some twenty-seven volumes. Jefferson knew Byrd's library and was impressed by it, for in 1773, when he began to plan a room for his own books on the second floor of his new house, he made a count of the volumes at Westover in order to calculate the space he would need for his own collection. Jefferson's archeological library eventually would contain classical works such as Clerisseau's *Monuments de Nismes*, Desgodetz's *Edifices Anciennes de Rome, Roma illustrata Donati, De la Faye sur la chaux des Romans*, Le Roy's *Ruins of Athens*, Piranesi's *Varie vedute di Roma antica ed moderna, Ritratto di Roma antigua* by Filippo de Rossi, Stuart and Revett's *Ruins of Athens*, and Robert Wood's *Ruins of Balbec*.

Trained in the law with its emphasis on logic, precision, and historical precedent, Jefferson discovered that archeology could be used as a critical tool to be applied to the prevailing provincial misunderstanding of the classical vocabulary, and its application to architecture sharpened Jefferson's appreciation of its strict principles. The taste for classical architecture was "single and sublime" and was "not the brat of a whimsical conception" if the ancient rules were adhered to. Turning his eye on the old capital building in Williamsburg, he noted that while the Doric order of the lower part of the portico was "tolerable just in its proportions and ornaments," the inter-colonations were too large, throwing the whole thing off. As for the upper portion of the portico, carried out in the Ionic order, it was "much too small for that on which it is mounted, its ornaments not proper to the order, nor proportioned within themselves. It is crowned with a pediment" that offended his intuitive sense of balance and his implacable devotion to authenticity because it was "too high for its span."

Jefferson was by no means the only Roman in Virginia in his concern for correct classical proportion. George Washington, who was building speculative town houses on North Capital Street in the new city of Washington in 1790, wrote his architect Dr. William Thornton that he hoped that "Rules of Architecture are calculated . . . to give symmetry, and just proportion to all the order & parts of the buildings, in order to please the eye." What made the state of architecture even sadder to Jefferson the critic was the fact that even considering the scanty resources of the colony there were ways that things could be done better. "To give these symmetry and taste, would not increase their cost. It would only change the arrangement of the materials, the form and combination of the members." Any additional expense could be offset by eliminating the "burthen of barbarous ornaments" that were improperly used to decorate the "misshapen piles."

When Jefferson attacked with a passion the existing state of native architecture in his *Notes on Virginia* in 1782, he sounded as if this were a call to an esthetic revolution. He declared that "the first principles of the art are unknown and there is scarcely a model among us sufficiently chaste to give an idea of them." The new order would be found in the archeological and architectural books. Their lavish plates with details of correct orders and "sufficiently chaste" examples of proportion and taste were to be ready and dependable sources for the architectural vocabulary of Monticello, Poplar Forest, the University of Virginia, and the other houses Jefferson either designed or influenced on the behalf of his friends, as at Bremo, the greatest Jeffersonian villa of them all.

In addition to Gibbs and Palladio, other authoritative books entered his library at an early date. These included Robert Morris's *Select Architecture*, published in London in 1755, a design book that was to prove useful in the initial planning of Monticello. It had been acquired in 1770 or 1771. In Morris's other book, *Architecture Improved*, there are a number of plans showing room relationships that are similar to those in Jefferson's first sketches for Monticello. William Chambers' *Chinese Designs*, published in 1757, was another source book that was acquired early. A "chinese temple" taken from Chambers appears as corner dependencies at the right angle of the terraces in the final plan of Monticello as an alternative design for the classical octagon pavilions. A note in the margin says, "I think I shall prefer to these Chinese temples 2 regular Tuscan ones. . . ." There probably were a number of other architectural books in Jefferson's earliest library but they cannot now be identified.

Precise, abstract, measurable, and with mathematically "correct" proportions, the elegant plates of these books were enough to inspire the methodical architectural student to critically dismiss the "rude misshapen piles" of colonial Virginia architecture. In his first trip outside of Virginia, traveling north to Annapolis, Philadelphia, and New York in 1766, the year before he was admitted to the bar, he extended his architectural observations and criticism. He was not impressed by what he saw on his travels. Since he was to begin the first tentative plan for Monticello the following year, his architectural awareness may have been heightened by anticipation. He wrote his friend John Page on May 25, 1766, to say that he found the town and port of Annapolis "extremely beautiful. The houses," he noted, "are in general better than those in Williamsburg but the gardens are more indifferent." As for Maryland's rather conservative Georgian capitol building, where he witnessed the celebration of the repeal of the Stamp Act, as well as other public buildings in the town, they were not "worth mentioning."

Jefferson's use of the octagonal form in the planning of space became a kind of Jeffersonian signature and appears earliest in the final plan of the first Monticello, and it is possible that he had remembered seeing similar elements as bay windows at Philadelphia and Annapolis. Or perhaps the genesis of this peculiar preoccupation with an unorthodox manipulation of living space had a more complex and unacknowledged origin in the architect's psyche. "His house plans in endless combinations of octagon and rectangle" may well have been fired, as Hyatt Mayor remarked, by "a kind of mathematical rage, a Procrustean cleaver for lopping life to make it fit, come what may, into the odd geometry of his rooms."

It was during this trip that he met in Philadelphia the distinguished Scottish doctor and classicist John Morgan. The young Virginian carried a letter of introduction to Morgan recommending the bearer as a "gentleman eminently worthy of your acquaintance." After completing his medical studies in Edinburgh and before moving to Philadelphia, Morgan had made the Grand Tour of the continent, follow-

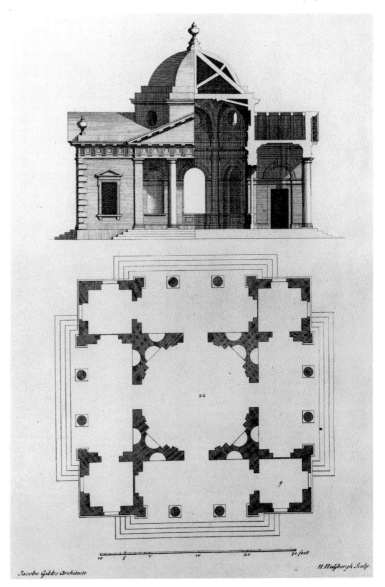

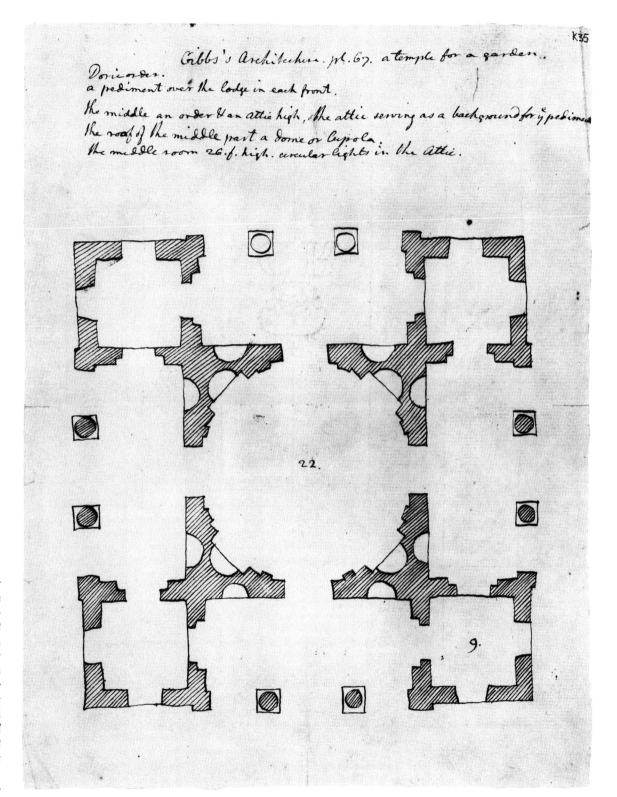

25, 26   Plan of a garden pavilion *(left) from Gibbs,* Book of Architecture *and Jefferson's copy of it (right). Gibbs described his garden pavilion as a "building of the Doric order in form of a temple, made for a person of quality and propos'd to have been placed in the center of four walks so that a portico might front each walk." Just where Jefferson planned to place his version of the pavilion at Monticello is not revealed in his notes or specifications.*

ing James Byers' "course of antiquities," a trip that would further develop the Scotsman's interest in painting and in antiquities. When he arrived in Philadelphia to found the Pennsylvania School of Medicine, he assembled a small art collection consisting of casts from the antique, paintings, drawings, and engravings. Morgan's library, containing a copy of Vignola's work on the orders of architecture, a seventeenth-century book Jefferson would find at last in Paris for his own library, must have inspired the young guest to a certain envy and admiration. There can be little doubt that the two men discussed the architecture of the antique world as well as the arts, since both subjects were well represented in the doctor's library. During his travels, Morgan had been to Vicenza and "visited several elegant palaces built by Palladio . . . and the Theatrum Olympicorum," of which he "acquired a pretty exact plate." Certainly the law student's encounter with the cultivated and well-traveled scientist must have made a lasting impression on Jefferson's esthetic education, as Kimball has suggested. In the accepted first scheme of Monticello, dated between 1768 and 1770, Jefferson provided niches in the drawing room on both sides of the entry door, perhaps to hold plaster casts such as the "Apollo of Belvedere" and the "Venus of Medici," reflecting the example of enlightened contemporary connoisseurship that had impressed him during his stay at Dr. Morgan's house, where he had seen copies from the antique.

In that early drawing of Monticello, with its clarity of line and fine shading of the solid elements, Jefferson's limited ability as a draftsman shows signs of improvement although his techniques did not evolve beyond that of a gifted gentleman-amateur. His draw-

ings do possess, nevertheless, an abstract, analytical, and painstaking quality that unmistakably conveys the designer's intentions. Much of what he wanted to communicate, however, was written out in detailed specifications giving references to published sources to be followed.

Self-taught in drawing and with no recorded mentors either in Williamsburg or Albemarle County, Jefferson, in his first drafting efforts, no doubt followed the example of his father, the surveyor and mapmaker. Along with the substantial estate that Peter Jefferson left his eldest son in 1757, he also bequeathed him his modest library and his mathematical instruments, including his surveying equipment. Surveying was a skill in the art of space description that Jefferson practiced and enjoyed all of his life. His ability to visualize and solve problems of space relations was undoubtedly developed from his early surveying experience when he began to record the farm properties he inherited on his father's death. There are numerous surveyed site plans of Monticello at different periods carried out under his direction and preserved in the Coolidge Collection at the Massachusetts Historical Society.

From his earliest notebooks, journals, and letters we know he had developed an unusually precise visual awareness that derived from his fascination with scientific observations. "He was possessed of a love of nature so intense," Edwin Betts wrote in his Preface to the published edition of Jefferson's Garden Book, "that his observant eye caught almost every passing change in it." As Randall put it in trying to establish this extraordinary facility in the broadest context of Jefferson's interests and abilities, "The eye of such a man looks at nothing, his ears hear

27 The Hermitage, *possibly by Theodore De Bruyn, c. 1770.* *This late-18th-century English country house near London was contemporary with the beginnings of Monticello. As a British citizen before the Revolution, Jefferson shared many of the values of the English gentry.*

nothing, his hand touches nothing, without collecting some of those facts which finally are grouped into systems to establish great truths in science or social economy." This ability to observe and to record accurately served him well in his architectural studies both in printed form and when analyzing completed buildings. His Garden Book in particular is a rich mine of examples of Jefferson's preoccupation with minute physical details, a concern that can be seen throughout his building and rebuilding of Monticello and later when he carried out his design for the University of Virginia.

While specific entries or comments on building are more scattered than the everyday records of gardening and farming, the evidence is there that the same "observant eye" was just as active as he noted, judged, analyzed, and compared buildings whenever he found something that interested him.

This was especially true in Paris and in his European travels, where he relentlessly explored the subject at every opportunity. Jefferson seems hardly ever to have been without a pen (or pencil, later in Europe), to note some small mechanical or design detail that might be of future use, although he never perfected the freehand sketch.

Elevations were especially difficult for him. His elevation of the first Monticello, however, with its central portico in two orders combined with the originality of a broad flight of steps—a design that has no specific ancient or modern prototype—is superior to that of earlier American draftsmen and has even been used as the cover of a recent study of neoclassical architecture.

Jefferson's years of academic study were prolonged and intensive, first at the College of William and Mary for two years, and then five years as an apprentice of George Wythe in the study of law. While his law studies were demanding—his grinding regimen outlined for Bernard Moore, listing eight different subjects "to employ" the student before eight A.M., is famous—there must have been some additional time to consider the principles of architecture. George Wythe's father-in-law Richard Taliaferro, an amateur gentleman-architect, probably designed the house where Wythe lived and that Jefferson the legal apprentice frequented, and it is unlikely that Jefferson would have missed the opportunity of discussing the subject with Taliaferro, whom Thomas Lee called "our most skillful architect." Thomas Waterman thinks that Taliaferro may have studied architecture in England before retiring to Virginia, and his experience and training would have been of the greatest interest to Wythe's young protegé from Albemarle County.

At the same time that he was formulating a political philosophy that would so profoundly shape the course of the colonial rebellion, his own conviction that the American cause was the cause of liberty and freedom from British tyranny also grew during these years. While his political vocabulary on behalf of the Revolutionary spirit was called into play early in his public career, after he was elected a member of the House of Burgesses in 1768, Jefferson also experienced his first conscious awareness of the larger symbolic purposes of architecture, which he called "the elegant art," in a new society that would be based on a different set of political, social, and cultural values from the inherited ones that were disappearing. At the close of the Revolution, he deplored the fact that "the first principles of art are unknown" in the new state of Virginia, there being no adequate models to set a standard for the new society to follow. Having had to organize his own course of study out of the thinnest of resources, he thought that the subject might at least be touched on at William and Mary by the professor of fine arts, a post he had urged on the college when he served as visitor while governor of the state from 1779 to 1781. Always the optimist, Jefferson lived with the hope that "perhaps a spark may fall on some young subjects of natural taste, kindle up their genius, and produce a reformation. . . ." The language is not unlike some of the passages found in his political documents of the Revolutionary period, thus linking the cause of political independence with an appropriate architecture, one that reflected the larger ideals of the New Republic.

As early as 1776, Jefferson had proposed the removal of the Virginia capital from the old colonial seat of Williamsburg to Richmond. Like Shadwell, Williamsburg would be no great loss, and the removal would effectively eliminate the "brick-kiln" architecture it represented, a style and model clearly inadequate and inappropriate for a modern republican state. As soon as the assembly had decided to establish a new seat of government at the fall line of the James River in 1780, Jefferson promptly introduced a bill in the House of Delegates to provide for new government buildings. Later when he was in Europe he finally had an opportunity to see firsthand the actual ruins of one relic of antiquity in southern France, confirming his earlier choice of the Maison

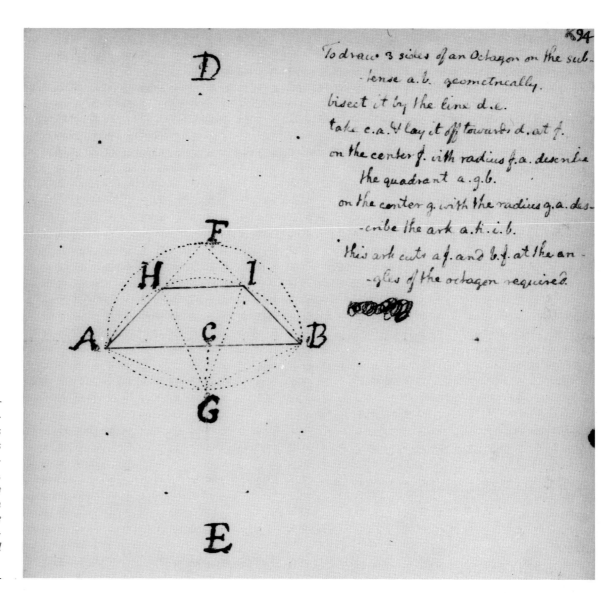

28 Page from Jefferson's building notebook, begun in 1770. *This page from Jefferson's notebook shows his method of calculating and drawing three sides of an octagonal space, a favorite shape that appears in many of his house designs. This theorum was worked out by Jefferson some time before he added the two semi-octagonal extensions to the original plan for Monticello.*

Carré as the model for the new capitol building in Richmond. In writing to James Madison from Paris in 1785, he underlined his selection of this "precious morsel of architecture left us by the antique world" as the inspiration for his design. In the same letter he made his famous declaration: "You see I am an enthusiast in the subject of the arts. But it is an enthusiasm of which I am not ashamed, as its object is to improve the taste of my countrymen, to increase their reputation, to reconcile to them the respect of the world, and procure them its praise." It was a declaration on behalf of the arts that runs with his declaration of political independence.

When it came to the laying out of the new seat of national government at Washington, Jefferson the statesman became even more aggressive in urging the highest possible standards in the planning and designing of the capitol and the other public buildings to serve the new nation. Again, his political abilities and leadership, which placed him in President

Washington's cabinet as Secretary of State, gave him a strategic position to insist on the higher functions of architecture; to encourage new forms of artistic expression that would match the new political idealism seemed a natural extension of his ambitions for the country he had helped to found. Again thinking of those limited, imperfect materials for study that he himself had had in Williamsburg of the 1760s he proposed to Washington that the government circulate inexpensive prints of outstanding architectural elevations and distribute them free to the citizens of nearby Georgetown in order to elevate their tastes and expectations. Writing to Washington, he reminded him that "while in Europe, I selected about a dozen or two of the handsomest fronts of private buildings, of which I have the plates. Perhaps it might decide the taste of the new town, were those engraved here and distributed gratis. . . . The expense would be trifling." His letters in January and March of 1791 to William Short in Paris to "pray get me by some means or other a compleat set of Piranesi's drawings of the Pantheon, & especially the correct design for its restoration" were probably related to his ongoing architectural propaganda activities in Washington. He had considered a possible "spherical" scheme for the new capitol building itself, with the Roman Pantheon serving as the impractical model. It was a form far more adaptable to the needs of a university library, even though the ancient monument with its all-embracing dome, commanding portico, and classical associations had an obvious appeal in symbolic terms for the idealistic government and its architect spokesman working at Monticello.

Throughout his life Jefferson was both a perfectionist and an idealist attentive to forms and things.

Given his insatiable curiosity, range of interests, and attempts to master every branch of knowledge, the mass of detail recorded daily in letters, journals, and diaries as "aides memoire" is at times obsessive, even painful. The farm and garden notebooks, recording all aspects of the complex systems of agriculture, botany, horticulture, and related subjects that went to the very heart of existence at Monticello, have at times a quality of desperation. It was as if the values and continuity of a threatened society were to be held together by the endless accumulation of statistical data in logical exactitude. Jefferson's minute calculations to determine, for example, if the interstices in cords of stacked wood represented in fact one-third of the total volume, can leave one with dismayed weariness. Or again, an entry in the Garden Book reads: "The circuit of the base of Monticello is 5¼ miles; the area of the base 890 acres. Within the limits of that base I this day tried the temperatures of 15 springs, 10 on the South and 5 on the N. side of the mountain, the outward air being generally about 75° of Farenheit." It is difficult to fathom why anyone would have gone to such trouble to determine what often appears to be useless trivia.

Aside from the abstract and even eccentric character of some of these observations on the most insignificant and seemingly irrelevant subjects, it represented a vital scientific passion that could be found in many individuals of the eighteenth century—both American and European—with claims to membership in the larger intellectual fraternity of the Enlightenment. It was characteristic of the universal man, as invented by the early Italian Renaissance, to study science, mathematics, and the fine arts as important aspects of his humanistic learning. Leon Battista

Alberti was probably the only Florentine to come close to the impossible goals of the ideal man of learning, and Jefferson shared many of Alberti's same aspirations and personal characteristics.

In Jefferson's prodigious intellectual activities, his efforts always to reach for perfection and to attempt to find the perfect solution advanced his understanding of all the phases of architecture—the plans, the manipulation of space, the mathematical calculation of proportions, and all of the details of the actual construction process. He remarked once that he could not be away from the building site at Monticello for more than an hour at a time, and it is no wonder considering the amount of supervision required and the depth and scope of his daily observations and calculations made while the house was being built. He noted, for example, in his Memorandum Book in 1769 at the beginning of the work: ". . . in digging my dry well at the depth of 14 f. I observe one digger, one filler, one drawer at the windlace with a basket at each end of his rope very accurately gave one another full employment but note it was yellow rotten stone with a great many hard stones as large as a man's head and some larger, or else the digger would have had time to spare. they dug and drew out 81 cubical yds in a day."

For all of this "morbid industry" of the perfectionist compiling and ordering apparently insignificant facts —an obsession, as Lord Clark has pointed out, that both Alberti and Jefferson shared—their intellectual motivation must have had similar roots in their early training and personal experience. It is the paradox of Jefferson the perfectionist that he created for himself and lived in a state of disruption, discomfort, and change, a condition of physical disorder that seems so alien to the image of the idealist we know through the letters and portraits. Yet Jefferson in his love of "putting up and pulling down," his deliberate compulsion to remodel any and every house he ever occupied, even if it was merely rented, must have given the domestic state of his personal life at times the unsettled quality of that of a frontier vagabond. Even before he finally completed the original plan of the first Monticello, he began in the summer of 1796 to tear it down, while his family was attempting to live in it. But to their dismay, when winter came the new walls had not been roofed except for the drawing room and Jefferson's bedroom wing. His great granddaughter Sarah N. Randolph, without recording the personal discomfort of her mother and other members of the family who were then living there, simply reported that ". . . he hoped to finish before the winter set in; but just as the walls were nearly ready to be roofed in, a stiff freeze arrested, in November, all work on it for the winter." The appalling living conditions at Monticello that winter may well explain Jefferson's complaint in a letter to Mary Jefferson on May 25, 1797, that he was "very slowly getting the better of my rheumatism, though very slowly indeed; being only able to walk a little stronger."

Six years later, in 1802, when Mrs. William Thornton, Jefferson's friend from Washington, visited Monticello, she reported that the house still was in an "unfinished state, though commenced twenty-seven years ago." Aside from the vagaries of the weather that often interrupted the work, the problem was the uncertainty of the designer in his scheme. "Mr. Jefferson has so frequently changed his plan, and pulled down and rebuilt so often that it had generally made the appearance of a place going to decay. . . ." When visitors were taken inside, Mrs. Thornton continues, "—Tho' I had been prepared to see an unfinished house, still I could not help being struck with the uncommon appearance & which the general gloom that prevailed contributed much to increase. —We went thro' a large unfinished hall, loose planks forming the floor, lighted by one dull lantern into a large room with a small bow and separated by an arch, where the company was seated at tea." Somehow the gloomy place gave Mrs. Thornton a distinctly uncomfortable feeling of "decay" and rootlessness, "the appearance was irregular and unpleasant."

Edward Thornton, who stayed at Monticello in October of the same year, found to his dismay the president living in what can only be described as romantic squalor. Thornton found the house "in a state of commencement of decay, Virginia being the only country as far as I know where the inhabitants contrive to bring these two extremes as near to each other as possible by inhabiting an unfinished house till it is falling about their ears."

When Sir Augustus John Foster, a young English diplomat, visited Monticello in 1804 he was surprised to find the pediment of one of the porticoes "supported on stems of Four Tulip Trees." But with an oblique reference to the eighteenth-century's fantasies about Adam's first house in Paradise, he found the trunks of the trees "as beautiful as the fluted shafts of Corinthian Pillars."

One visitor as late as 1809, who expressed his surprise at the unfinished state of things, was told by the retired president that since architecture was his delight, "and putting up and pulling down one of his

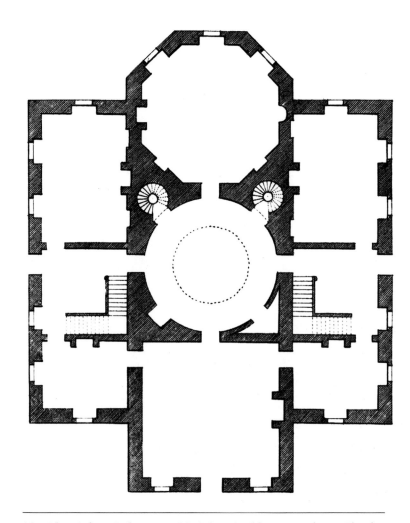

29 *Plate 2 from Robert Morris's* **Select Architecture** *(above). The plan may have suggested to Jefferson the octagonal salon that projects from the middle of Monticello's rear facade.*

30 *Jefferson's plan for garden pavilion* *(right). Jefferson was fascinated with the abstract forms of small garden structures, and this plan for a domed octagonal house would have made a perfect Jeffersonian retreat.*

favorite amusements," he hoped that it would continue to be unfinished at least during his lifetime.

Such uncompleted and disorganized arrangements could just as easily have been remarked upon by visitors to Jefferson's houses in Philadelphia, Paris, the President's House in Washington, or the Governor's Palace in Williamsburg, all of which underwent

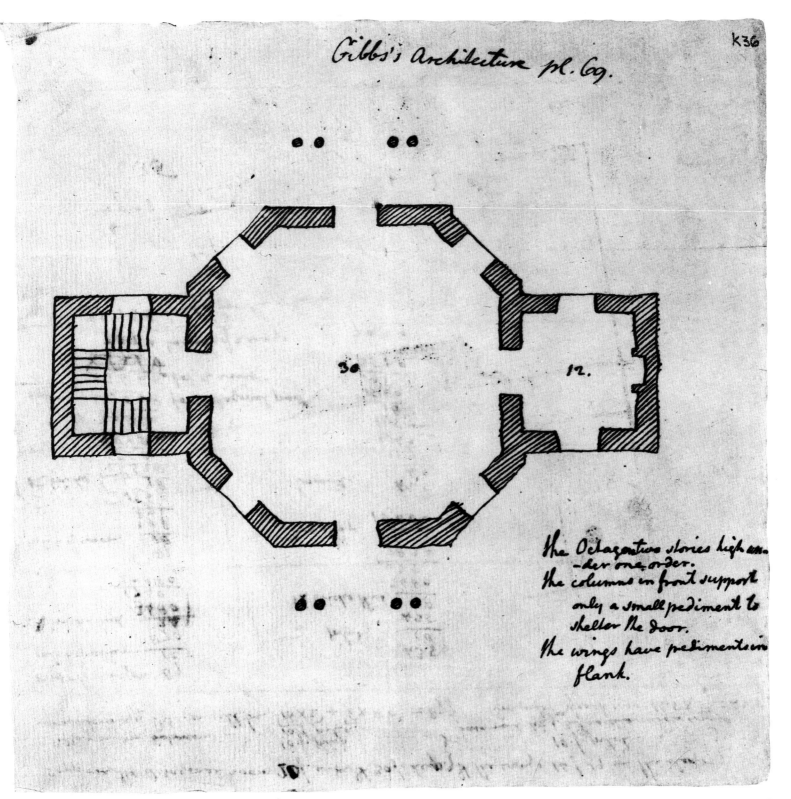

36

12.

The Octagon two stories high un-
-der one order.
the columns in front support
only a small pediment to
shelter the door.
the wings have pediments in
flank.

35

alterations according to his plans during his stay to satisfy his "favorite amusement" and always to accommodate a new style of living not provided for in the old arrangements.

Without venturing too far onto the uncertain terrain of psychological biography, and especially as to how it relates to Jefferson's attraction to building and to architecture, there are, however, conditions of Jefferson's early life as an architect that invite speculation. Certainly no other contemporary American with a similar passion for architecture comes close to the full-scale, personal, creative involvement that Jefferson displays. The Marquis de Chastellux remarked that Jefferson was not only the architect of Monticello, he "was often one of the builders." By participating in the building process he was able to master the common and established vernacular lan-

31 Octagonal end of two-story drawing room at Farmington, designed by Jefferson. *The plan of the addition to the existing house of George Divers was drawn in 1802, indicating the continuing professional interest Jefferson took in architecture even while serving as President.*

guage, a basic condition for the development of a true architecture adapted to local climate, materials, and construction skills. And certainly no contemporary ever willingly subjected himself or his family to such chaotic living conditions over such an extended period of time in order to satisfy his building obsession. If Mrs. Bayard Smith recorded the secondhand comment attributed to Jefferson accurately, that he had created what may be thought of as unpleasant living conditions chiefly for his own amusement, then his mania seems all the more self-centered. When laid against his expressed desire for peace and quiet amongst his adoring and adored family, and his constant reference to Monticello as a retreat or Elysium far removed from "the circle of cabal intrigue and hatred," the actual conditions brought about by his putting up and pulling down, that prevailed at least until he finished (or stopped working on) Monticello in 1809, are difficult to explain.

There was throughout Jefferson's early childhood and on into his student days an unsettled quality of restless moving about and of seldom staying in one place for long, beginning with his family's move to Tuckahoe when Jefferson was not yet two-years old. He was to claim in his autobiography that the journey to Tuckahoe and his arrival there carried on a pillow was his first conscious memory. Later there were long periods away from his family, when at the age of nine he was sent to board at Dover Church with the Reverend William Douglas, then with the Reverend James Maury—"a correct classical scholar" —and still two more years at the College of William and Mary, where he lived in rented rooms. In 1763, Jefferson wrote of his unsettled life as a student in Williamsburg, giving us the first reference to his life-long obsession, when he confided that he wanted to build a house "to prevent the inconveniency of moving my lodgings for the future." But it would be "no castle" he assured his friend, "only a small house which shall contain a room for myself and one for you. . . ." By this time he had left the college to study law with George Wythe, the distinguished Williamsburg lawyer.

Whatever the roots of Jefferson's deeper conflicts regarding the repeated upheavals he would bring about over the years at Monticello—in contrast with his abiding desire to achieve an ideal state of tranquility in his living arrangements—the contradiction is apparent. It is a contradiction that must be taken into account when attempting to sort out the factors that caused him to devote so much of his creative genius to housing his own complex self, and at the same time attempting to satisfy his high standards of order, proportion, and authenticity of detail as laid down by the earlier architects whom he admired.

It is a commonplace observation to say that Monticello with all of its idiosyncrasies, gadgets, and unresolved problems more nearly reflects the personality of its designer than any other house in America. Yet if Monticello stands "as one of the most civilized houses ever built," as William Pierson has written, it is surely because it was built by and for one of the most civilized, sensitive, and complex intellects who as a self-made architect became his own client. By exploring in some detail the long, intricate, uninhibited experiment that finally produced the historical house, we can begin to grasp some of the more intimate and subtle dimensions of Jefferson's remarkable personality and genius.

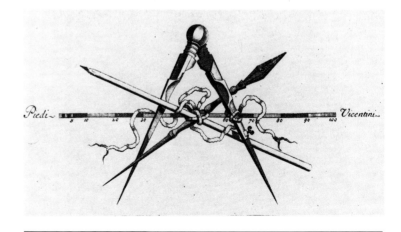

32 Pens and architectural tools. *The cartouche is from Scamozzi's edition of Palladio's* The Four Books of Architecture.

THE FIRST
MONTICELLO

33   The first building completed at Monticello. *Jefferson moved into the South Pavilion in the fall of 1770, and it served as his bachelor's quarters while work progressed on the central portion of the house.*

IN THE GRAY, OVERCAST, MIDDAY LIGHT of early
October, 1786, a carriage returned to Paris
from the Porte St. Denis with a lonely, depressed, middle-aged Virginian, now the
American minister to France. That morning, accompanied by his friend Pierre d'Hancarville the archeologist, he had insisted on traveling to the edge of
the city to say a final goodbye to Maria Cosway, who
was returning to London after a visit to Paris, where
she had captured Jefferson's heart. Shortly after he
had arrived back at his house at the Grille de Chaillot
"more dead than alive . . . and rent into fragments by
the force of my grief," Jefferson sat down before his
hearth in the Hôtel de Langeac and wrote his celebrated love letter to Mrs. Cosway, who was then head-
ing north to London and with no immediate plans to
return to Paris. Known as "My Head and My Heart,"
Julian Boyd calls it "one of the notable love letters in
the English language." Using an eighteenth-century
conceit of a dialogue between the cool, rational head
and the emotional sentiments of the heart, Jefferson
reveals in his passionate letter a deeply anguished
man tormented and torn by "the divided empire" of
his complex, riven heart and mind.

No doubt the pall of the wet October day had put
in relief the recollections of the first time he met the
beautiful, exotic, languorous Maria, a woman of
twenty-seven who had been introduced to Jefferson
by young John Trumbull. If only that first day they
met had been "as long as a Lapland Summer day,"

34 View from Monticello. *"From its lofty but gradual elevation, the morning was beautiful; the sun beamed forth in all his majesty; the birds warbled
sweetly around us, the air was pure, balmy and elastic; and when within sight
of the house, we paused for sometime to contemplate the divine scene thrust
upon our view."*

35 Orchard, Monticello. *Jefferson set out trees even before work was begun on the original house in 1769.*

the forty-three-year-old widower wrote, as he recalled their first afternoon together inspecting the Halle aux Bleds, the crowded, noisy new grain market in the middle of Paris. An audacious new piece of architecture with a giant dome 130 feet across and constructed with wooden ribbing and glass, the light-flooded Halle had attracted wide attention, and Jefferson had been drawn to it as he was to virtually every new building then going up in the French capital of Louis XVI.

The setting of the new grain market seems an unlikely place for the beginning of a romance, but in fact dramatic chateaux, pavilions, folies, parks, firework displays, and garden settings in and around Paris would provide the exotic backdrop for the couple as their affair developed in the autumn days following that first meeting. According to the Heart in the celebrated letter, it was always the practical Head and its insatiable interest in buildings and new architectural designs that set the stage for the doomed affair, causing "the present distress." The meeting at the teeming grain market filled with shouting buyers and sellers, ". . . was not the consequence of my doings," Jefferson's Heart declared. "It was one of your projects which threw us in the way of it. . . . It was you remember and not I," the Heart reminded the always practical Head, "who desired the meeting at LeGrand and Molinos [architects of the new market]. I never trouble myself with domes and arches. The Halle aux Bleds might have rotted down before I should have gone to see it. But you forsooth, who are eternally getting us to sleep with your diagrams and crochets, must go and examine this wonderful piece of architecture. And when you had seen it, oh! it was the most superb thing on earth!"

Later in the startling self-portrait, Jefferson's Heart, now all sentiment and passion, turns to thoughts of "our dear Monticello" with the hope that the Heart's description will prove tempting enough to lure the cosmopolitan Mrs. Cosway there to discover for herself "those delightful places! Those enchanted Grotto's! Those Magnificent Mountains, rivers, &c. &c.!"—a world that Maria Cosway would never see. It had been two years since Jefferson had left his incomplete mountain aerie in Albemarle County for Europe's "vaunted scene," and his Heart's recollection for Maria's benefit inspired a description that must have drawn on memories of his earliest visits to that virgin mountaintop. There transfixed in a reverie of nature, the boy would immerse himself in the spectacular solitude, removed and above

36 Orchard at dawn, Monticello. *Archeological investigations over the past several years have enabled Monticello's gardeners to replant original varieties of fruit trees in the same locations that Jefferson chose more than two hundred years ago.*

the everyday confusion of the family plantation at Shadwell, with all of its distractions and interruptions set out in its stolid frontier disorder along the banks of the Rivanna. But luminous Monticello: "where has Nature spread so rich a mantle under the eye? Mountains, rocks, rivers. With what majesty do we there ride above the storms! How sublime to look down into the workhouse of nature, to see her clouds, hail, snow, rain, thunder, all fabricated at our feet! and the glorious Sun, when rising as if out of a distant water, just gilding the top of the mountains and giving life to all nature!"

The ecstasy of affection and desire the description reveals leaves no doubt that it had indeed been drawn from the writer's deepest emotions. And it was the same passionate, romantic, impractical Heart that had dictated the selection of the site for the house in 1768, when the young lawyer—"the Head"—had returned from Williamsburg to Charlottesville to begin the practice of law and generally assume the role of a rich colonial grandee, establishing an estate on his inherited land at the very western edge of the British Empire.

The language of the Head and Heart letter can be read on several levels. Revealing the portrait of a divided personality beneath the disguise of the eighteenth-century metaphor for the dialogue, the penetrating self-examination helps us understand many of his remarkable accomplishments and creations, including the design and building of Monticello through all of its phases. Romantic and realist, poet and pragmatist, democrat and aristocrat, Jefferson consistently upheld the most advanced notions of political and social organization as the uniquely American ideal, while at the same time maintaining

44

an establishment founded upon a system of slavery that in many ways reflected the most reactionary values of British and European societies. In his manners, his speech, his agrarian values, his table silver, his domestic staff, his equipage, his aloofness, his nonchalance, Jefferson was, as John Peale Bishop has observed, an aristocrat down to the curve of his calves, in spite of the fact that he could not trace the genealogy of the Jefferson family beyond his grandfather. His repeated and unqualified declarations of love for Monticello and dedication to the quiet, agrarian life of a Virginian planter must be set beside the obvious pleasures of city life that he discovered dur-

37 **Thomas Jefferson** *by Jean-Antoine Houdon. Jefferson's bust by his friend Houdon was first exhibited at the Louvre in the Salon of 1789, just before Jefferson returned to the United States.*

ing his years in Paris. As Dumas Malone has written, those five years of rich, stimulating, sophisticated urban living were probably the happiest of his entire life. Indeed, when he left Paris in 1789, he was confident that he would return after a few months' visit in the United States.

It is not surprising then, given the complex texture of Jefferson's genius and creative personality, that his own intensely personal house, its setting and furnishings, would suggest some of the same ambivalent conflicts that lay masked beneath the bold, even arrogant head we see in the Houdon bust. It is no wonder that Monticello has few architectural equals when measured by the extraordinary dimensions of its creator's personality.

Three years after reaching his majority, when he received from his father's estate some 5,000 acres, he was introduced to the practice of law at the bar of the General Court of Virginia in 1767. In his first full year of practice, he registered in his Memorandum Book, 1767–1770, sixty-eight cases on which he had worked. While he continued to live at Shadwell with his mother, his law practice kept him traveling to court sessions in the neighboring counties. Yet, as the entries in his Garden Book for that year record, he was already developing an interest in gardening that closely paralleled his growing interest in architecture. Both flowers and vegetables were sown and cultivated under his direction, and a wide variety of ornamental and fruit trees also were planted. On August 3, 1767, the entry in the Garden Book reads: "inoculated common cherry buds into stocks of large kind at Monticello." It is the first mention of Monticello in Jefferson's writings, and it is altogether appropriate that it appears first in his garden journal.

**38   Maria Cosway, *self-portrait engraved by Valentine Green.* *Jefferson was a forty-three-year-old widower when he met the attractive, talented English artist in Paris through John Trumbull.*

The hillside where he had planted his new orchard was just below the site already chosen for the house he was now determined to build, although the precise moment when he selected the romantic and altogether improbable and impractical spot is not recorded. As Marie Kimball and others have pointed out, it was a gesture suggesting a romantic, unorthodox impulse without precedent in America or even in England. It is difficult to think of a contemporary precedent in all of Europe for such an adventuresome, independent decision involving the siting of a new house, where a high hilltop was selected without at least some older, fortified structures dictating the choice. In a way the mountaintop was a microcosm and symbol of the American continent itself, stretching in its unencumbered vastness to the west beyond the Blue Ridge Mountains and Jefferson's new horizon.

Literary sources probably played a part in the choosing of Monticello's picturesque location. Among the books that Jefferson bought in 1765 were the *Works* of William Shenstone, that romantic gardener, farmer, and poet who had developed his Yorkshire farm, The Leasows, into a celebrated estate that he called a "ferme ornée." The second volume of the *Works* contained Shenstone's essay "Unconnected Thoughts on Gardening," along with Dodsley's "Description of the Leasows." A map and description of the landscaped farm with its various scenes, prospects, and walks was appended as a guide. Appropriate poetic inscriptions were carefully worked into the layout. Even though Jefferson was to be quite disappointed with Shenstone's creation when he finally saw it with John Adams in 1786—"the architecture has contributed nothing," he noted in his travel journal—it may well have been an early and stimulating source for the young lawyer's evolving and by no means clearly established plans for his own picturesque estate on the edge of the American wilderness.

Given the unlimited range of choices for a house-site on the Rivanna estate of 2,650 acres where Shadwell stood, or on the rest of the lands that Jefferson had inherited, the choice with all of its drawbacks must be considered chiefly for its psychological appeal. Quite aside from the spectacular views that Monticello enjoys in all directions, Jefferson's daily rides over his vast property and in the neighborhood throughout his life would have satisfied most appetites for esthetic, lofty prospects and views without building a small village and plantation-center on the impractical hilltop that he finally selected. To the Marquis de Chastellux the fact that Jefferson had personally selected the precise location was almost as significant as his having built the house itself. "For although he already owned fairly extensive lands in the neighborhood," Chastellux wrote in his celebrated description of the first Monticello, "there was nothing, in such an unsettled country, to prevent him from fixing his residence wherever he wanted to. But nature so contrived it, that a sage and a man of taste should find on his own estate the spot where he might study and enjoy her." Jefferson's poetic habitat did not end with its walls and columned porticoes, but rather the whole complex of buildings, gardens, orchards, and fields was to resonate, in its active confrontation with nature, with the surrounding countryside of wooded hills, valleys, mountains, rivers, and plains stretching to the horizon. For all of its practical drawbacks, hardships, and expense— "He appeared," Malone has written, "to be flying in the face of common sense"—Jefferson never once expressed a regret for his decision.

The selection of the mountaintop was breathtakingly original and immediately impresses every visitor to Monticello. Even a Mrs. Drummond, who lived in Williamsburg and never visited there, appreciated the startling, poetic quality of the setting from the

39 Villa Pisani, by Andrea Palladio. The portico of this villa was adapted by Jefferson in the final elevation of the first version of Monticello. He translated classic principles and proportions into forms dictated by the local climate, materials, and craftsmanship of Virginia.

few lines in the Miltonic Stile. Thou wonderful Young Man, so piously entertaining, thro out that exalted letter. Indeed," Mrs. Drummond concluded, "I shal think, Spirits of an higher order, inhabits Yr. Aerey Mountains. . . ." Although Jefferson's letter to Mrs. Drummond inspiring her reply is missing, the reference to "the Miltonic Stile" conjures up a letter laced with evocative paraphrases of Milton's description of the Garden of Eden.

But for mortals, including Jefferson and his workmen and slaves who were to be responsible for the building and rebuilding of the house and grounds over the next forty years, "spirits of an higher order" might well have been useful in overcoming the monumental physical handicaps that the mountaintop presented.

Andrea Palladio understood the practical as well as the esthetic and psychological issues involved in selecting the ideal place to build a house and discusses it in Chapter XII of his Second Book, called "Of the Site to be chosen for the fabrichs of Villa's." Before coming to any question of the design of the villa, Palladio, in the utmost practical terms, briefly describes the life of a villa, a life that Jefferson and any other Virginia gentleman of the eighteenth century would have understood completely. First of all, the country villa was the center of a way of life based on the art of agriculture and where by industry and careful management one naturally improved one's estate. It was also a place where the daily walks and horseback rides restored one's physical and mental strength that has been "fatigued by the agitation of the city." Above all the villa was a place where "private and family affairs are chiefly transacted." Surrounded by an adoring family and "virtuous friends"

picture Jefferson conveyed in a letter he had written in 1771 asking her to send some plant and orchard material for his new establishment. "Let me recollect Your description, which bars all the Romantic, Poetical ones I ever read. . . . no pen but Yrs., cou'd (surely so butiful describe) espeshally, those

40   Elevation study by Jefferson, c. 1770. *In this early study for the first Monticello, Jefferson carried the important classical entablature of the Doric order, from Gibbs'* Rules for Drawing, *around the entire body of the house. He preferred cut stone for the exterior decoration, but it was too expensive.*

41 Elevation study by Jefferson, c. 1771–72. *This study for the final version of the first Monticello was never completed, but it shows Jefferson's reference to Palladio's Villa Pisani in the two orders for the portico, Doric below and Ionic above. A visitor to Monticello in 1780 wrote that "the Governor professes a noble spirit of building . . . according to his own fancy."*

who shared one's intellectual and esthetic interests, one "could easily attain to as much happiness as can be attained here below," a sublime state of affairs and perfection that Jefferson at his Monticello aspired to and strove for throughout his mature life. It was no wonder that Jefferson so willingly absorbed not only Palladio's architectural theories but his moral principles as well, for the ideal villa life in the Veneto of the sixteenth century, as described by Palladio, was with minor modifications easily translated into the Piedmont vernacular of Jefferson's eighteenth-century Virginia. The Byrds, the Lees, the Pages, and the Randolphs were, after all, not that different from the clients Palladio had , Venetian aristocrats living and managing their farms and estates in the

42 Plan study by Jefferson, c. 1768–70. *This early study of Monticello shows a cruciform plan with a two-story central block. The note, "The pediments should be in height two ninths of their span," indicates that Jefferson was already dedicated to Palladian proportions based on his studies.*

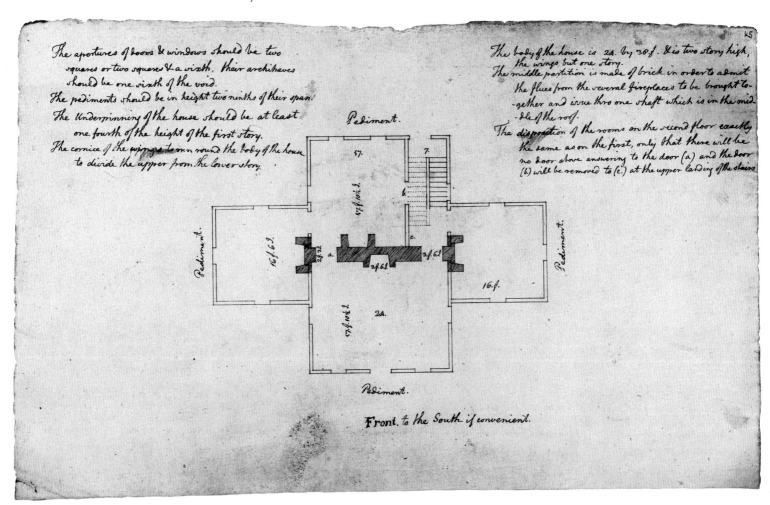

Veneto. The Virginian aristocracy, like the earlier Italian, saw to it that their estates were productive and dominated by an administrative center in order to supervise the operation. Appropriate service facilities and staff quarters were grouped nearby. It was Palladio's unified, harmonious solution to the design and organization of these building types that had appealed to Virginians even before Jefferson's time, through the influence of the English Palladian movement and its preoccupation with the architectural problems of country estates. Even though Palladio did recognize the improved climate of "elevated and cheerful places where the air is . . . purged of all ill vapours and moistures," nowhere did Palladio or his ancient Roman sources suggest a mountaintop as a prime site for a country house except when it was absolutely necessary. Perhaps it was Jefferson's enlarged American sense of space that translated Palladio's "monticello" into a Virginia mountain on a scale quite different from the small Italian hills Palladio had in mind when he wrote his treatise. If the obviously practical considerations of staying in the center of the estate could be ignored, then, according to Palladio, the banks of a river would be the first choice because it combined both elements of beauty and utility. Transportation was readily available, as was, equally important, water to be used for the pleasure and kitchen gardens, they being the "sole and chief recreation of a villa."

If a river is out of the question, the next choice for a house site would be on an "elevated and cheerful" place, so long as there was ample supply of good water "limpid and subtle . . . which makes good bread and in which greens are quickly boiled." But the existence of an ample supply of water at Monticello,

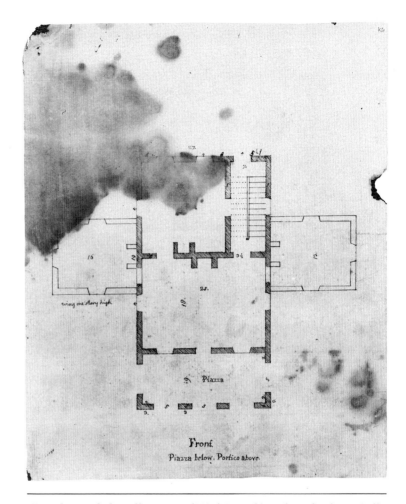

43 *Plan study by Jefferson, c. 1768–70.* In this early study of Monticello, the young architect begins to show greater skill in his draftsmanship. In a note he calls for, "Piazza below. Portico above," on the front elevation, and he may have planned classical pediments on all four sides, as in fig. 42.

that fundamental, decisive element in picking a country house site until the advent of modern water systems, was not one of Jefferson's overriding priorities in his determination.

From the very beginning there was a water shortage at Monticello. In the summer of 1769, when he began to manufacture bricks by the thousands, the

51

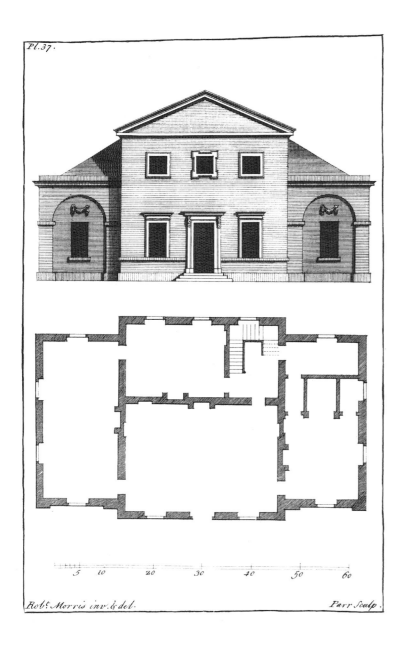

44 *Plate 37*, **Select Architecture by Robert Morris.** *Morris's design for "a little Building intended for Retirement" appears to be the source for an early study for Monticello. Jefferson was familiar with Morris's published works, and he had owned one of his books as early as 1770.*

springs on the side of the mountain were inadequate to support the operation. The new well that had been dug was not yet supplying water, so it had to be carried a considerable distance from other sources.

In the Memorandum Book, 1776–1820, the notes only hint at the continuing problems of maintaining a sufficient water supply for the Monticello household and the staff that lived there. The springs were never reliable, and the original well was hardly much better. Jefferson noted on February 23, 1778, "the water is returning into the well at Monticello having now been dry for 13 months." It was an old story that was regularly noted in the Memorandum Book: 1791, "the well has failed this year"; 1797, "the well has failed this summer"; 1799, "the well has got very low this summer (which was dry), so as not always to furnish clear water for drinking nor water for washing." It was not until after the alterations and rebuilding during the first decade of the nineteenth century, that a water collecting system of cisterns was finally installed after a water collecting table for each roof area was meticulously worked out by the system's designer/engineer.

The uncertainty of the water supply was not the only shortcoming to Monticello. Timber had to be cleared from the hillsides and the ground leveled. There was also the problem of building and maintaining the long, steep roadways up the mountain. The chronically bad road conditions were remarked upon by more than one visitor over the years. "We continued on rather poor roads and reached, at 3 o'clock in the afternoon, the home of Governor Jefferson," Baron von Closen wrote in his journal in 1780. Sir Augustus John Foster, in his record of his visit in 1804, noted "the disagreeable Ford to Cross

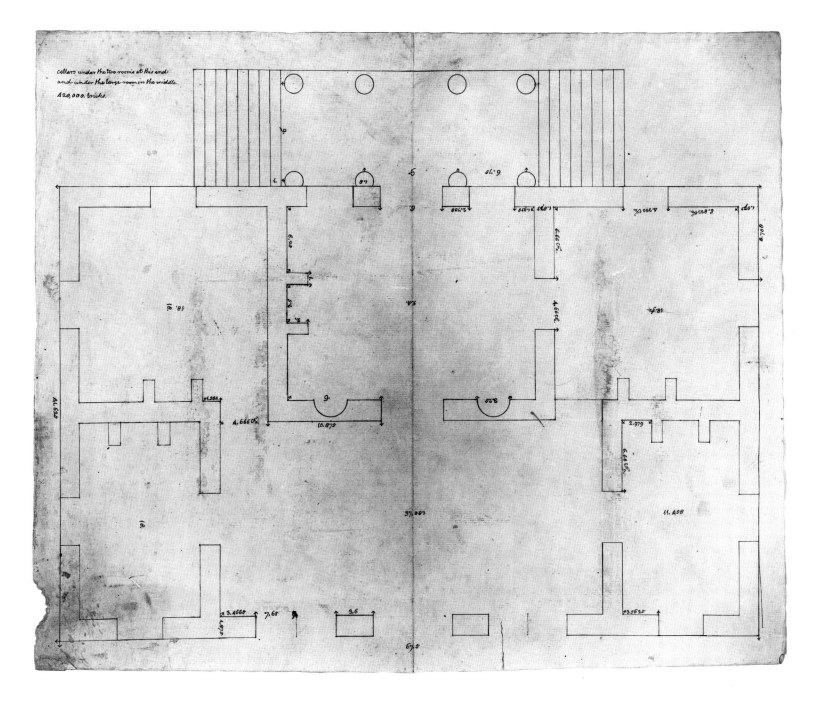

at the North River," near Monticello, "which lamed one of my horses" before even beginning the winding ascent. Mrs. William Thornton had actually gotten out of her carriage and walked the last three-quarters of a mile for fear that the road could not be followed in a rain storm. The situation of Monticello

45 *Plan study by Jefferson, made before the fall of 1770. This study for the first Monticello is taken from Palladio's Book 2, Plate 41, a plan that also has L shaped service wings. There are no stairs indicated in this plan, suggesting that Jefferson was not contemplating a second story at this time. The ornamental niches in the back walls of the front center room were carried over into the final version of the plan for the first Monticello.*

53

might be "grand and awful," Mrs. Thornton wrote, but it was "far from convenient or in my opinion agreeable."

On May 15, 1768, one month after his twenty-fifth birthday, Jefferson made a contract to level the top of his little mountain across the Rivanna River and above his widowed mother's house, Shadwell. The decision was a triumph of his imagination, his eye, and his heart over all of the apparent difficulties and persuasive arguments the head could muster: "May 15, Agreed with Mr. Moore that he shall level 250 f. square on the top of the mountain at the N.E. end by Christmas, for which I am to give 180 bushels of wheat, and 24 bushels of corn, 12 of which are not to be paid until corn comes in. If there should be any solid rock to dig we will leave to indifferent men to settle that part between us." The building of Monticello was underway, and it marked the real beginning of Jefferson's architectural career, the opening lines of his architectural essay and autobiography.

Nine months later, on February 5, 1769, the newly elected member of the House of Burgesses wrote from Shadwell to Thomas Turpin explaining to him that he would be unable to supervise the legal studies of Turpin's son because "my situation both present and future render it utterly impossible." The reasons were obvious. Work at Monticello was taking every spare moment left from his travels connected with his growing law practice and attending to his duties in Williamsburg. By the following November, he wrote with eager anticipation of his move from Shadwell, "I propose to remove to another habitation which I am about to erect and on a plan so contracted as that I shall have but one spare bedchamber for whatever visitants I may have." The

"habitation" is the earliest reference to Monticello in Jefferson's correspondence.

The first small bachelor's retreat may have been modest and constricted—the dimensions were eighteen feet by eighteen feet—but it was only just a beginning. The fact that this structure survived all of the subsequent changes and remodelings over the next forty years, becoming the southwest pavilion at the end of the western extremity of the enfolding terrace, says a great deal about the careful thought that Jefferson had given to the overall scheme from the beginning. It was a scheme that would tenaciously maintain its relationship and scale to the mountaintop and to the surrounding panorama through all of the subsequent experimenting, enlargements, and piecemeal changes.

One of the early changes was to abandon the first layout of the terraces, which were connected to the main house by open arcades and were to form an enormous rectangle enclosing what is now the west lawn. These wings were to contain all of his offices, storage facilities, and stables in a grandiose Palladian gesture, a gesture unrealized on such a scale even by Palladio's rich Venetian clients in the sixteenth century. The two L-shaped terraces that were retained in the final designs carried an office corridor running the entire length beneath the house.

Work on the south outchamber, the young architect's first constructed design, was started in the autumn of 1769. In his Memorandum Book, he carefully noted that "four good fellows, a lad and two girls of ab! 16," could on a cold, snowy day, "dig a cellar in mountain clay three feet deep, eight feet wide and sixteen and a half feet long." Prior to construction, George Dudley, a brick maker of Williamsburg, was hired, and in nearly three weeks he had produced forty-five thousand bricks in kilns on the site. Jefferson had already carefully considered the size of the brick to be made by measuring the bricks at Rosewell. The first bricks at Monticello were 7½

47 *Intermediate plan study by Jefferson of the first Monticello, 1768–70.* *The thickness of the walls of the central portion of the house indicates that it was to be two stories while the rooms on either side were to be one story with attic. The narrow stairs at the side of the entrance was a favorite device used by Jefferson.*

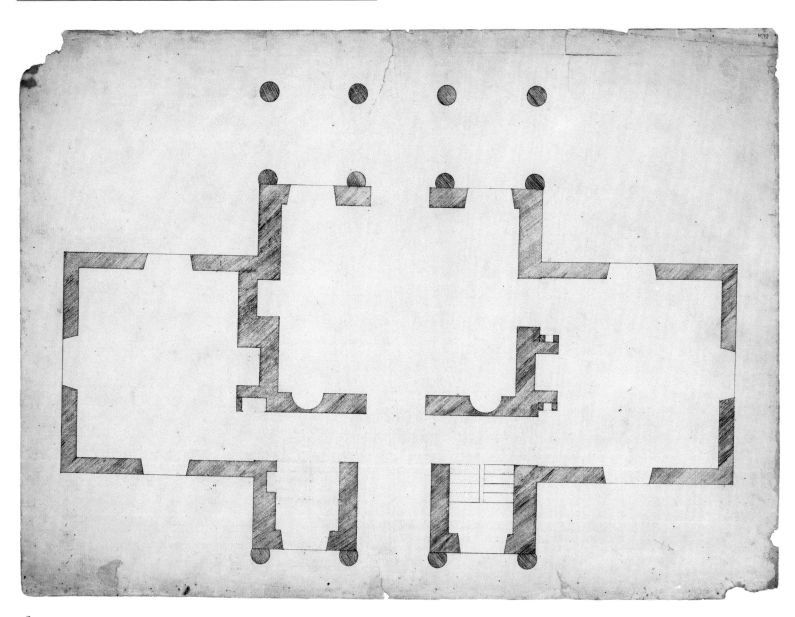

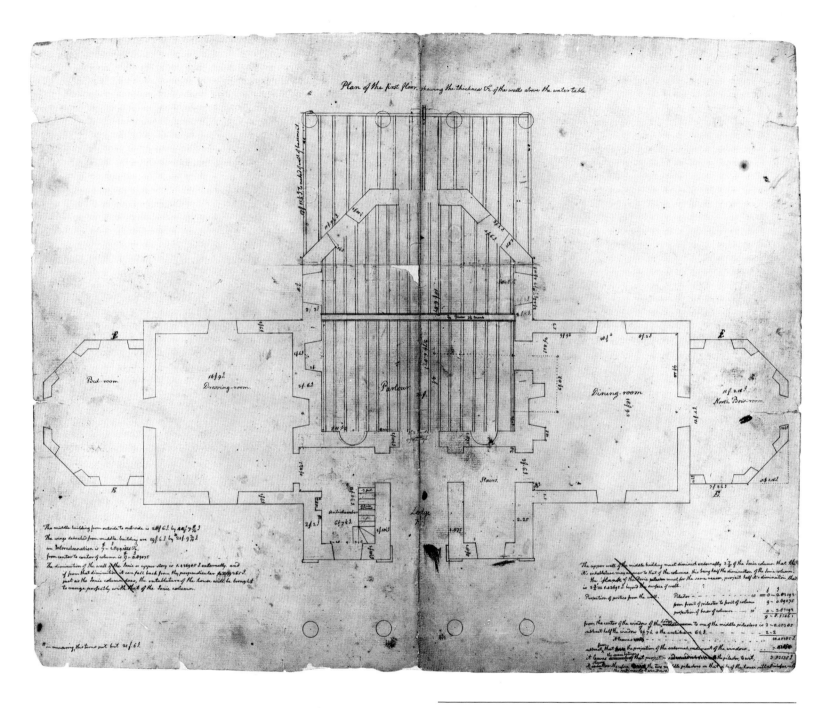

48 First adopted plan of Monticello, completed some time prior to spring, 1771. In this plan, octagonal projections were added to the original drawing, and pilasters were substituted for engaged columns. The entry was flanked on both sides by a stairwell. Jefferson here called the tea room the "North Bow-room."

by 2½ inches, a size that falls within the range of Virginia bricks of that period although of a smaller scale than at Rosewell, where the house itself was much larger.

In the spring of 1770 the work moved ahead rapidly even though he had to spend several weeks in Williamsburg, where he was beginning to deal with the difficult political issues concerning the colonies' rights of self-determination. It is not without significance that the testing of the twenty-seven-

year-old lawyer's political principles and his understanding of America's emerging political existence paralleled his architectural apprenticeship at his

49 *West portico. The parlor bay survives from the first Monticello.*

50 *East portico. The stone columns were moved to their present location from the original house in 1803 during the remodeling. Painted white in the late 19th century, they have been restored to their original stone.*

mountain laboratory in Albemarle County.

Precisely when he made his first preliminary and amateur drawings for the main block and service wings at Monticello cannot be determined. Frederick D. Nichols believes that the earliest studies may date from 1767, a conclusion based on some calculations Jefferson jotted in his pocket account book of that year. The earliest surviving sketches are unexceptional, the work of an inexperienced gentleman-amateur groping his way along and exploring those building ideas then popular in the colonies. The work on the preliminary plans continued until 1770, while the basic construction on the foundations of the house and dependencies proceeded. His main reference books were the distinguished baroque architect James Gibbs' *Rules for Drawing the Several Parts of Architecture* and *Book of Architecture*, Robert Morris's *Select Architecture*, and Leoni's *The Architecture of A. Palladio in Four Books* (English edition of 1715 or 1742, or both). As he refined his interpretation of these sources and settled on the scheme of the two-story central block with two one-story wings—a plan that seems to have come from Morris's *Select Architecture*—his studied concern for the correct proportions of the classical details became more apparent. The proportion of the pediments and the carrying of the cornice around the entire body of the house to divide the upper from the lower story indicate a growing sophistication in the handling of classical vocabulary within the Virginian vernacular of country house architecture. One of the more advanced plans during the preliminary phase is close to one found in Book 2 of Palladio. The classical loggia with its niches is reminiscent of Mount Airy, but, as Kimball has pointed out, the boldly projecting portico is a direct result of Jefferson's careful study of Palladio's treatise rather than an adaptation of contemporary Virginian models.

The final drawing for the elevation, with its central portico in two orders—Doric below supporting, as in Palladio, the more refined Ionic above—reached by broad steps, has no direct precedent even though scholars have repeatedly noted its obvious references to Palladio. In the details of the upper and lower orders, the architect followed Palladio's plates of Doric and Ionic orders precisely. The portico itself represents a departure from the standard Anglo-Palladian convention of using it merely as a decorative frontispiece applied over the main entrance and indicating the central axis. Jefferson has instead recognized its logical, functional possibilities by architecturally expressing the gable end of the central block. The first floor consisted of an entry hall, parlor, dressing room, dining room, and two small octagonal room projections balanced at either end, one a bedroom in the south bow and the other a room off the dining room.

After the small brick "outchamber" was finished and plastered in the summer of 1770, and even though work on the main house had just begun, Jefferson was able to move to his laboratory on November 26, 1770. In the following February he wrote to James Ogilvie in London giving a few details of his rustic new life. "I have lately removed to the

---

51 Octagonal projection, southwest corner. *This corner survives from the first version of Monticello, where on the final plan it was indicated to be a bedroom off a large dressing room. In the second Monticello, the octagonal projection became Jefferson's "Cabinet," or study, and the adjacent room became his bedroom, with his bed positioned between the two rooms.*

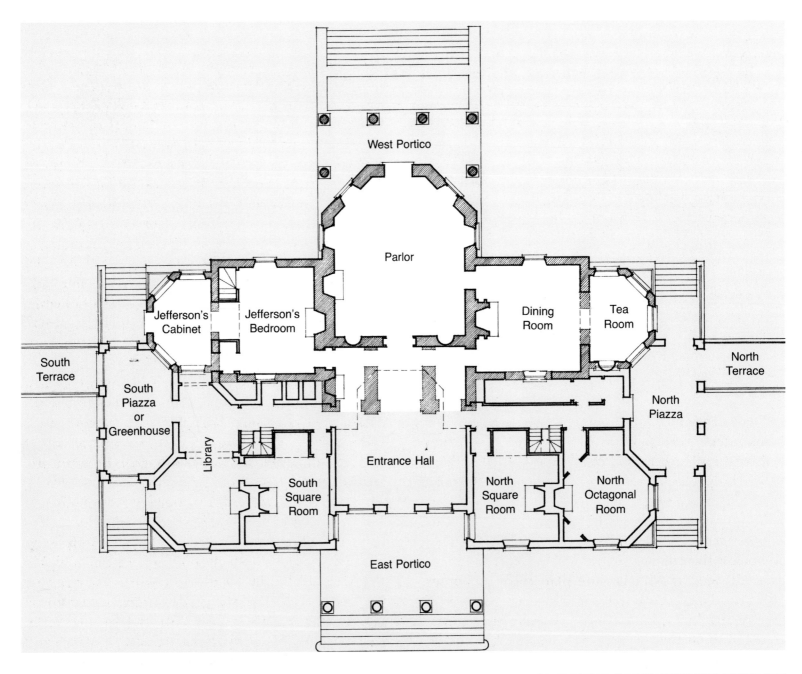

West Portico

Parlor

Jefferson's
Cabinet

Jefferson's
Bedroom

Dining
Room

Tea
Room

South
Terrace

North
Terrace

South
Piazza
or
Greenhouse

North
Piazza

Library

Entrance Hall

South
Square
Room

North
Square
Room

North
Octagonal
Room

East Portico

mountain from whence this is dated. . . . I have here but one room, which like the cobler's, serves me for parlour for kitchen and hall. I may add, for bed-chamber and study too. My friends sometimes take a temperate dinner with me and then retire to look

52 Floor plan of the enlarged version of Monticello. *On this plan, the walls of the original house are shaded to distinguish it from the later additions. Even though it appears that Jefferson merely duplicated the original rooms to enlarge the house, close study suggests a completely new orientation of the spaces according to their public and private functions.*

53 *Conjectural view of the east front of the first Monticello. Some schol-ars doubt that the second-story portico was ever built before Jefferson began his remodeling of the house.*

for beds elsewhere."

Some time prior to the fall of 1770, the first study of the general layout on the carefully leveled plateau shows the projected terraces forming a rectangular space to the west of the main block, which is centered near the eastern edge of the graded area. The two long service wings have been suppressed on either side below the edge of the central lawn enclosing an area 250 feet by 500. On the plan Jefferson notes with proud exactitude that the boundary circumfer-ence of the home lot with semicircular ends meas-ured "3715.88 feet or 1238.62 yards." The scheme leaves no doubt that the designer was a man who could deploy and manipulate a large-scale plan spread horizontally over a vast and difficult terrain, taking advantage of all of the spectacular views while at the same time accommodating a remarkably effi-cient staff and service operation hidden from sight.

The house itself was not large, but the interplay between the architecture and nature created a feel-ing of articulated space that seemed well propor-tioned to the majestic countryside spread below in all directions. The radical reversal of the Anglo-Palladian convention of a court-of-honor between extended wings and the placing of the service wings beneath the flat-roofed terrace walks imaginatively solved the practical problems of servicing the house without blocking the views with lateral extensions, as one sees, for example, at Mount Airy and Blandfield. By placing the domestic work areas of kitchen, bak-ery, and brewery on the south side of the hill while using the north exposure for stables and storage, Jefferson may well have been also thinking of the importance of solar orientation.

The self-portrait in the letter to Ogilvie of an aus-tere idealist nurturing his independence in a one-room cottage, remote and aloof, surrounded with little more than his books and an occasional friend was, like most self-portraits, only partially accurate. In fact, the periodic need to withdraw to a simple, solitary retreat removed from daily pressures, distrac-tions, and temptations was always an aspect of Jeffer-son's complex emotional and intellectual life even when he was in the thick of things. In Philadelphia there would be the small windowless study-retreat he built at the end of the garden of his rented house on High Street. "The object of the last was," he wrote to the owner, "that I might have a place to retire and write in where and when I wished to be unseen and undisturbed even by my servants, for this purpose it was to have a skylight and no lateral windows. . . ." Apparently he went too far in his search for privacy, finding the structure fit only for a storage room when it was finished because the contractor failed to put in

63

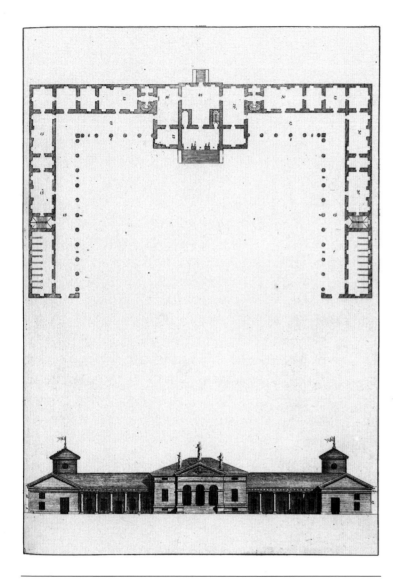

54   Plate 41, Book 2, Palladio. *Jefferson developed his ideas for the service wings at Monticello from Palladio's design for a villa shown here extending right and left and turning sharply to form a great U-shaped court.*

the skylight. In Paris there was his monk's cell in the Hermitage of Mont Calvaire outside of the city, where Jefferson the diplomat would occasionally retire in order to restore his spirit in an atmosphere of plain living and high thinking. When he wrote to Maria Cosway of the "gloomy monk sequestered from the world," removed from "unsocial pleasures in the bottom of his cell," he spoke from firsthand knowledge. After Monticello was completed, the superb little Palladian villa retreat at Poplar Forest was built by Jefferson on his lands in Bedford County so that he might satisfy this deep personal need to escape into a solitude removed from the steady procession of visitors that complicated his life at Monticello. At Monticello, he was "so engrossed by business of society," he complained to his friend Doctor Benjamin Rush, that he could only correspond "on matters of urgency." But at his retreat, "in the solitude of a hermit," he had the leisure as well as a disposition "to attend to my absent friends."

Even though he already had loftier house plans in mind and on paper the year he first moved into the small bachelor quarters at Monticello, in 1770, the appeal that the simple life had for him is again hinted at in a letter to John Page at Rosewell. Their mutual friend Dabney Carr had recently married, and his rustic domestic establishment "in a very small house, with a table, half a dozen chairs and one or two servants" made him one of the happiest men in all the world. "He possesses," Jefferson reported, "truly the art of extracting comfort from things the most trivial . . . with an utter neglect of the costly apparatus of life. . . ." Jefferson may have envied his friend's homely family life devoid of "costly apparatus," but it was not the kind of existence that would serve his own emotional and esthetic needs, no matter what he said to the contrary. Even in the elegance of his house in Paris he enjoyed the fantasy of living

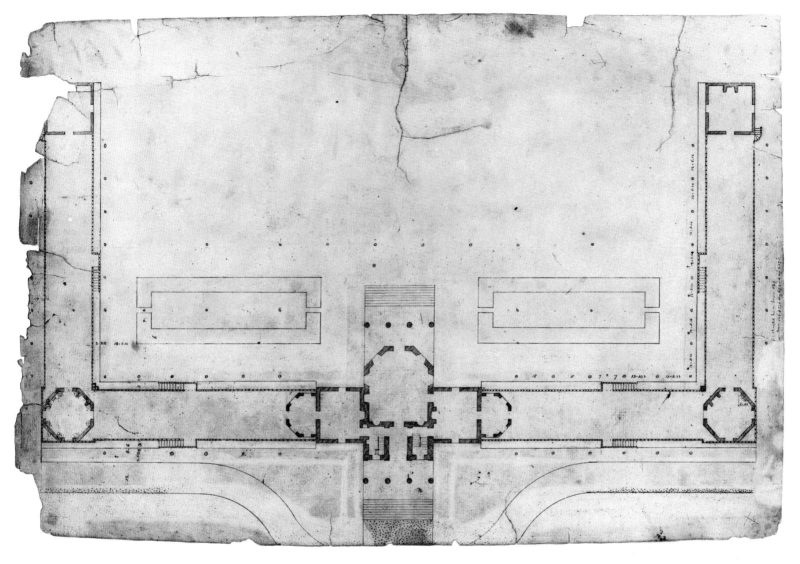

55 *Final plan for the first Monticello and its proposed dependencies, before August, 1772. The proposed octagonal pavilions shown at the right angles of the terraces were abandoned by Jefferson for an unobstructed view of the countryside, and the formal flower beds on the west probably were never laid out.*

the rustic life. To a Virginian friend he wrote from Paris, "I had rather to be shut up in a very modest cottage, with my books, my family and a few old friends, dining on simple bacon, and letting the world roll on as it liked, than to occupy the most splendid post which any human can offer." He had, after all, ordered yards of "deepest yellow" striped silk the summer before and other "costly apparatus" for his establishment, including three dozen glass tumblers, two looking glasses, one dozen plates, probably of pewter, and one dozen each of knives, forks, coffee

cups and saucers. Recent archeology at Monticello confirms the quality of the appointments of the young squire's table.

The breathtaking possibilities of the shifting perspectives seen from the heights he had selected for

56 South terrace. *Built on the roof of the below-grade service wing, the terrace continues at a right angle above the arcade and the sheltered offices on the south side of the hill.*

Monticello already gripped Jefferson's imagination, an imagination that fully matched its natural grandeur. Beyond the immediate house and its dependencies, a romantic, overcharged vision of a transformed landscape, a pastoral make-believe world of temples, towers, and statuary extending on all sides and beyond the embrace of the outstretched wings

of the house to the north and south, was beginning to take shape.

By the summer of 1771 he had fallen in love with Martha Skelton, whom he had first known while a student at William and Mary, and perhaps as early as February of 1771 had made plans to marry the wealthy widow on the first day of the next year. In his letter to Ogilvie the previous fall he confided that he had thoughts of marriage and he needed to expand his quarters to get "more elbow room this summer." At the end of the Memorandum Book for 1771, and on the eve of his marriage, Jefferson wrote out a remarkable private reverie conjuring up a picturesque landscape at Monticello in the most advanced English style and of monumental proportions. At ease with great spaces and inspired by his reading of Milton, Pope, Addison, Shenstone, and probably Thomas Whately's *Observations on Modern Gardening*, a book just published the year before in 1770, Jefferson, in his notes, projected a program of painterly sequences of embellished nature on the most advanced and ambitious scale in an attempt to translate the English picturesque landscape into an American setting. That his somewhat sentimental landscape plans—dotted with temples, deer-parks, burial grounds, urns on pedestals, ornamented springs and grots—exceeded his resources is not surprising.

Choose out for a Burying place some unfrequented vale in the park, where is, 'no sound to break the stillness but a brook, that bubbling winds among the weeds; no mark of any human shape that had been there, unless the skeleton of some poor wretch, Who sought that place out to despair and die in.' let it be among antient and venerable oaks; intersperse some gloomy evergreens. the area circular, ab! 60 f. diameter, encircled with an untrimmed hedge of cedar, or of stone wall with a holly hedge on it in the form below. [He makes a drawing of a spiral on the margin to illustrate this.] in the center of it erect a small Gothic temple of antique appearance. appropriate one half to the use of my own family, the other of strangers, servants, etc. erect pedestals with urns, etc. the passage between the walls, 4 f. wide. on the grave of a favorite and faithful servant might be a pyramid erected of the rough rock-stone; the pedestal made plain to receive an inscription. let the exit of the spiral at (a) [this "a" refers to spiral diagram] look on a small and distant part of the blue mountains. in the middle of the temple an altar, the sides of turf, the top of plain stone. very little light, perhaps none at all, save only the feeble ray of an half extinguished lamp.

Except for the clearing where the single two-story brick pavilion clung to the side of the steep slope above a newly planted orchard on the south side of Monticello, the newly married Jeffersons were met by a bleak setting covered with three feet of snow

57 Service wing. *As Margaret Smith reported in 1809: "The north and south fronts present arcades, under which are cool recesses that open in both cases on a flowered terrace, projecting a hundred feet in a straight line, and then another hundred feet at right angles, until terminated by pavilions."*

58 Final plan of the basement and dependencies, before August 4, 1772.
Even though Jefferson completed this plan for the sunken service wings or dependencies before the fall of 1772, the north wing would not be finished until 1799 and the southeast "all weather passageway" was not begun until 1801. The rooms directly beneath the house were devoted to storage and to cellars for wine, rum, and beer, as well as an armoury. Under the terraces, there were kitchens, smoke room, offices, laundry, stables, and servants rooms, taking advantage of the drop of the hill on either side.

when they arrived unexpected on that cold night of the 26th of January, 1772. The experience of entering "the horrible dreariness of such a house" without heat and with servants asleep, was often recounted by Jefferson's descendants and may have been compared with other discomforts at Monticello that became chronic over the years during the slow and

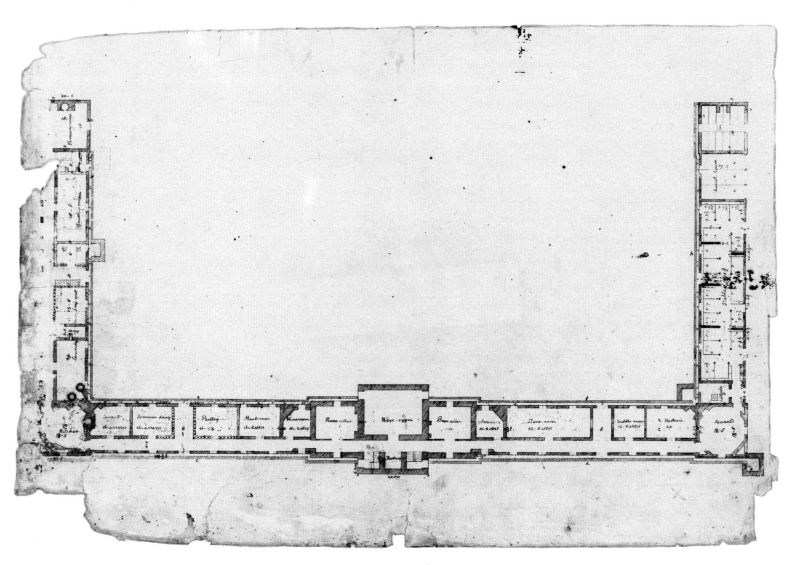

agonizing process of building and remodeling.

The work on the main house was well underway in the winter of 1771–72 when the foundations and basement were finished, following the original plan but without the octagonal projections. These were added later to take advantage of the unobstructed view over the terraces now determined to be placed eventually below the grade of the lawn and facing outward and down the mountain. But just how much of Monticello was even marginally habitable beyond the southwest pavilion when Jefferson arrived with his bride is a matter of conjecture. The northwest or dining room wing was to be the first part completed, and Marie Kimball believes that it may have been enclosed if not finished that first winter.

The summer of 1772 saw slow but steady progress under Jefferson's direct supervision following a three-month trip to Williamsburg. He had hoped to have all of the molded architectural elements made in stone, but the limited skills of local stonemasons required that this work be done in England. The estimate for the custom stonework supplied by the London mason William Gates included "a Doric pedestal . . . the order entire of which should be 22½ feet." This measurement corresponds to the proportions calculated from Gibbs' *Rules for Drawing the Several Parts of Architecture* and had been included in Jefferson's earliest surviving elevation.

Calculating and designing as the work progressed, Jefferson ordered from his English agents a number of building materials and furnishings that could not be secured in the colonies. These included sheet lead, cartridge paper for walls, and papier-mâché ornaments for ceilings in the principal rooms. The Memorandum Book of 1769 records the ordering of "a Scotch carpet 17 f. 3 i. sq." That same year he began to subscribe to the fashionable London journal, *The Gentleman's Magazine*. It was at this time that he drew up a list of desiderata for "Statues, Paintings, etc.," apparently with the intention of securing good academic copies and casts for the house and possibly the gardens. If such a collection had been assembled, it would have made Monticello one of the first art galleries in the western hemisphere.

Like his other romantic ambitions to decorate his hillside with Greek, Gothic, and Chinese temples and a triumphal column that was to be higher than Trajan's, Jefferson's dream of having a private art collection in his new house on the western edge of the Virginia colony far outran his abilities to realize these flights of imagination. These aspirations, however, cannot be dismissed merely as the passing fancies of a young, naive enthusiast, though he was that, too. They represent a part of his personality, his "passion," his "taste," which he openly acknowledged, as when he wrote to James Madison from Paris declaring his enthusiasm for the arts. It expressed his pride to run before his own time and place. Nowhere is his "running before the times" more apparent than in the earliest plans, memoranda, and notebooks recording his initial planning of Monticello. Certainly few if any of his fellow countrymen could begin to grasp let alone conceive of many of the tastes and enthusiasms he harbored and cultivated. "He had," as Malone has remarked, "set himself upon a mountain in more ways than one." Later, during those heady years in Paris when he confessed his enthusiasm for the arts to Madison, he began to collect ideas for the second Monticello he would build on his return to Virginia. His enthusiasm and eye eventu-

59 Passageway, south entrance (left). This passageway runs beneath the house above and links the service areas below the terrace walks on either side of the hill. Pliny called such an arrangement a "cryptoporticus," and it was widely used in Roman villas. William Pierson has suggested that Jefferson may have been familiar with the one surviving at Hadrian's Villa at Tivoli through engravings.

60 Present wine cellar (above). Monticello's wine cellar is directly below the dining room. Dumbwaiters on both sides of the fireplace were used to lift bottles to the floor above.

61 Stable stall (right). Work on the North Terrace, where stalls for horses, carriage rooms, an icehouse, and a laundry were located, was begun in 1801. The North Pavilion, balancing Jefferson's initial construction on the south, was not completed until 1809.

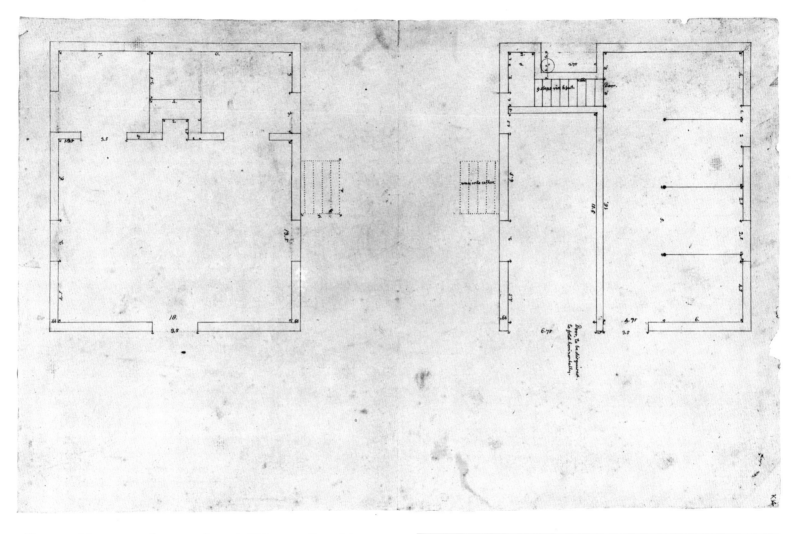

ally would accumulate a virtual library of architectural ideas to inspire the designing of the new public buildings in Richmond, the new capital of Virginia, and the even newer capital city of the United States at Washington. Somehow the new nation's architecture had to have in it a "ring of eternity" and to manifest the ideals expressed in its great, revolutionary documents and laws. The best building examples that civilization had to offer must be the model. The

62 Plan study by Jefferson for South Pavilion, c. 1770. *This early drawing was done for Jefferson's bachelor's quarters, a building that eventually became the South Pavilion of Monticello. Stalls for four horses are conveniently located on the downhill level, below the apartment.*

same standards on a more modest scale should be upheld by the nation's statesmen in their private houses. Although he never said this in so many words, the message was clear.

We do not have many details of Jefferson's married life at Monticello during the decade of the seventies, but as with Washington at Mount Vernon the Revolution did not seem to interfere much with the work on the house. In December of 1774 Jefferson wrote that he was expecting fourteen pairs of window sashes with glass from England, but the Resolution against Importation that he had supported was threatening the shipment. The number of windows ordered corresponds with the fourteen windows in the "middle building" and south wing, suggesting that at least this portion was enclosed from the weather by this time. The final scheme of the second floor, reached by a small stair to the right of the entry "Lodge" above the parlor, was to be a library with a room on either side. When Jefferson first installed his library in August of 1773, it must have been on the lower floor because his growing book collection already represented over twelve hundred volumes and the library on the second floor was not yet completed. The making and laying of brick continued after the Declaration of Independence and during the crisis of the Revolution. In 1778, Jefferson contracted for the stone columns for the east portico from William Rice. When the British troops later arrived in pursuit of Jefferson, who was now governor of Virginia, the house was still far from finished.

For Martha Jefferson, and her growing family responsibilities during the war years, the unfinished state of the house, creating endless domestic inconveniences, must have been a trial. Littered with stacks of bricks that had been molded and fired on the site, along with lumber, building rubble, and scaffolding left in place on the unfinished walls from one season to the next, the grounds would have given Monticello an unsettled look, a metaphor of the unfinished state of the country itself. Dumas Malone's observation that "the house at Monticello was not for some time a convenient one" is surely an understatement. In fact it was a chronic condition that gainsays Jefferson's professed need for a quiet, calm, tranquil atmosphere of privacy to live in. For most of his domestic life at Monticello the state of things must have been quite the opposite.

Two years after his marriage, Jefferson's wealth had been greatly increased by the inheritance of his wife, whose father had left her an estate of over eleven thousand acres of land as well as other property. This material increase in his own estate enabled him to pursue his architectural projects with even greater ambition. Still there was much that was incomplete when the Marquis de Chastellux visited Jefferson after the war in 1782. The upper portico

---

63 South Pavilion. *The South Pavilion, shown in relationship to the service wing below and the west portico of Monticello on the upper level, was built nearly forty years earlier than its counterpart on the north.*

of the Ionic order shown in the drawings probably was never carried out, as there is no record of the work's being ordered nor of its being dismantled at the time of the remodeling begun in 1796.

None of the dependencies beyond the first pavilion was completed until after 1800, when the terrace offices finally were built. These two L-shaped service wings that connected to form an axial corridor beneath the house followed closely a plan in Book 2, Plate 41, of Palladio. Space was allotted to kitchens, pantry, meat room, summer dairy, smoke room, buttery, beer cellar, rum cellar, and wine room. Offices, stables, and a few rooms for house servants were also included. Since there were a number of fireplaces in the basement area on the south, some solution for chimneys projecting onto the terrace had to be found. Jefferson's experiments on paper included the possibility of sending the smoke up through the hollow columns of corner pavilions. Another plan called for a chimney in the form of a large obelisk with holes near the top to emit the smoke. Iron pipes running underground to discharge the smoke at some distance from the house were also considered. The design for the finished chimney was straightforward and in the form of Palladio's Doric pedestal. Drawings for the molded bricks of the chimneys were drawn full scale in order to guide the brickmaker in the making of this detail.

---

64 Kitchen. *The kitchen was located beneath the right-angle turn of the South Terrace, a good distance from the main house in case of fire. Food cooked for the family meals was carried by servants through the passageway underneath the house to the north side, and then it was taken up a small staircase into the narrow passageway that runs through the center of the north wing, and from there it was taken into the dining room.*

The roofs of these offices or dependencies were flat and formed terraces level with the main house. At each elbow of the terrace, "corner temples" were considered. The drawings show a pair of small octagonal structures, but beneath them are traces of earlier ideas that have been erased. Kimball was able to sort out these changes by referring to the Building Notebook where Jefferson has identified one square as a "chinese temple" taken from "Chamber's Chinese designs, VI, 2." It would have been an awkward two-storied pavilion with four columns on a side. Following this reference Jefferson wrote, "I think I shall prefer to these chinese temples 2 regular Tuscan ones, of the height of the outchamber, i.e. the column and Entabl 15f. 6I., the module 21¼ I." Below this note Jefferson's imagination conjured up yet a third inspiration: "prefer to both the Monoptery in Vitruv. pa. 143 but of Tuscan order with 8 columns of 26⅔ I. diam." An additional note specified that this temple should be "composed of a circular colonnade taken from Perrault's Vitruv. pl. 34 and 35. . . . base and capital to be taken from Palladio Pl. 11, architrave and frieze Pallad. Pl. 12 right hand figure." The octagonal structures that were finally settled upon in the drawing were taken from yet another source, that of Lord Burlington's estate at Chiswick following the design of the small garden temple by William Kent.

---

65 South Terrace. *One of the problems with placing the kitchen and smoke room beneath the South Terrace was that of venting smoke up through the terrace. After considering a number of fanciful design alternatives, including the discharge of smoke some distance from the house through iron pipes and a chimney shaped like an obelisk and 22½ feet high, Jefferson finally settled on a handsome if conventional chimney in the form of Palladio's Doric pedestal.*

66 *Marquis de Chastellux.* *The marquis had been a commander in the French Army in America. In 1782 he visited Monticello with great delight and later wrote "that Mr. Jefferson is the first American who has consulted the fine arts to know how he should shelter himself from the weather."*

Even though there may be some esthetic question raised by these obtrusive structures in relationship to the central placement of the main house and the overall scheme of the connecting terraces on either side, we have no clearer picture of Jefferson's creative approach to the evolution of architectural ideas than in these corner temple projects and to other pavilions considered for the gardens. There is a freshness and sense of freedom with the classical architectural vocabulary that parallels his equally open, experimental approach to political issues during the decade of the American Revolution. We can follow his ideas as he plays with one eclectic solution after another, the problems posed serving as design exercises as much as functional structures actually to be built. In the remodeled and expanded version of Monticello, the memory of these early experiments enabled him to invest his architecture with a dynamic, vital quality that allowed him to transcend the academic chill one so often finds in neoclassical buildings of the time.

By 1782 most of the interior of the original house was completed though probably not finished with the proposed classical decorations. No further work would be done on it for another fourteen years while Jefferson was abroad or serving as a member of Washington's cabinet. The first Monticello as it appeared in 1782, riding aloof and singular above the surrounding countryside, seemed to visitors and especially Europeans partial to the ideals of the American Revolution to be the perfect habitat for one of the chief actors "in the theater of the New World." The fact that it was still a work in progress seemed symbolically appropriate. This was certainly the Marquis de Chastellux's admittedly biased conclusions when he first saw it in 1782. Chastellux, an aristocrat, a member of the French Academy, and a commander in the French Army in America, could not have been a more sympathetic observer of the style of life the American farmer and statesman was creating for himself on the western edge of the American settlements.

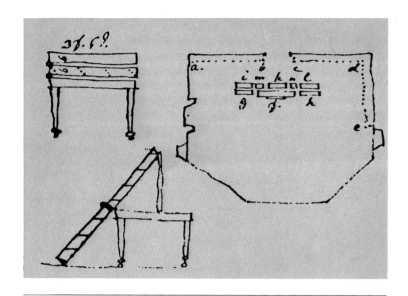

67 Sketch by Jefferson of arrangements for his library, c. 1789. Jefferson's plan for the second-floor library of the first Monticello includes a design for a folding table that can be made into library steps. In the remodeling of the house, the library was moved to the first floor.

Chastellux first saw the house "preëminent in these retirements" at some distance from the main road as he approached from the east, a visual consideration Jefferson may have had in mind when he moved the main portion of the house in the final layout so that it would be seen from the eastern approach. On an early plan, a note indicated that the orientation could "Front to the South if convenient," again demonstrating Jefferson's pragmatic approach to planning. While marveling at the imagination and daring of a builder who would have selected this precise spot, Chastellux finally arrived at the front door of Monticello, a name he thought too modest for the lofty situation, which Jefferson himself had "preferred."

"The house of which Mr. Jefferson was the architect, and often one of the workmen, is rather ele-

gant, and in the Italian taste, though not without fault; it consists of one large square pavilion, the entrance of which is by two porticos, ornamented with pillars. The ground floor," he continued, "consists chiefly of a very large, lofty saloon which is to be decorated entirely in the antique style; above it is a library of the same form, two small wings with only a ground floor and attic story are joined to this pavilion and communicate with the kitchen, offices, etc. which will form a kind of a basement story over which runs a terrace." Jefferson obviously showed Chastellux his proposed plans since the terraces would not be completed for years to come.

The marquis explained that such a detailed description was necessary for the reader's understanding and in order to "show the difference between this house" and any other house in America; "for we are safe to aver," he continued in admiration, "that Mr. Jefferson is the first American who has consulted the fine arts to know how he should shelter himself from the weather." Chastellux was not over sensitive to the way the house functioned, but he was impressed by the way it reflected the range of interests of his tall, red-headed host who was not yet forty but who had accomplished so much. Here was "an American who without having quitted his own county, is at once a musician, skilled in drawing, a geometrician, an astronomer, a natural philosopher, legislator and statesman." Blest with "a mild and amiable wife, charming children of whose education he himself takes charge, a house to embellish, great provisions to improve, and the arts and sciences to cultivate. These are what remain to Mr. Jefferson after having played a principal character in the theater of the New World."

During his visit with Jefferson, who enjoyed cultivating international friends with intellectual tastes even in his student days at Williamsburg, the marquis had spent evenings conversing with his host over a bowl of punch on every possible subject, from natural philosophy and poetry to the fine arts. "For no

68 *Jefferson's drawing for the Ionic entablature of the study, c. 1775.* *The detail for this drawing is taken from Palladio, Book 1, Plates 18–22, and the entablature was intended for the large library situated above the parlor of the first Monticello. These architectural elements were destroyed when the upper floor was removed in preparation for the building of the dome room. Jefferson's precise dimensions are noted in the upper right-hand corner.*

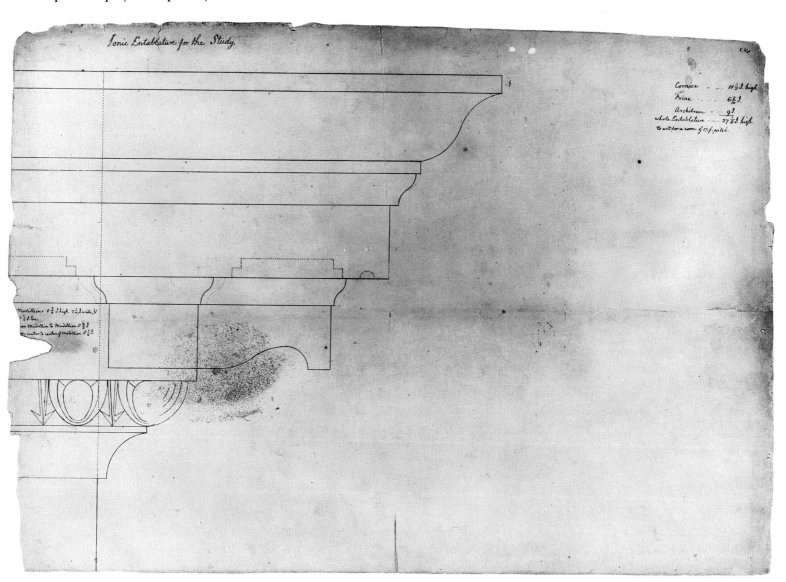

object had escaped Mr. Jefferson; and it seemed as if from his youth he had placed his mind, as he had done his house, on an elevated situation from which he might contemplate the universe."

But Jefferson's idyllic world that Chastellux thought he saw in the heady atmosphere of talks of art, books, and science—"a conversation always varied and interesting. . . . Sometimes natural philosophy, at others, politics or the arts were the topics"—was a distorted picture that did not fully convey the harsher realities of daily life at Monticello. Not only was the work on the house exasperatingly slow and probably further delayed by Jefferson's frequent absence, there was the constant threat of sickness and death that had carried off friends and family without warning. Only three of his children born during his ten years of marriage had survived infancy, and Mrs. Jefferson, laboring under increasing depression and debility, was again advanced in pregnancy when Chastellux arrived. Four months later, after the birth of her last child, Martha Jefferson died on September 6, 1782. Jefferson was destroyed. Only a few months after the Frenchman's visit, he would write a relative: "This miserable hand of existence is really too burdensome to be borne, and were it not for the infidelity of deserting the sacred charge left me . . . all my plans of comfort and happiness reversed by a single event and nothing arising in prospect before me but a gloom unabridged with one cheerful expectation." Who can doubt that the bitterness of this loss, and its association with the first Monticello as a poignant reminder of those happier days of family life, had played a part in the decision to completely transform the house beginning in 1796, after Jefferson's long stay in Paris and Philadelphia.

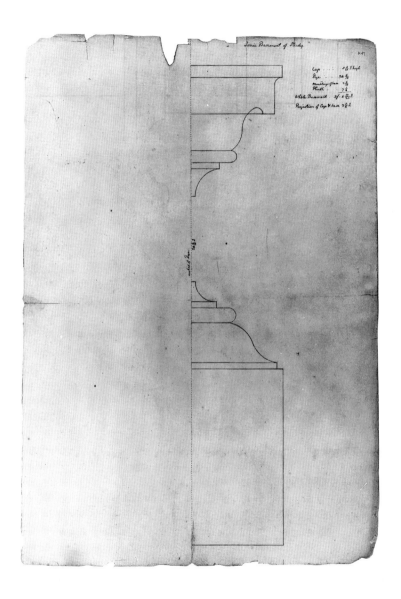

*69 **Jefferson's full-scale drawing for the Ionic "Basement" of the study, c. 1775.** A working drawing, this was, along with the other detailed plans illustrated, prepared by Jefferson as a guide to the master builder and his carpenters in copying correct classic orders for Monticello. These drawings are among the earliest surviving American architectural plans prepared for such purposes.*

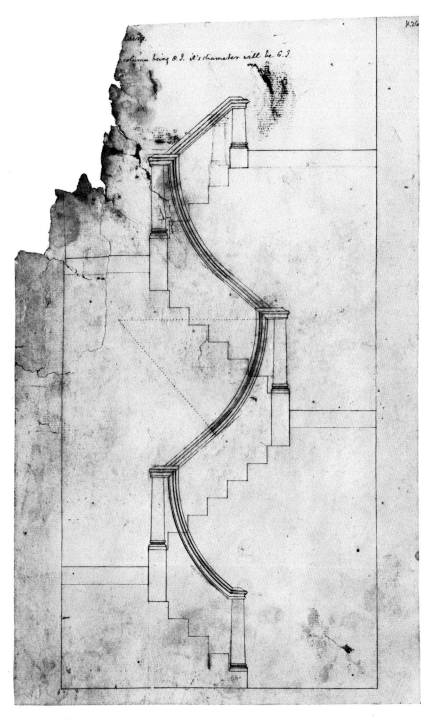

columns being 8.9. it's diameter will be 6.9.

K.26

The first Monticello, as the Marquis de Chastellux rhapsodized, was indeed a radical architectural departure from anything that had been built in the American colonies before the Revolution. But other critics have thought the floor plan "cramped and awkward." Hyatt Mayor found Monticello and many of Jefferson's other house plans unsettling, with spatial relations that seemed to grow out of "a kind of mathematical rage." Some have been troubled by a seeming lack of coherence in the internal arrangements that resulted from the long trial and error approach to the design. In contrast, Poplar Forest was built from a single plan and without later alterations.

Fiske Kimball, who more than any historian advanced the studies of successive generations of Jefferson scholars through the monumental publication of the architectural drawings in 1915, saw in the "academic correctness and superior convenience of Monticello" its importance to the classic revival movement at the turn of this century. Jefferson in his use of ancient sources was, as a revivalist, "the most Roman of the Romans," and Kimball thoroughly approved.

A few critics have concluded that the original Monticello and its successor were something more than just an experimental architectural laboratory, which was certainly true. In the aggressive determination of Monticello's remarkable siting, Jefferson

70 Jefferson's drawing for the interior stairs of the first Monticello, c. 1775. Jefferson probably did this drawing around 1775, the year that the second story to Monticello was begun, on the eve of the Revolution. Ironically, the paper Jefferson used for the drawing, one of eighty-three different types identified by Fiske Kimball among Jeffersonian documents, carries a watermark of the arms of England with the crown sunk in the ribbon.

sought an active confrontation with raw nature and with all of the implications this special tension would provide the formal architecture that would follow. Through his successive studies, it becomes apparent that Jefferson recognized the dangers as well as the creative opportunities posed by the physical circumstances of his "preferred" decision to place his house on the mountain. As we have seen, he accepted and modified the limitations of the site without losing the obvious esthetic, emotional, and symbolic values embodied in his original designs, and at the same time he created a house that would also meet the practical, social, and emotional needs of himself and his family. How well he accomplished his objective can be seen in the experimental way he worked through the successive preliminary plans, groping at first as a pedantic amateur among his books but emerging finally in full command of his medium.

As G. E. Kidder Smith has pointed out, Jefferson took a conventional Palladian feature, the service wings of kitchens and storage rooms, and then brilliantly placed them for maximum efficiency beneath the main house and the terraces, where the staff could function without interfering with the family's domestic life. In this way Jefferson anticipated Louis Kahn's theory of room arrangements on the basis of "the serving versus the served."

---

71 Jefferson's drawing of balusters for the stairs of the first Monticello, c. 1775. *This detail was drawn one-third actual size to aid his carpenters in creating precisely the effect he desired. Thin and elegant, even this relatively minor detail of his house was not overlooked by the young politician–architect, and it suggests a sensitive eye that was drawn to the refined elements of design. This preoccupation also was expressed in Jefferson's furniture, silver, and even window treatment.*

Not satisfied with the dull, commonplace, rectangular rooms of most colonial Virginia houses, he settled on the unusual polygonal interiors and projections that give a sophistication to the interrelationship of rooms not even to be found in the revered Palladio. That he had also helped himself creatively to European architectural sources, such as Gibbs and even more importantly Robert Morris along with Palladio and Vitruvius, while at the same time expressing disdain for contemporary British architecture generally, displays a maturity and confidence that rose above his avowed colonial prejudices. He had indeed evolved as a highly professional architect out of the gentleman-amateur training he had imposed upon himself, equipping his critical faculties to question and to break when necessary with firmly entrenched building styles and attitudes that had dominated the colonial American architecture up to his time. Even in the case of traditional materials and structural methods he adopted, Jefferson was able to invest his red brick walls and white plaster and wood interiors with an understanding and appreciation of their peculiar qualities that often raised the results to the level of poetry.

72 **Interior stairway.** *Elegant and yet quite serviceable, this is one of a pair of stairs Jefferson placed in inconspicuous passageways on both sides of the center axis of the house, so as not to interfere with the overall scheme of room relations. The stairs connect below with the underground service passage, providing protected circulation between the offices located beneath the terraces and all floors of the house.*

73 **South side of the West Portico.** *The octagonal salon that projects from the middle of the rear facade survives from the first Monticello and had no precedent in colonial America. It may have been inspired by a similar plan of a villa designed by Robert Morris.*

THE SECOND
MONTICELLO

74 Thomas Jefferson, *by Gilbert Stuart, 1805. Known as the "Edgehill Portrait," this likeness hung at Monticello and was repeatedly reproduced during Jefferson's lifetime. It was later adopted as the official image by the government for stamps and currency, and is now owned jointly by the Thomas Jefferson Memorial Foundation and the National Portrait Gallery.*

I N DECEMBER OF 1793, after a diplomatic sojourn of five years in Paris and three in Philadelphia while serving in Washington's cabinet, the Secretary of State abruptly resigned and returned to his farm in Virginia. Even though repeatedly he had let himself be drawn into public service and away from Monticello—beginning with his election to the colonial House of Burgesses at Williamsburg in 1769 and ending with the second term of his presidency in 1809—Jefferson was outspoken in his preference for tranquil retirement at his Virginia estate over the drudgery of public office. At the close of his second term he wrote: "The whole of my life has been a war with my natural tastes, feelings and wishes. Domestic life and literary pursuits were my first and my latest inclinations, circumstances and not my desires led me to the path I have trod." One may wonder whether Jefferson's career that had required him to be away from Monticello during his most active years was exclusively and solely a matter of fate and circumstances beyond his control. The gap between his professed desires and the actual conditions that took him away for longer periods than he was there is inexplicably wide and difficult to explain as circumstances entirely beyond his control. Against this dichotomy and inconsistency between his nature and the actual circumstances of his life in exile, it is also fair to consider more closely the equally paradoxical discrepancy between Jefferson's manifest emotional

75 Monticello from the northwest. *The portico and dome on the west facade were completed in 1809, after Jefferson had demolished the existing second floor on the first Monticello. The portico is two columns deep and projects boldly outward onto the lawn, but it is checked by the vertical accent of the dome above.*

76 Construction of the Hôtel de Salm, *artist unknown, 1786. The Hôtel de Salm, which Jefferson watched under construction in Paris, was one of the many new buildings that fascinated the architect–statesman. He wrote the Comtesse de Tessé that he was "violently smitten" with it. The Roman style of its French Neoclassicism in rationality of plan and innate dignity appealed to him very much.*

and psychological need for solitude and privacy on the one hand, and his restless, willful passion to repeatedly disrupt his domestic existence wherever he lived by remodeling his quarters at every opportunity.

In June 1793 he wrote to James Madison anticipating his retirement from public life: "The motion of my blood no longer keeps time with the tumult of the world. It leads me to seek happiness in the lap and love of my family, in the society of my neighbors and my books, in the wholesome occupations of my farms and my affairs, in an interest or affection in every bud that opens, in every breath that blows around me, in an entire freedom of rest, of motion of thought—owing account to myself alone of my hours and actions. . . ." At the same time that he confided his feelings to Madison, Jefferson was planning his escape from the confinement of working "within four walls," serving time as a member of Washington's cabinet. His sensitive, restless intelligence was also meditating the radical alteration of the first Monticello, to transform it into a house that would be far different from its predecessor. It was a building program that would continue with repeated interruptions for the next sixteen years, half of which he would spend in Washington as president.

The fabric and grounds of Monticello unquestionably had suffered during Jefferson's absence of ten years in Paris and Philadelphia, and sections of the original plan remained unfinished, such as the extended arms of the service wings. The Duc de la Rochefoucauld-Liancourt was struck by the neglected state of the house when he visited Monticello in the summer of 1796. Rochefoucauld noted, however, that its owner had "resumed the habits and leisure of private life," and that he was "now employed in repairing the damage occasioned by this interruption and still more by his absence; he continues his original plans, and even improves on it, by giving to his buildings more elevation and extent."

As early as November of 1792 Jefferson had written from Philadelphia to his workman Stephen Willis to prepare the new foundations:

Having long ago fixed on the ensuing spring for the time of my retiring to live at home, I did, when there the last fall, endeavor to put things into a train for resuming building. this winter is employed in getting framing, limestone, & bringing up stone for the foundation of the new part to be first erected. the demolition of the walls wherein the present staircase is run up, & of the antichamber (about 60,000 bricks) will, with 20,000 new bricks which I

77 Chiswick Villa, London. *Chiswick's designer William Kent had drawn upon Palladio, as had Jefferson, but the American architect's simpler taste and appreciation of vernacular materials produced quite different results in Virginia. Nevertheless, the resemblance between Monticello and the west entrance of Chiswick is striking.*

pocess, suffice I hope for the first summer's construction, building to the water table with those. I shall begin about the first of april to dig my cellars, & then do the stone-work, and as far as I can judge I shall be in readiness after that to do the brick-work. . . . I am extremely anxious to do the part of my house meditated this summer if possible. my operations of the subsequent years will be more certain. . . ."

Ultimately, the alterations and additions would more than double the depth of the original house, with a new suite of rooms and entry hall paralleling those already built and separated by narrow, transverse corridors. The central focal point would be the new entry hall leading through double glass doors into the old parlor beyond to the west. On the eastern

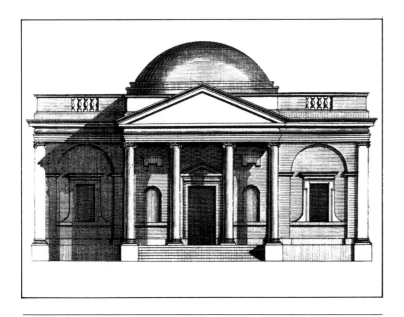

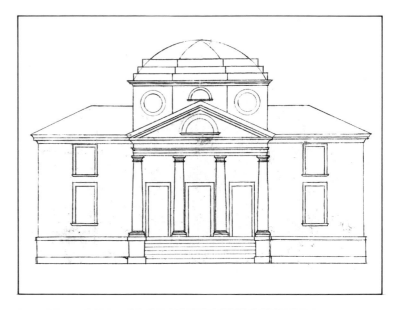

78 *Plate 43,* **Select Architecture,** *by Robert Morris. This "Garden or Summer-House" designed by Robert Morris has many elements in common with Jefferson's design for the west front of Monticello. The pedimental enframement of the central door of Morris's design is identical to that at Monticello.*

79 *Jefferson's elevation for an unidentified town house, c. 1800. This drawing is not for Monticello, despite the resemblance, but probably was done for a house to be built in Philadelphia. Its design is related to Monticello's remodeling and to Jefferson's design for Barboursville.*

facade the original portico of stone columns was to be moved farther east to its new (and present) position. At either end of the house, doubling the octagonal bays permitted Jefferson to unify them by placing an arcaded loggia between that led out onto the north and south terraces. Narrow stairs, alcoves for beds, the sideboard space in the dining room, and a number of closets were placed along the corridors in order to maintain the illusion that the house was now only one story, although a number of bedrooms would be tucked in on a mezzanine floor. The second floor of the original structure, with its library room and the flanking attics, was demolished. The removal of the original second story and the decision to build a dome over the existing parlor—an idea

that was imported from Paris—required a completely new design for the western portico. Six bedrooms were fitted into the new second floor and three more on the floor above, on the level with the dome room.

Contemporary French architecture and particularly the newer work of architects such as Claude-Nicolas Ledoux, Jean-Francois-Thérèse Chalgrin, and Pierre Rousseau attracted Jefferson's eye during his stay in Paris. "Were I to proceed to tell you how much I enjoy their architecture . . . I would want words," he confessed to his friend Charles Bellini in the fall of 1785, hardly more than a year after his arrival in France. Sculpture, painting, and music also had a special attraction for the "savage" from the New World. Whenever he could and wherever his diplomatic errands would take him, he never missed the opportunity to observe and study the design and construction of the local buildings that caught his attention. "Architecture," he wrote in his travel notes to two young Americans, John Rutledge and Thomas Shippen, "[is] worth great attention . . . in every space of twenty years . . . houses are to be built for three-fourth of our inhabitants. It is, then, among the most important arts; and it is desirable to introduce taste into any art which shows so much."

While Jefferson was in Paris, the Hôtel de Salm, designed by Rousseau and now the Palace of the Legion of Honor, was being built, and its design made an immediate and apparently deep impression on him. "Violently smitten" was his own characterization of his first impression of the elegant house placed above the banks of the Seine in the middle of Paris (in a letter to Mme. de Tessé). Both the massing of the low octagonal dome and the strong horizontal one-story lines of the second version of Monticello clearly recall the river front of the house Jefferson had studied for hours from a perch in the Tuileries Gardens as it was being built across the way. Jefferson's use of the balustrade running completely around the house above the powerful line of the entablature, as he had seen at the Hôtel de Salm, further dramatized the horizontal plane. It also unified the separate parts of the new and extended mass. "He intends that [the house] shall consist only of one story, crowned with balustrades," Rochefoucauld noted in 1796. "A dome is to be constructed in the center of the structure. The apartments will be large and convenient; the decoration, both outside and inside, simple, yet regular and elegant." The designer was not daunted by the problem of continuing the line of

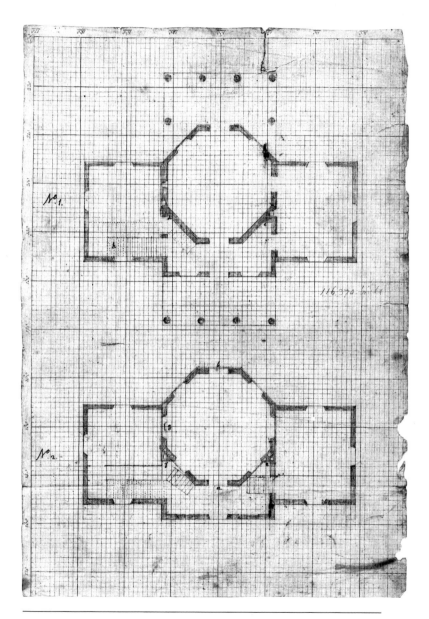

80 Jefferson's plan study for an unidentified town house, c. 1800. *These drawings for the first and second floors of the town house in fig. 79 are related to Jefferson's plans for Barboursville, a house he designed for one of his neighbors in 1817, combining the elements of a dome and a large octagonal drawing room. Barboursville was built without the dome that Jefferson planned for it, and the place is now in ruins following a fire in 1888.*

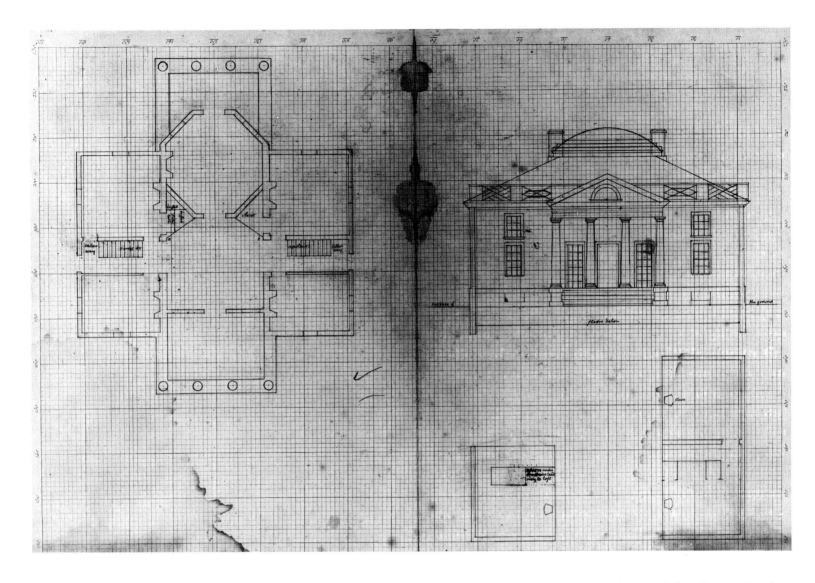

81 Jefferson's plan and elevation for Barboursville, Orange County, 1817. *Friends of Jefferson were occasionally successful in persuading the former president to design their houses after his return from Washington. His neighbor James Barbour was pleased to receive such a plan and agreed with the architect that the workmen should study Monticello before beginning. "To that end," he wrote on March 29, 1817, "I have directed them to repair to Monticello . . . to see your building and receive such verbal explanations as might facilitate their labors."*

the balustrade around the base of the dome. In that section between the portico and the house itself, interrupted by the dome, he simply installed thin profiles of the three-dimensional balustrades that read correctly from the ground.

The interlocking mass of the dome above the one-story portico on the western front gives a monumen-

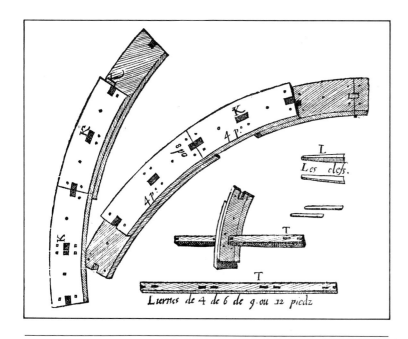

82   *Detail from* **Nouvelles inventions pour bien bastir et a petis fraiz** *by Philibert de l'Orme, Paris, 1561. This construction detail showing the French architect de l'Orme's method of piecing together the elements of the ribs for a dome was followed by Jefferson at Monticello.*

tal quality to the house that is unmatched in any other American house. It also establishes a coherence that belies the complexity of the revised scheme. "Monticello, according to its first plan," declared the Duc de la Rochefoucauld-Liancourt, "was infinitely superior to all other houses in America in point of taste and convenience. But after having expanded his architectural studies beyond books to the architectural models of Europe the new Monticello," he declared, "will certainly deserve to be ranked with the most pleasant mansions in France and England." Other visitors were also impressed by the new plans. "If carried out as according to the plan laid down," Isaac Weld wrote in his travel journal, "it will be one of the most elegant private habitations in the United States."

Even before Jefferson had written in the spring of 1796 to William Giles that he had "begun demolition of my house," adding with characteristic optimism that he hoped "to get through its reëdification in the course of the summer," he was making plans to construct the dome over the central west front. Inspired by the Temple of Vesta illustrated in Palladio's *Four Books of Architecture*, it was the first dome to be erected over an American house. Hemispherical forms had long fascinated Jefferson, and as early as 1770 he had experimented with the combination of dome and octagon in a proposed plan for a chapel. Robert Morris and Palladio were drawn upon for inspiration and direction in this experimental exercise. A few years later he designed a domed garden pavilion or outchamber for Monticello, taking a plate from William Kent's *Designs of Inigo Jones* as a model. The cap of the dome, however, came from Palladio's illustration of Bramante's *Tempietto*. An alternative garden temple design taken from Gibbs' *Book of Architecture* was also made at the same time. The scale of

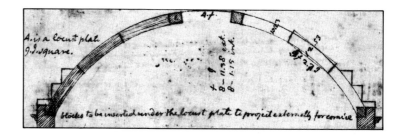

83 *Jefferson's drawing for the construction of Monticello's dome, c. 1796. The drawing illustrated is a detail on a page of Jefferson's notebook for remodeling, which he began in November, 1796. He notes that there will be thirty ribs to the dome and that each will take 63 feet of plank.*

Gibbs' dome, the stepped sides used as a structural technique to compensate for the outward thrust, and the bull's-eye windows place Gibbs in the genealogy of this most original element in Monticello's composition. All of these historical references and continuities seemed to have a special meaning for the architect, and some may have been quite personal. The fact that the light wood sides of the structure echoed the Halle aux Bleds carried a further autobiographical note as a souvenir of that first afternoon he had spent in Paris with Maria Cosway in the late summer of 1786.

At about the same time the dome was started at Monticello, Jefferson drew up plans and specifications for an unidentified town house that closely resembles the Monticello west portico. He strongly recommended Philibert de l'Orme's structural system for the dome, writing that "nothing is more simple than this structure, and it is so cheap that it is used for barns in France. a very coarse & uninformed carpenter is making mine, who never heard of a dome before."

After lowering the walls of the original second story with its seventeen-foot ceilings to ten feet, Jefferson stepped the lower part of the exterior dome after the ancient model and following the Temple of Vesta in order to compensate structurally for the great outward thrust of the dome at its base. For the construction of the dome itself, and adapted to his octagonal plan, he used the system devised by the sixteenth-century architect de l'Orme published in *Nouvelles Inventions pour bien bastir et à petis fraiz* (Paris, 1561). Jefferson had acquired a copy of the book when he was in Paris. The construction of the dome from assembled wooden ribs—"the same principles [of]

85 Dome from roof of the south wing. *In preparation for building the dome on the existing Monticello, Jefferson removed the entire second floor of the structure. His library, which had been situated above the parlor, was moved to the first floor and installed in the newer part of the south wing, opposite Jefferson's study. This remodeling led to minor design problems created by the dome, and Jefferson's attempts to resolve them led to interesting solutions, as where the balustrade cuts into the molding of the window frame.*

the wheat market of Paris"—was remarkably simple, enabling his carpenter James Dinsmore to build it without difficulty. The dome was begun in 1800, and in 1805 a single sheet of glass large enough to cover the oculus opening of four and one-half feet was finally put in place. For the interior details of the new dome room, Jefferson had once again turned to Palladio, using the illustration of the attic story of the arcade attached to the Corinthian Temple of Nerva Trajan as the model for the bold base moldings and cornice. It was a remarkable modern adaptation of classical sources to an American interior.

Jefferson referred to the interior of the dome as his "sky-room," but the use of the room during his lifetime is unclear. When Margaret Bayard Smith visited Monticello in 1809, she wrote that her host "took us to the drawing room in the dome. It is a noble and beautiful apartment," and if it were finished and used, ". . . it might be the most beautiful room in the house." At the time that it was built, the library of over four thousand volumes that had been housed in the original space was removed to Jefferson's rather more cramped library-study in his private suite. The dome room would have made a splendid library if the floor could have carried the load, but access was too difficult and there was no heat, although Jefferson had ordered a Swedish stove for the isolated room similar to the model that the Earl of Buclan had sent him earlier. The fact that the domed space was separated by flooring from the parlor beneath and did not function inside as in Palladio's Villa Rotunda is a compromise that critics have found difficult to explain.

To return to the main floor and to glance again at the changes in the new room arrangement, aside

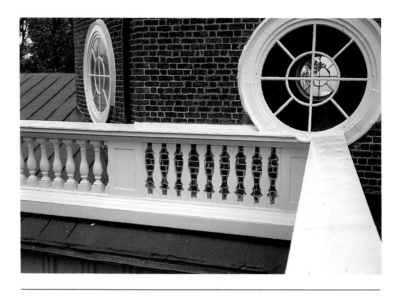

86 Dome windows and balustrade. *Another design problem caused by the dome was the necessity of continuing the balustrade around the entire house, as planned by Jefferson. Where necessary, he simply applied flat profiles of the balusters against the dome, creating the illusion of its continuation.*

from the spacious entry hall that emphasizes the main axis of the house as it opens into the parlor beyond, the new rooms on either side of the hall appear merely to duplicate the original ones. But here one must study carefully the rooms according to their public and private functions. The "rooms of entertainment," as Jefferson called the hall and parlor (which the English referred to as rooms of parade), together with their porticoes and axial doorways created within their unified spatial volume the central core of the house. The primary importance of this space is underlined both visually and functionally. The height of the ceilings of the two central rooms, furthermore, corresponds to the top of the exterior entablature that encircles the house, giving further emphasis to the composition.

87 *Detail of the cornice designed for Monticello's dome. Even in areas hardly visible from the ground, Jefferson insisted on careful copies of classic moldings that he selected from Palladio or other architects who had studied the ruins of antiquity.*

The dining room and tea room on the right and Jefferson's bedroom–sitting room on the left are of almost equal importance, as is indicated by ceiling heights identical to the hall and parlor. These rooms can be entered from both the hall or the parlor, giving further unity to the social function of this suite of public rooms. For greater privacy, Jefferson's bedroom is entered only from the hall through a door in the extreme left corner. Mrs. Smith immediately grasped the "public" quality of the central space when she visited Monticello in 1809. "Its general effect is imposing. You enter the hall through wide folding doors, which we never saw closed, and whose ever-open portals seemed indicative of the disposition of the master. . . . After a momentary pause, we passed into the drawing room through doors so wide as scarcely to separate it from the hall. . . ." Even

when Jefferson was not there to receive guests, apparently the three principal rooms could be viewed by uninvited visitors. George Gilmer recalled being ushered into Monticello in 1809, the last year of Jefferson's presidency, without any apparent introduction. "Three rooms of his house were left open, to be shown to strangers who might visit the place," he reported later.

The internal relationship of this coherent central volume is superbly articulated on the western facade by the slight set-back of the two octagonal bays on either side of the portico. In order to accommodate the bedrooms on the mezzanine, Jefferson stacked them in "two tiers" as he had seen done in the new Parisian houses, where narrow stairs were used similar to those he would adapt to the rather cramped service spaces of Monticello. As he wrote to a friend, "In particular all the new and good houses are of a single story. That is of the height of 16. or 18. f. generally, and the whole is given to rooms of entertainment; but in the parts where there are bedrooms they have two tiers of them from 8. to 10. ft. high each with a private staircase. By these means great staircases are avoided, which are expensive and occupy a space which would make a good room in every story." It may have been these spatially separated vertical room arrangements on either side of the two-story hall and parlor that had prompted Mrs. Smith to call the house "peculiar." This observation may also have stemmed from the subtle discrepancy between the absolute symmetry of the exterior and the fact that no two of the internal spaces are exactly identical. Jefferson's four-room suite on the left side of the main floor—bedroom, cabinet, library, and the enclosed loggia—flow together into one continuous space. The open wall for the suspended bed emphasizes the continuity between the rooms. The loggia placed between the two octagons to unify the exterior served Jefferson as a botanical laboratory and greenhouse.

The corresponding rooms on the opposite side of the hall on the first floor are identical in placement and general shape, but the space is perceived differently because of adjustments that completely alter the relationship between the spaces. Only the dining room and tea room, with the same ceiling heights, function as one continuous space. This is underlined by the fact that the tea room only can be entered through the large arched doorway from the dining room. The two guest bedrooms that are entered by separate doors from narrow passageways are quite separate and private, in keeping with their function.

In both the first and second versions of Monticello, Jefferson adhered closely to the principles and grammar of classical design. In the first Monticello, the austere symmetry both inside and out, dictated by the Palladian principles, reduced the functional necessities to a minimum. But in the second version, while classical precepts continue to be followed in the exterior symmetry and the strict axial arrangements, there is a new boldness, flexibility, and sophistication in the handling of the classical vocabulary. More complex domestic needs are also accommodated. On the east side of the house, the sense of movement into the interior space is heightened both by the recessed space beneath the portico and the three tall round-head openings. These large glazed windows and door all but dissolve the barrier of the wall separating the porch from the interior, allowing the two spaces to flow together. This is especially evident

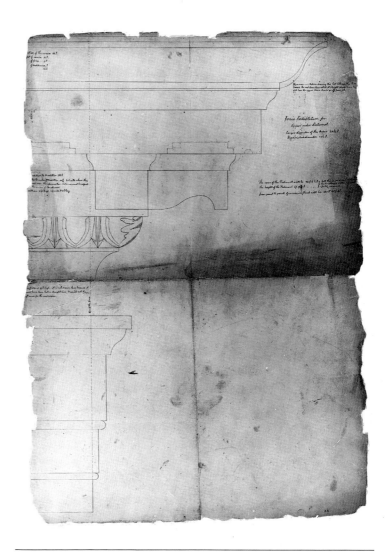

88 Jefferson's working drawing for an exterior entablature, 1775. Following the Ionic order, Jefferson created this detailed drawing for the use of his carpenters in making the cornice beneath a pediment. He notes the dimensions of the pediment but adds, "this is on a supposition the bricklayer makes his work perfectly accurate."

at twilight or at night when the hall is lighted and animated with people inside, drawing a visitor immediately into its inviting space.

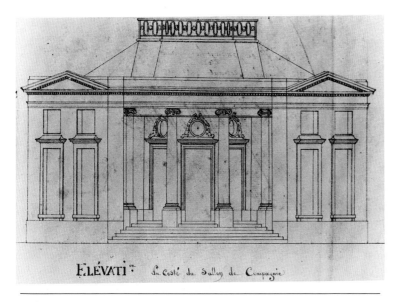

89 Elevation for the villa of the Duc de Chartres at Monceau, 1769. *Jefferson's admiration and close study of the latest styles of Parisian architecture had a considerable impact. The placement of the attic windows directly above the main ones in this villa is a device Jefferson used at Monticello.*

On the garden side of the house to the west, the momentum of the thrust continues as one is drawn out onto the lawn by the projection of the central core through the octagonal room and the deep portico completed in 1804. Looking back to the house, however, one finds that this strong east–west movement has been balanced by the vertical emphases created by the concentrated accent of the central dome, which becomes the dominating motif of the house. The tall, elegant, triple-hung windows of the public rooms on the garden side, unlike the more conventionally proportioned windows on the east front, extend to the floor, establishing a sense of the tall rooms behind. To accommodate the two-story tier of bedrooms on the opposite side of the house, the windows are also arranged in tiers, with the small

attic windows placed directly above those serving the first floor. The location of the second floor is established by the simple entablature that has been placed on the top of the first-floor windows. Jefferson may well have seen this tiered window treatment in the pavilion built by the Duc de Chartre in the Parc Monceau only a few years before he arrived in Paris.

All of these arrangements and details so carefully designed and orchestrated with such skill were the work of a mature architect. Beyond that, Monticello also served Jefferson's complex range of interest from art to natural history in the organization of its various functions. Its classical decoration provided a constant reference to the architecture and civilization of the ancient world, a fitting background for the classical literature piled up in the library and drawn on in daily correspondence and conversation. Using Palladian and classical sources, each public room has been embellished with a theme taken from a particular order but adjusted to fit precisely the scale of the individual room. The tendency in American country houses of the late eighteenth century had been toward a simplification of interior decoration through the elimination of superfluous embellishments. The ideal neoclassical interior communicated a restraint, an austerity that avoided the "barbarious ornaments" with which the buildings of Williamsburg were "sometimes draped," as Jefferson the young architectural critic had noted earlier. "Sufficiently chaste" models of architectural decoration inside or out did not exist, he complained, leaving no doubt about his own taste.

Sumptuous wall decoration of rooms was not uncommon in the grander Virginia houses of the eighteenth century. For example, painted and marbleized

90 Window, east facade. The treatment of the bedroom windows on the mezzanine floor of Monticello is similar to what Jefferson had admired in Paris. The ceiling height of the first-floor bedrooms is only slightly more than half as high as the public rooms in the center of the house, particularly the parlor, entrance hall, and dining room.

woodwork of the drawing room at Marmion in King George County (now removed to the Metropolitan Museum) dates back to the 1760s and is one of the finest surviving colonial interiors. The walls above the dadoes of Marmion are paneled and richly painted with a full entablature at the ceiling. The chimney breasts are also paneled the full height of the hall and other rooms. The overmantels in these rooms consist of a rectangular center surrounded by four

square and four long panels. This same wall treatment was also followed at Tuckahoe. The Randolph house, which Jefferson knew intimately, has fine wall paneling that Thomas Waterman traces to plans of Joseph Moxon's *Mechanick Exercises* published in London in 1703. As at Stratford, the Randolph-Tazewell House at Williamsburg, Sabine Hall, and a number of other Virginia houses, room paneling, mantels, and archways were given architectural importance by the use of the typical Georgian pilaster described in William Salmon's *Palladio Londonensis* and illustrated in several of the plates. The full-height Corinthian pilasters in the east parlor at Tuckahoe are unfluted and have curiously joined caps, confirming Jefferson's observation that no workman could be found in the colony capable of drawing and executing a proper order.

Design books gradually became more widely available in the Virginia colony, as the centers progressed, and their influence can be seen in interior decorations as well as in the overall architectural planning. When Jefferson in his own way turned to these published sources for the inspiration to finish the rooms at Monticello, he was working in a well-established tradition even though the results would be far different.

As early as 1730, William Byrd had consulted Gibbs' *Book of Architecture* for the design of the monumental marble mantel in the great drawing room at Westover. It is not only the mantel but the superb design of the paneling and the elegant plasterwork of the ceiling that make Westover's parlor one of the finest interiors of the early Georgian Period. The techniques of decoration that Jefferson was to use at Monticello in combination with the classical details

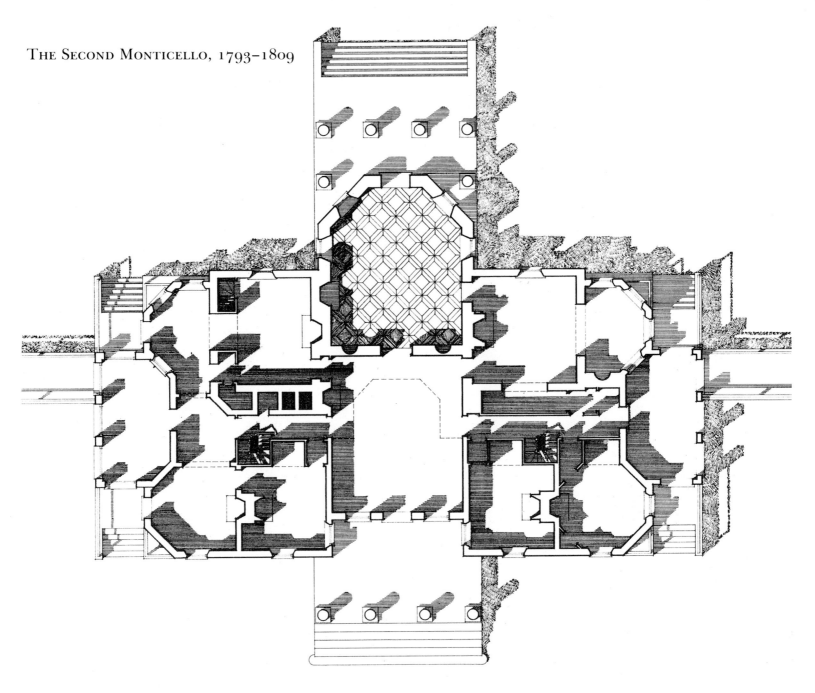

of the woodwork were used to great effect in a number of the eighteenth-century Virginia houses. Plaster and papier-mâché embellishments, for example, were cast and then set in the ceilings by trained craftsmen rather than being modeled in place. At Mount Vernon, Washington ordered papier-mâché ornaments for a ceiling decoration in 1757. Jefferson's Memo-

91 Perspective drawing of Monticello's first floor. *This drawing shows the layout of the rooms on the first floor after the house was remodeled. The parlor with its parquet floor drawn in scale, the two rectangular rooms flanking it, and the semi-octagonal extensions on either side constituted the main floor of the original house. In the remodeling, the house was doubled in depth, and the stone columns on the east front of the house were moved out to their present positions on the East Portico. Notice the placement of the pair of stairs in the center of the wings, off narrow passageways.*

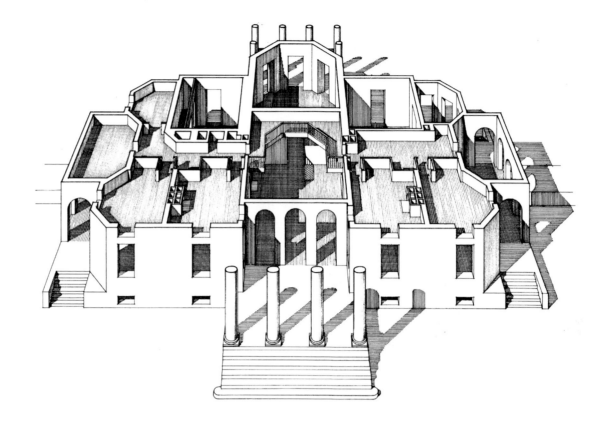

92 Perspective drawing of Monticello's second floor. *The second-floor, or mezzanine, plan reveals six bedrooms with access to a central passageway that crosses the entry hall as a low balcony. Besides the public rooms, Jefferson's private suite also benefits from the full height of this floor for its ceilings. The bedroom windows on the second story are only half the ceiling height.*

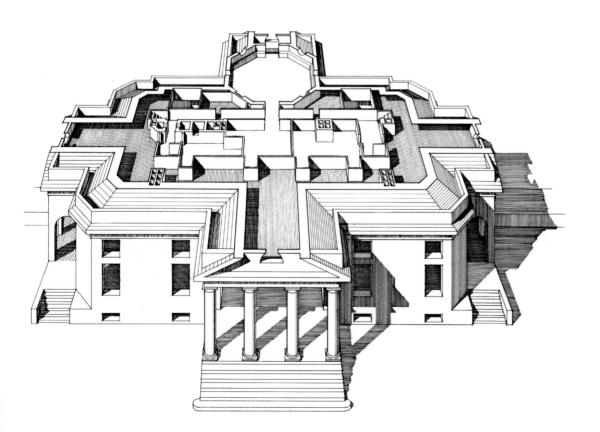

93 Perspective drawing of Monticello's third floor. *The habitable space on the third floor of Monticello consists of three small bedrooms and the large dome room. The small stairways open on a narrow passageway in the center of the third floor, and this is the only access to the dome room, a very imposing space that eventually became a storeroom.*

randum Book records that he had similar plans to enrich the ceiling of Monticello's original dining room with "papier mâcheé . . . Divided into 6 x 2 compartments and resembling as much as may be Gibbs' rules for drawg. pl. 58. upper figure, & Palladio B 4. Pl. 26 fig. C. D. F." The earlier plaster ceiling decorations at Westover had followed the French Rococo designs fashionable in England in the mid-Georgian period, with their rod-and-ribbon at the corners and large scrolled ornaments with leafage, masks, and roses on each side. By the 1770s the deliberate use of plaster as a finish for the walls of a major room rather than wood paneling appears to great effect at Mount Vernon, where the elaborate mantel is accentuated by the magnificent enriched plaster ceiling and frieze. It was at Kenmore, the Fielding Lewis house in Fredericksburg, Virginia, that the major rooms of a Virginia mansion were first finished in an elaborate plaster decoration rather than in the more traditional wood paneling popular in Georgian England. In the seventeenth century Inigo Jones had eliminated paneling from his buildings as a decorative feature and, as in Italy, had used plaster to carry out restrained ornamentation. Jones believed that he was following in the Palladian tradition rather than the contemporary style of later baroque Italian architects who used the walls and openings for exuberant decoration of high-relief plasterwork.

Kenmore's drawing room, with its plaster ceiling

*94 **Monticello from the southeast.** This view shows the newer part of the house, with the East Portico. The blank wall in the octagonal projection backs up a floor-to-ceiling bookcase in Jefferson's library. The greenhouse was created to link the new semi-octagonal corner with the original one, and a window of Jefferson's study looks into it.*

in four-corner motifs with two matching circular features in the center, represents the best piece of plaster decoration in America. Inspired by a number of high Georgian English sources, it reflects a type of conservative interior design that Jefferson identified as hopelessly reactionary if not downright un-American. For Jefferson, the classical rules of proportion and decoration that informed his criticism of English Georgian architecture and its colonial Virginian adaptations as "the most wretched style I ever saw," could be applied to the inside as well as to the outside of a house.

In his plans for the decoration of the main rooms at Monticello, Jefferson showed himself to be both a Palladian classicist and an American eclectic. In scale and ornamentation none of the internal spaces are exactly alike even though symmetry appears to be the overriding principle, but, as William Pierson has observed, once he had been introduced in Paris to the sophisticated "flexibility and logic of French rational planning he never again saw architecture as only a matter of applied theory derived from books." In 1822 Jefferson wrote to his ornamentalist William Coffee, who was working on the new buildings of the University of Virginia, regarding the private versus the public use of classical ornaments. "You are right in what you have thought and done as to the Metops of our Doric pavilion. more of the baths of Diocletian are all human faces, and as are to be those of our Doric pavilion. But in my middle room at

95 Entrance, East Portico. *Except for the stone columns, everything on the eastern side of Monticello was built in the remodeling of the original house. The four small windows above the larger ones on the first floor illuminate four bedrooms, tiered above the north octagonal room, the north square room, the south square room, and Jefferson's library.*

companied the Marquis de Lafayette on his visit to Monticello in 1825, wrote that "throughout this delightful dwelling are to be found proofs of the good taste of the proprietor, and his enlightened love of the arts." As a skilled reader of the classical grammar of design and decoration and with a discriminating eye, Levasseur carefully noted each room's decorative scheme, reflecting on his host's impeccable classical taste and his professional concern for the smallest detail. "The interior of the house is ornamented in the different orders of architecture, except the composite; the vestibule is Ionic; the dining room Doric, the drawing room Corinthian and the dome Attic." He was also impressed that the ornamentation of each room had been executed "in true proportion as given by Palladio." Jefferson's French guest, even with his sophisticated architectural tastes, was clearly taken with the provocative and sensitive design of Monticello, which was both a philosopher's pavilion retreat and a functional house built to serve an extended "family" of married children, grandchildren, and a continuous flow of guests—relatives, friends, and strangers. Margaret Bayard Smith counted twelve members of the immediate family seated at dinner when she visited Monticello in 1809. The members of Jefferson's extended family in residence varied from year to year but it included children, grand-

96 East Portico. *Jefferson installed a compass on the portico ceiling that registers the wind direction through the action of his weathervane on the roof. The clock has a second face immediately inside and above the entry, where weights mark the day of the week as they descend the wall.*

97 East Portico. *This view shows the entablature and pediment corner of the East Portico, above an original stone column from the first Monticello.*

Poplar Forest, I mean to mix the faces and ox-sculls, a fancy I can indulge in my own case, altho in a public work I feel bound to follow authority strictly."

Even though he would firmly adhere to the rules of proportion and detail of classical design, he drew freely on classical French inspiration for the decoration of friezes and mantels, with their griffins, bacchanalia, and urns. Auguste Levasseur, who ac-

children, his two widowed sisters, Mrs. Marks and Mrs. Carr, as well as the latter's six children, all of whom were there to greet him when he retired from the presidency in 1809. After this date, the permanent Monticello family included Martha Jefferson Randolph, her husband Thomas Mann Randolph, and their eleven children. Maria Jefferson Eppes, her husband John Wayles Eppes, and their son were in residence from time to time. Monticello's highly personal requirements made it not only the most imaginative, original house in America, but it would be difficult to find a close counterpart in Europe.

It is in the fascinating array of household inventions that the classical idiom of grandeur is instilled with a personal intimacy and warmth reflecting Jefferson's richly human genius and practical American curiosity. These gadgets, which appeal so strongly to the modern visitor who seems to relate more to this pragmatic side of Jefferson's personality than to the original architectural expressions of the house, were largely taken for granted by contemporary visitors, who rarely commented upon them. In 1804 Sir Augustus John Foster was amused to be shown some of Jefferson's mechanical "knicknacks," including the revolving coatrack placed in the recess at the foot of the bed, which could be turned with a long stick. The bed itself, placed in what the English visitor described as a "Door way" and open to the rooms on either side, also impressed him. Above the bed, left-over space was economically used for off-season clothes storage, and it was fitted out with three decorative portholes above the bed to provide ventilation.

Apparently Jefferson himself liked to work with his hands and kept a room with a carpenter's workbench and a large assortment of tools. "This, as be-

ing characteristic, is worthy of notice," his friend Margaret Smith wrote following her visit in 1808, "the fabrication with his own hands of curious implements and models, being a favorite amusement." His discriminating hand and a craftsman's sense of how things go together and function can be seen in his fine early drawing for the stairway for the first house. The fact that the stairs were to be located in an inconspicuous place did not diminish their creator's concern for their delicate detail and scale. The carefully shaped balustrades betray the understanding of a first-class cabinetmaker.

In 1780, one of his German prisoner friends, who had been captured while serving in the British army and then held in Charlottesville, worked with Jefferson to make a compass for the ceiling of the drawing room at Monticello. He left the following assessment: "The Governor possesses a Noble Spirit of Building, he is now finishing an elegant building projected according to his own fancy. In his parlour he is creating on the ceiling a compass of his own invention by which he can know the strength as well as the Direction of the Winds. I have promised to paint the Compass for it." In the remodeling, the weather vane was moved to the ceiling of the front portico where the face of the clock made it easy for Jefferson to record his meteorological observations. The clock in the front hall, with a second face located over the door that tells the days as its operative weights fall through openings into the basement, is celebrated. Visitors who have heard the hour strike may think a washtub has been banged, but, in fact, the sound comes from a Chinese gong used in China to "announce the approach of certain mandarins in their visitations thro' the streets." It was ordered by Jefferson in 1792

98 *Plate 2, "Ordre Dorique: au Théatre de Marcellus a Rome," from Fréart de Chambray's* Parallele de l'Architecture. *Jefferson used four plates from this volume in working out the classical details for his drawings used in the decoration of Monticello.*

and finally arrived in 1797, after prolonged correspondence and delays.

The dining room with its monumental, sunlit proportions is misleading since the room is not very large. The need for servants to have space in which to serve meals properly was reduced, however, by the dumbwaiters and other serving arrangements. Jefferson had an aversion to the presence of servants in the dining room during the long and intimate conversations that frequently took place there. A brief glimpse of those conversations is suggested in a passage from the Marquis de Chastellux's description of his visit. "I recalled with pleasure that as we were conversing over a bowl of punch, after Mrs. Jefferson had retired, our conversation turned on the poems of Ossian. It was a spark of electricity which passed rapidly from one to the other; we recollected the passages in those sublime poems which particularly struck us. . . . In our enthusiasm the book was sent for, and placed near the bowl. Where by their mutual aid, the night far advanced imperceptibly upon us." His deep need for privacy was also reflected in his own suite of rooms. "While he was a-writin' he wouldn't suffer nobody to come into his room," Isaac Jefferson, a Monticello slave, recalled in his dictated memoirs. "When he wanted anything he had nothin to do but turn a crank and the dumbwaiter would bring him water or fruit on a plate or anything he wanted." Isaac was referring to the dumbwaiter on either side of the mantel in the dining room, where bottles could be brought up from the wine cellar below. Another serving arrangement consisted of shelves attached to the back of the door opposite the stairs leading down into the kitchen passageway. Food placed on these shelves could be passed into the dining room with-

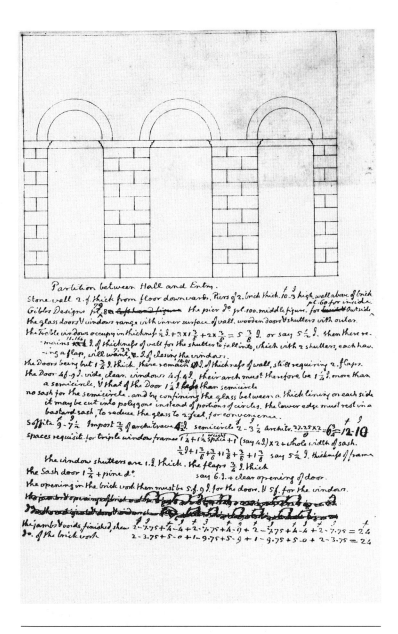

99 *Jefferson's drawing for the entry wall beneath the East Portico. The rusticated stonework shown in the drawing was carried out in sand applied to fresh paint. This drawing appears in Jefferson's notebook for remodeling that he began in November, 1796, and the meticulous calculations beneath it are typical of his method of working out designs.*

out the servant entering and disturbing the guests and their host.

Before moving into the gardens, orchards, and grounds beyond the house, something needs to be said about the importance of natural light and its effect on the main rooms, where light from the windows and skylights play over the spaces with their richly molded pedimented doorways, friezes, and entablatures. The introduction of light into architectural space particularly fascinated architects of the late eighteenth century. Larger windows began to appear, and in greater profusion. Ceilings were opened up with skylights, and clerestory windows were widely used. Solid door entries were surrounded with shimmering glass side-lights and overhead transoms. Doors themselves became panels of glass. Gables were penetrated with large fanlights that enable light from above to reach interior halls and staircases. French architects, in particular, experimented with ways to animate the interior space by bringing in light through more sophisticated engineering. The dome of the Halle aux Bleds with its glass panels placed between delicate ribs enthralled Jefferson when he visited the new building. A project to use a similar wood-ribbed and glass dome actually appears in Jefferson's anonymous entry in the design competition for the President's House in 1792.

Benjamin Henry Latrobe, Jefferson's Surveyor of Public Buildings, shared Jefferson's enthusiasm for the introduction of light but was more professionally restrained when the president insisted on an imperfectly engineered glass-paneled ceiling in the manner of the Halle aux Bleds for the new House Chamber in the Capitol building. The memory of the Halle aux Bleds and the sunlight pouring into its interior in a most unclassical fashion seemed to obsess Jefferson, and he was unrelenting in his demand that Latrobe incorporate a similar roof over the House of Representatives. Not only did Latrobe feel that the light would be too intense at times but he was also concerned that "condensed vapor would shower down upon the heads of the members from the 100 lights." When leaks did appear and Latrobe once again suggested abandoning the plan, Jefferson remained adamant.

It was during this period that work on the remodeling of Monticello proceeded with plans for the installation of skylights over the dining room and Jefferson's bedroom. He was determined to light each space according to its function. The dome room's oculus was fitted out at this time with a large, expensive piece of crown glass even though the room was off-limits to most visitors and rarely would be seen. It was another detail of light that the perfectionist architect insisted upon. Jefferson seemed to recognize the importance of light to architecture and to space as a basic constituent to be manipulated. In the dining room and in his bedroom, where windows could be placed in only one outside wall and without bay projections, the introduction of light at the ceiling level enhanced the significance of the space by dramatizing the heights of the rooms. "He is a great advocate of light and air," Colonel Isaac Coles wrote to General John Cocke in discussing Jefferson's role in the design of Bremo, Cocke's house. "As you predicted he was for giving you octagons. They were charming. They give you a semicircle of air and light." Coles also recalled Jefferson's adherence to the "Italian" rule that windows should represent at least one-third of wall space.

The white dome of Monticello dominates and completes the flattened top of its mountain. With its many entrances and large windows, the gentle and intensely personal architecture, classical in design, Roman in spirit, and yet utterly American, the house fulfilled both the practical and emotional needs of its builder. At the same time, the horizontal lines of the house and the landscape intersect and coincide in an orchestrated relationship with remarkable effect. Nature itself, in all its vastness and wonder and seen through the doors, windows, and skylights, is a physical presence within the rooms, a presence that reminded its occupant of the metaphysical implications the forces of nature play in our daily lives and especially in the life of one who attempted to live the ideal agrarian existence of a farmer, dependent on its vagaries.

One visitor, the Reverend Henry C. Thweatt, has left us a description of a storm that occurred while he was visiting Monticello in 1826, capturing the feeling of nature's mysterious participation in the architecture itself, a confrontation with the elements that

100 Plate from Alberti's L'Architectura, 1565. *Jefferson's design for the east entry wall resembles this plate, another example of the architectural references to the past subtly worked into Monticello's fabric.*

dramatized the role that light and shadow plays.

. . . the weather being unusually warm for the season a violent storm of wind, rain, thunder & lightning suddenly came up presenting . . . quite a novel & terrific scene. The cloud was below resting seemingly about midway up the slope of the mountain on the west side, its bosom . . . with elemental strife pouring forth . . . torrents of rain while the furious wind, flashing lightning & crashing thunder . . . all let loose at once . . . on the dwelling that crowned the summit of the mountain where overhead all was bright & clear. The sun shining in great splendor without the least mist which contrasted with the dark storm cloud below . . . we were in a room walled on every side but one with glass (being a projection or wing of the main building). The glass consisted of large thick plates two feet or more in width and nearly the full height of the room set in frames of wood—with shutters outside to be closed when desired & serving especially as a protection against hail and for the relief & comfort of its occupants. . . . On this occasion however, the storm came up suddenly and unexpectedly that there was not time to close the blinds till we found ourselves of what we most dreaded—and then none—neither servants or visitors were willing to venture outside to close the shutters. . . .

This scene of indescribable terror continued near . . . an hour during the silence of death [that] pervaded the room. Not a word had been spoken . . . during the whole. At length as the storm subsided . . . I ventured to ask Mr. Jefferson if it was not often unpleasant to him . . . to be thus exposed to such violent & terrible storms . . . and if during the present one he had not felt a good alarm— that for my part I had never before during my life been more frightened. . . . With his usual placid look & soft, tone of voice he answered, "I was not in the least alarmed my son but silently enjoyed the solemn grandeur & awful sublimity of the scene. I have witnessed many such here & elsewhere and always on like occasions endeavor as best I can to realize the presence, power & majesty of the almighty Being. . . ."

Or, putting it even more poetically, Jefferson had written the following to Maria Cosway in urging her to visit Virginia: "With what majesty do we there ride above the storm. How sublime to look down into the workhouse of nature to see her clouds, hail, snow, rain, thunder, all fabricated at our feet!"

When the storm cleared, the water calmly dripped from the portico onto the steps that led to the lawn and at its edge through the ancient forest to the Blue Ridge mountains and west toward the unknown future of American destiny, a destiny that the Reverend Thweatt's host had so profoundly shaped as architect and leader of the New Republic in its formative years. But the influence that Jefferson had hoped to have on his fellow citizens in their domestic economy, their esthetic values as a part of the pursuit of happiness, and in their personal relationship with nature itself was another matter. Those heroic ideals would soon be replaced, were in fact already being replaced, by an industrialism that would make Jefferson's belief in the self-contained working farm that Monticello represented obsolete. Monticello, that most civilized piece of domestic American architecture, so thoroughly intertwined with the life and values of its creator, itself would slip into a steady decline after Jefferson's death until rescued by a later and sobered generation in the twentieth century who realized that it still had something to teach a post-industrial society.

---

101 Entrance hall, looking west toward the parlor. The low balcony above joins the north and south wings on the mezzanine floor, where there are six bedrooms. In Jefferson's time, the entrance hall was his museum and was crowded with Indian artifacts, mastodon bones, natural history specimens, antlers of moose, elk, and deer, artworks, and curios from Lewis and Clark's expedition to the Northwest.

103   Ceiling medallion, entrance hall (left). *The Federal eagle surrounded by stars holds the chain in its claws for a chandelier.*

104   Frieze detail (below), *from Les Edifices Antiques de Rome, by Antoine Babuty Desgodetz. Jefferson relied heavily on the work of Desgodetz in designing the decoration for Monticello.*

105   Jefferson's drawing for the entrance hall entablature, c. 1805 (bottom). *This full-scale drawing is based on Palladio's Ionic order and includes Jefferson's design for a panel.*

102   Entrance hall, looking east from balcony (facing). *"You enter the hall through wide folding doors, which we never saw closed, and whose ever-open portals seemed indicative of the disposition of the master." Jefferson's seven-day calendar clock hangs above the entrance, operated by weights along the walls.*

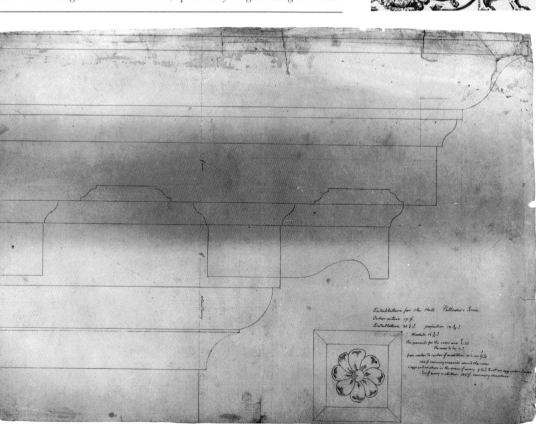

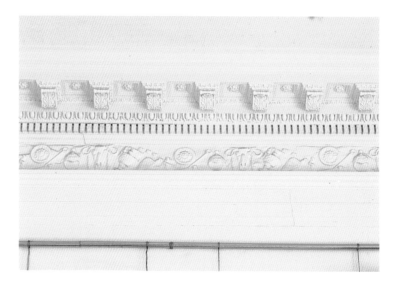

106 The parlor, looking east (left). *The central door of the parlor, linking this room with the entrance hall and the front door of the house beyond, serves to accent the central axis of Monticello. "An apartment like this," a visitor noted in referring to the central hall, "extending from front to back, is very common in a Virginian house; it is called the saloon, and during the summer is the one generally preferred by the family, on account of its being more airy and spacious than any other."*

107 Detail of parlor entablature (top right). *The brass picture rail at the bottom of the entablature was installed on the north and south walls of the parlor to carry the weight of the numerous paintings that hung in the room.*

108 Frieze detail (above). *The frieze in the parlor was taken from Desgodetz's* Les Edifices Antiques de Rome.

109 Jefferson's drawing for the parlor entablature (right). *This full-scale drawing is taken from Palladio's Corinthian order, with modillions and dentils, and was done at the time of the remodeling, 1784–96.*

110 Jefferson's drawing for the modillions in the parlor entablature (below). *In this full-scale drawing of a modillion, its volute has been cut out to serve as a template in producing this decoration for the parlor.*

111 Parlor, northeast corner (facing). *In this view, one can see into the dining room, and beyond that into the tea room. The mirror is one of a pair flanking the east parlor entrance and covering plastered-over niches from the original Monticello.*

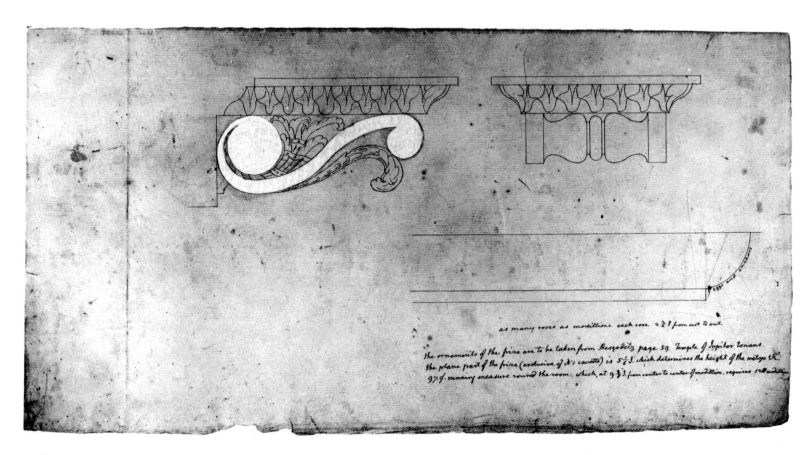

112 *Plate from* **Parallele de l'Architecture,** *by Fréart de Chambray* *(left). For the dining room entablature, Jefferson was guided by Chambray's plate "Ordre Dorique: A Albane pres de Rome." However, in the frieze he alternated the rosette with an ox skull.*

113 *Dining room, looking south (below). The door on the left leads into the entrance hall, and the one on the right goes into the parlor. Open panel doors on both sides of the mantel give access to dumbwaiters used in bringing bottles up from the wine cellar. As Margaret Smith reported, "The table was plainly, but genteely and plentifully spread, and his immense and costly variety of French and Italian wines, gave place to Madeira and a sweet ladies' wine. We sat till nearly sun down at the table, where the dessert was succeeded by agreeable and instructive conversation."*

114 Dining room, window pediment and entablature (above). The decoration of architectural elements in the dining room is bolder than in the other public rooms. Notice that the rosettes and skulls in the entablature frieze are repeated beneath the pediment crowning the only window in the dining room. In contrast, the two doors in the south wall have a rather simple enframement.

115 Jefferson's drawing for the cornice in the dining room (right). This full-scale working drawing was done in 1775, or later, and it shows the treatment of the bottom surface of the cornice. This is visible in fig. 114, above the frieze. Jefferson may have taken this treatment from Fréart de Chambray, but he has substituted diamond shapes for rosettes in the panels.

118 *Jefferson's drawing for the base of the dining room dado* (left). *Even though the cause of the revolution was taking more and more of Jefferson's time, he continued with his drawings for Monticello.*

119 *Jefferson's elevation for the north wall of the dining room* (below). *It is one of the few interior elevations that Jefferson did in his notebook for remodeling begun in November, 1796.*

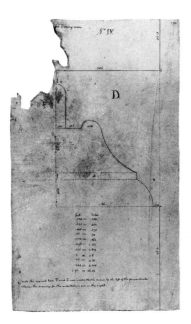

116 *Dining room, arched opening in east wall* (above). *The arch leading into this alcove/passageway is identical to the one in the north wall of the dining room that leads into the tea room. Jefferson's servants brought the food into the dining room through this passageway.*

117 *Jefferson's drawing for the cap of the dining room dado* (left). *Drawn about 1775, this full-scale section of the dado molding is meticulously noted with measurements to the hundredth of an inch.*

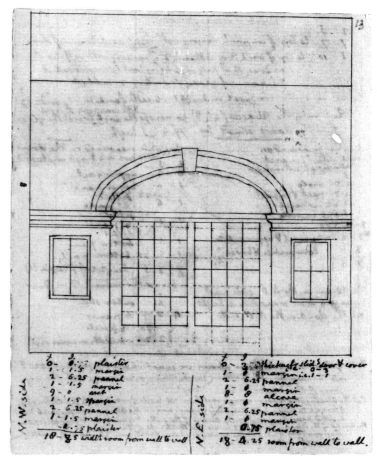

120 Dining room, looking toward tea room. *Jefferson's elevation in fig. 119 matches this view, except for the absence of windows in the side walls. The tea room is separated from the dining room by a double set of sliding doors that offer insulation in winter.*

121   Tea room (left). In Jefferson's time, this was known as his "most honourable suite" since he adorned its consoles and walls with the likenesses of his heroes and contemporaries. Inventories suggest that the room was crowded with furniture as well. The busts of Franklin, John Paul Jones, Lafayette, and Washington are reproductions of the Houdon originals that Jefferson had bought in Paris.

122   Cornice detail, tea room (above). In the tea room decoration, Jefferson returned to Fréart de Chambray for inspiration. Using a frieze similar to that in the adjoining dining room, he eliminated the ox skull and used only rosettes, even on the underside of the cornice, which has diamond shapes repeated in the other room.

123   Jefferson's bed, in the south wall of his bedroom (facing). The door on the right opens on a stairway up to the area above his bed, where clothes were stored out of season. The portholes for ventilation lend a special decorative effect to the room, illuminated from a skylight above.

124   Jefferson's cabinet room, seen beyond his alcove bed (below). Jefferson, third president of the United States, died in this bed on July 4, 1826, the fiftieth anniversary of the signing of the Declaration of Independence, at the age of eighty-three.

127 **Greenhouse** (*facing*). *In the remodeling of the first Monticello, when the semi-octagonal projections at the ends of the house were duplicated in the addition to the building, Jefferson joined them with arcades, one of which became the greenhouse.*

128 **Greenhouse, seen from Jefferson's cabinet** (*below*). *Above an open volume of Palladio—Jefferson's "bible"—a window in his cabinet looks onto the glass-enclosed piazza that served as the architect/gardener's greenhouse and birdcage. The Palladio plate shows an entablature treatment that is similar in many ways to the cornices in both the dining room and the tea room.*

125 *Frieze detail* (*top*), *from* Les Edifices Antiques de Rome *by Antoine Babuty Desgodetz. Jefferson chose this frieze to adapt for the decoration in his bedroom, and it can be seen beneath the mantelpiece in fig. 126.*

126 **Mantelpiece, north wall of Jefferson's bedroom** (*above*). *The red brocade bed hangings with gold tassels above Jefferson's bed alcove are reflected in the French mirror that hangs above the mantel. Opposite several books once owned by Jefferson is the terra cotta bust of his granddaughter Anne Cary Bankhead that was executed by William Coffee about 1820. This fireplace was the only source of heat in the combined bedroom and study.*

129 Library, seen from Jefferson's study (*above*). *In grouping his suite of private rooms—bedroom, cabinet/study, and library—across the south end of the house, Jefferson created this open space that ties them together. Access to the glazed south piazza, or greenhouse, is through the open doors to the right.*

130 Jefferson's library, looking east (*facing*). *Several thousand books were stored in this room and elsewhere throughout the house during Jefferson's lifetime. The south pavilion was used for some of the overflow. George Gilmer was there in 1809 while Jefferson was away, and he wrote that although the library room was locked "the window-blinds were thrown back, so that I could see several books turned open upon the table, the ink stand, paper and pens, as they had been used when Mr. Jefferson quitted home."*

131 South side of Monticello, viewed from terrace *(preceding spread). The lower floor of the south end of the house was Jefferson's own suite of rooms—starting on the west with his bedroom and cabinet, the glazed piazza that was his greenhouse in the center, and to the east his library, marked by the solid wall needed for shelves.*

132 Detail of south pediment and balustrade *(left). Jefferson's eye for detail is superbly demonstrated in the meeting of pediment, balustrade, and entablature at this corner. The small attic window of a bedroom has been deftly incorporated into the frieze.*

133 Detail of entablature, north piazza *(below). The classical decoration of the north piazza was taken from Fréart de Chambray's* Parallele de l'Architecture, *Plate 3, "Ordre Dorique au Termes de Diocletien à Rome." Jefferson was also to use this decoration for Pavilion I of the University of Virginia, as well as other details that first went into Monticello's design.*

134 Alcove bed, north octagonal room (above). *Jefferson saw alcove beds in Paris and adopted them for his houses in Philadelphia and Poplar Forest as well as at Monticello. As Mrs. Thornton noted in 1802, "When we went to bed we had to mount a little ladder of a staircase about 2 feet wide and very steep into rooms with the beds fixed up in recesses in the walls—the windows square and small turning in pivots. Everything has a whimsical and droll appearance."*

135 Detail of The Column House, Désert de Retz (right). *Jefferson and Maria Cosway visited the Désert and may have seen the fashionable alcove beds that closely resemble those he later introduced in Virginia.*

136 Dome room (*facing*). *"It is a noble and beautiful apartment," wrote Margaret Smith of the dome room, but it "was not furnished and being in the attic story is not used." Its purpose is unknown, but Jefferson would have agreed with Philip Johnson's remark that "The worst thing about building something is to have to think of a reason for doing it."*

137 Dome, above west portico (*above*). *References to the architects de l'Orme, Gibbs, Kent, Palladio, and Morris are seen in this single grouping of design elements.*

138 Cornice and molding details above door, dome room (left). Jefferson's orchestration of the classical vocabulary in an original way was never better than in this design passage.

139 Doorway, dome room (bottom left). Though few guests ever saw it, this doorway, held in place by the classical baseboard on either side, is one of the most beautiful entries in the entire house.

140 Baseboard, dome room (above). Monumental in scale and elaborately capped, this baseboard in what Jefferson also called his "Sky Room" was inspired, according to his own notes, by Plate 18, "Attic from temple of Nerva Trajan," in Book 4 of Andrea Palladio's Four Books of Architecture, published in 1570, a major source of classical Roman design.

141 Circular window, dome room (facing). Jefferson was very much concerned with the vistas from Monticello, even to the extent of placing the house's dependencies below grade level. He planned to build a dramatic observation tower on top of Carter's Mountain, visible through the window and nearly half a mile away.

THE
LANDSCAPE

142 The vegetable garden. *A fresh and abundant supply of vegetables was essential to the welfare and health of the Monticello establishment. The first vegetable garden was laid out in 1774, on terraces just above the orchard. The plot was 80 feet wide and 668 feet long.*

IF THE YOUNG THOMAS JEFFERSON, the political and social visionary, held exalted hopes for the future of the American people, he was prepared to lean into that future from a spectacular perch. The placing of Monticello on the first rise of the Southwestern Mountains—had Jefferson done nothing else—would have established him as one of our most inspired early landscape architects. The authoritative commitment with which he went about preparing the top of the low mountain, known from earliest childhood, enabled him to establish the center of a personal world he would gradually create to his own imaginative specifications over the next forty years. Native stands of majestic timber that encircled the sides of the mountains remained—"the noblest gardens may be made without expense. We have only to cut out the superabundant plants"— except where he placed the lawn, orchards, two gardens, and roundabout drives, until his death. He repeatedly wrote to friends and told visitors of the constant stimulus this "sublime," awesome scene gave to his imagination through its changing moods and seasons. Pope's estate at Twickenham was said to have had a special "genius" worthy of its creator, and the genius of Monticello's environment, which Jefferson constantly consulted, joins Voltaire's Ferney and Monet's Giverny to give new resonance and meaning to Pope's admonition to "consult the Genius of the Place in all; That tells the Waters or to rise, or fall."

The spot that Jefferson had selected—remote, noble, and proudly commanding spectacular views in all directions—identifies his imagination as much with the romanticism of the late eighteenth century as with Pliny's classical scenes of the Italian countryside. The extent to which his youthful fantasies were fired by the extravagant literary imagery of the period can be seen in the continuation of a passage in the Memorandum Book of 1771 recording his thoughts on the landscape planning for the new estate.

. . . at the spring on the North side of the park.

a few feet below the spring level the ground 40 or 50 f. sq. let the water fall from the spring in the upper level over a terrace in the form of a cascade. then conduct it along the foot of the terrace to the Western side of the level, where it may fall into a cistern under a temple, from which it may go off by the western border till it falls over another terrace at the Northern or lower side. let the temple be raised 2.f. for the first floor of stone under this is the cistern, which may be a bath or anything else. the Ist story arches on three sides; the back or western side being close because the hill there comes down, and also to carry up stairs on the outside. the 2^d story to have a door on one side, a spacious window in each of the other sides, the rooms each 8. f. cube; with a small table and a couple of chairs. the roof may be Chinese, Grecian, or in the taste of the Lantern of Demosthenes at Athens.

the ground just about the spring smoothed and turfed; close to the spring a sleeping figure reclined on a plain marble slab, surrounded with turf; on the slab this inscription:

> *Hujus nympha loci, sacri custodia fontis*
> *Dormio, dum blandae sentio murmur aquae*
> *Parce meum, quisquis tangis cava marmora, sommum*
> *Rumpere; si bibas, sive lavere, tace.*

---

143 Aerial view of Monticello from the west. *Directly in front of the house is the great lawn, bordered by the serpentine walk, and below that the first roundabout. As Mrs. Thornton wrote in 1802, "There is something grand and awful than convenient in the whole place. A situation you would rather look at now and then than inhabit."*

near the spring also inscribe on stone, or a metal plate fastened to a tree, these lines: "*Beatus ille qui procul negotiis, Ut prisca gens mortlium, Paterna rura bobus exercet suis, solutus omni foenore; Forumque vitat et superba civium*

144 Thomas Jefferson *by Charles-Balthazar-Julien Fevret de Saint-Memin, 1804. Jefferson, at sixty-one, was approaching the end of his first term as president, and the remodeling of Monticello was well advanced, when the French artist Saint-Memin drew this profile.*

Potentiorum limina. Liget jacere modo sub antiqua ilice, modo in tenaci gramine: Labuntur altis interim ripis aquae; Quernuntur in silvis aves; Fontesque lymphis obstrepunt manantibus, somnos quod invitet leves." plant trees of Beech and Aspen about it. open a vista to the millpond, river, road, etc. qu, if a view to the neighboring town would have a good effect? intersperse in this and every other part of the ground (except the environs of the Burying ground) abundance of Jessamine, Honeysuckle, sweet briar, etc. under the temple, an Aeolian harp, where it may be concealed as well as covered from the weather.

This would be better.

the ground above the spring being very steep, dig into the hill and form a cave or grotto. build up the sides and arch with stiff clay. cover this with moss. spangle it with translucent pebbles from Hanovertown, and beautiful shells from the shore at Burwell's ferry. pave the floor with pebbles. let the spring enter at a corner of the grotto, pretty high up the side, and trickle down, or fall by a spout into a basin, from which it may pass off through the grotto. the figure will be better placed in this. form a couch of moss. the English inscription will then be proper.

> *Nymph of the grot, these sacred springs I keep,*
> *And to the murmur of these waters sleep;*
> *Ah! spare my slumbers! gently tread the cave!*
> *And drink in silence or in silence lave!*

The ground in General

thin the trees. cut out stumps and undergrowth. remove old and other rubbish, except where they may look well. cover the whole with grass. intersperse Jessamine, honeysuckle, sweet briar, and even hardy flowers which may not require attention. keep in it deer, rabbits, Peacocks, Guinea poultry, pigeons, etc. let it be an asylum for hares, squirrels, pheasants, partridges, and every other wild animal (except those of prey). court them to it, by laying food for them in proper places, procure a buck-elk, to be, as it were, monarch of the wood; but keep him shy, that his appearance may not lose its effect by too much

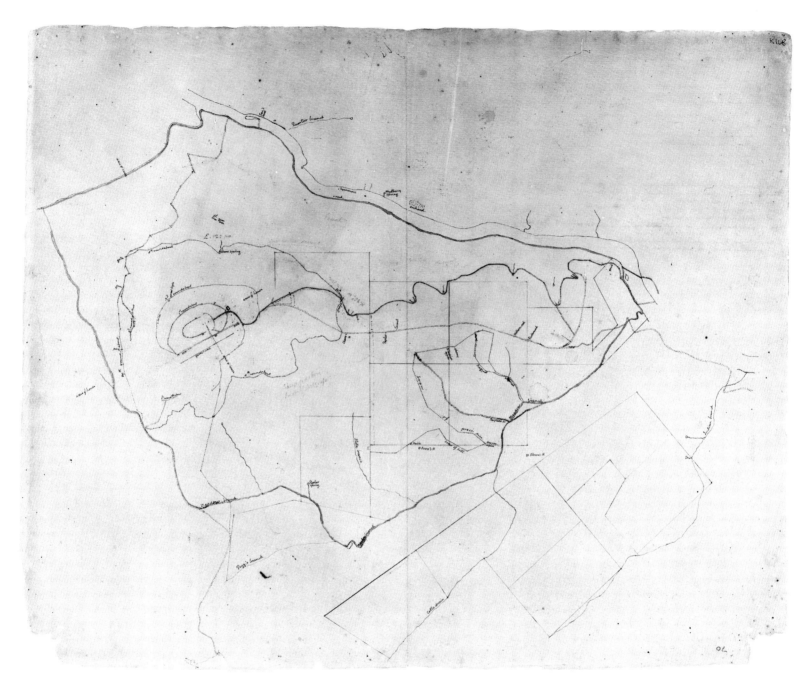

familiarity. a buffalo might be confined also. inscriptions in various places, on the bark of trees or metal plates suited to the character or expression of the particular spot.

benches or seats of rock or turf.

145 General plan of the Monticello lands, 1806. *Jefferson's plan of the estate shows the location of the house and grounds in relation to the Rivanna River, and the long, twisting road leading up to the house is clearly delineated, along with springs, branches, and even individual trees of note.*

The conventional account of the origins of the picturesque landscape garden of the English school of the eighteenth century places important emphasis on the significance of painting and especially the landscape views of Claude Lorraine and Salvator Rosa. "All gardening is landscape," said Pope, and English garden enthusiasts have insisted that their first observations of nature came from paintings. But in Britain's American colonies there were no calm and idyllic Claudian canvases or Rosa's romantic wildernesses of roaring torrents, twisted trees, and rock dells to inspire Virginia gardeners and to make

146 Jefferson's survey of Monticello, 1803. This map of Monticello, "with house and offices," shows the routes of the four roundabouts with which Jefferson encircled his mountain. Mulberry Row, the site of the plantation's industries, was the straight road to the south of the house where weaving, nail-making, blacksmithing, and joinery were carried out.

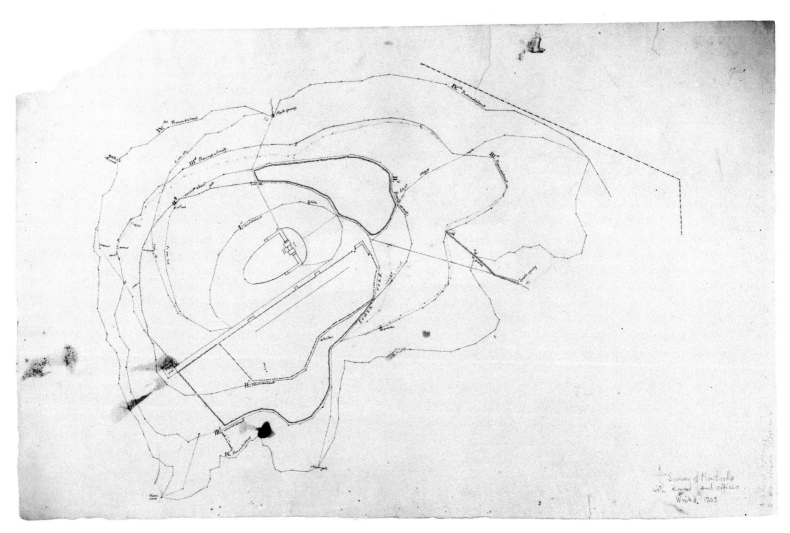

them realize how an artist's perception can improve nature. Like his contemporaries in Europe, Jefferson the student of classical poets probably derived his appreciation of nature first of all from ancient literary descriptions of Arcadia by Virgil and Homer. Later European poets that he read and knew well—Tasso, Shakespeare, and Milton—celebrated the same heroic scenes of glades, woods, streams, and meadows that could well have served as elevated descriptions of the Virginia countryside in which Jefferson grew up. The obvious hint of these literary inspirations in the jottings of his Memorandum Book, as a guide to his landscape plans, evokes some of the imagery of these romantic and poetic sources. The "unfrequented vale in the park, where is no 'sound to break the stillness but a brook, that bubbling winds among the weeds'"; "the small Gothic temple of antique appearance"; the marble slab with its Latin inscription; the aeolian wind harp hanging under a

pavilion; all conjure up visions of a literary ideal rather than a scene drawn from a painting by Claude or Gaspard Poussin.

It was during this same period of mental landscape planning that Jefferson made his tracings of garden temples from Gibbs, the plans for the Chinese pavilions at the corners of the L-shaped terraces on either side of the house, and the drawings for unusual towers designed to be used as observation points and "eye catchers" in the distant landscape. It was one of these projects that included the proposal for a triumphal column higher than that of Trajan's in Rome.

An early plan of the first Monticello shows two formal, rectangular flowerbeds on either side of the west portico, a conventional, formal architectural treatment of the lawn immediately around the house. Jefferson would have seen similar geometric garden treatments at Williamsburg, Mount Airy, and possibly at Rosewell, where the layouts followed the dictates of John Jones' translation of A. F. Dezallier d' Argentville's *The Theory and Practice of Gardening* published in 1712. It was Jefferson's first garden book, which he purchased when he was twenty-one, but its codification in plans and descriptions of the classical garden inspired by Andre LeNotre had little appeal to a young man raised in the exhilarating natural setting—hills, river, mountain, and woods—of the Virginia countryside. As early as 1765, he had read William Shenstone's *Works* describing the Englishman's ornamental farm near Birmingham called The Leasowes. Shenstone's informal accommodation of landscape esthetics with the practical activities of agriculture was an approach that made sense in the American environment. Joseph Addison's suggestion that a whole estate could be turned into a "kind of garden" was easily visualized in virgin eighteenth-century Piedmont. A plan of Shenstone's farm was reproduced in the book, and Jefferson was sufficiently impressed to include it in a basic library recommended to Robert Skipwith in 1771. Thomas Whately, whose *Observations on Modern Gardening* he also owned, said that The Leasowes represented a perfect picture of Shenstone's mind, "simple, elegant and amiable," an accolade Jefferson himself might have used to describe his own landscaping aspirations at Monticello.

Both Shenstone and Whately were to have a significant influence on Jefferson's evolving landscape ideas, particularly when the grounds were extensively redesigned during the first decade of the nineteenth century. When Jefferson and John Adams made their English garden tour together in 1786, following Whately's itinerary, Jefferson wrote that he "always walked over the gardens with his book in my hand," noting carefully "the particular spots he described . . . and saw with wonder, that his fine imagination had never been able to seduce him from the truth." Whately's description of the elements of the integrated landscape in which architecture was carefully balanced must have impressed Jefferson. "Nature, always simple," Whately wrote, "employs but four materials in the composition of her scenes, ground, wood, water and rock. The cultivation of nature has introduced a fifth species, the buildings requisite for the accommodation of men."

Just as he had combined a practical understanding of building with his bookish study of the rules of architecture, Jefferson also learned the basic journeyman skills of surveying, inheriting his father's surveying and drafting equipment, which he was able to put to use when the work on the new house began. He also learned from his father how to read the topography as a mapmaker, allowing him to focus on the landscape forms—the land, rivers, forests, hills, and mountain ranges—with an eye expert in reading the physical evidence of his natural environs.

The other passion—it seemed to transcend mere skill—that further equipped Jefferson to carry out large-scale gardening projects was his love of planting, cultivation, and the carrying on of all the countryman's activities as a farmer, with a scientific discipline that enabled him to study the minutest details of botany and horticulture in a professional way. It was an enthusiasm throughout his life, one

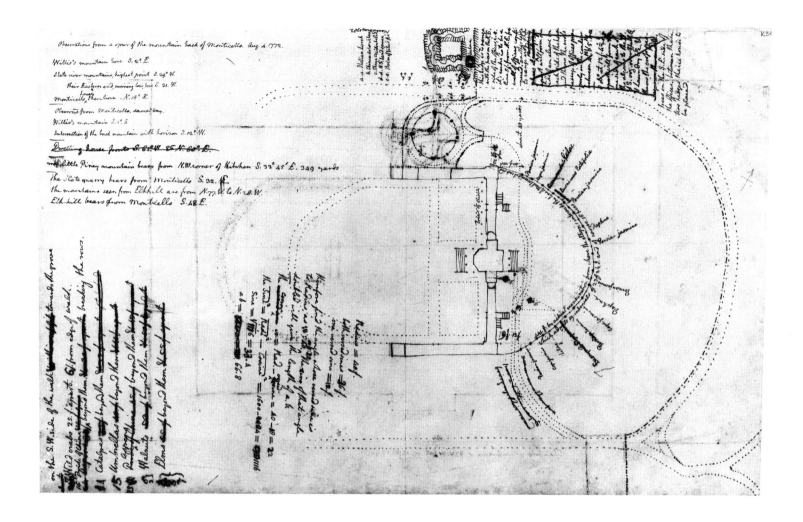

148 Jefferson's general plan of the Monticello grounds. *According to Frederick D. Nichols, Jefferson initially drew this plan before May, 1768. It was a working drawing and was changed and altered over the years, as is clear from all of the emendations.*

that he repeatedly acknowledges in his letters. At the close of his term as Secretary of State, with his thoughts turning to the prospect of the quiet rural life of Monticello, he wrote to Washington, "I return to farming with an ardor which I scarcely knew in my youth and which has got the better entirely of my love of study." After he had completed the rebuilding of Monticello, with its new garden layouts, he confided to the painter Charles Willson Peale that if heaven had given him a choice of a profession or calling, it would have been as a gardener and farmer. "No occupation is so delightful to me as the cul-

ture of the earth and no culture comparable to that of the garden."

By 1769, with the top of the mountain leveled and actual construction underway, we get a clear picture from the Garden Book of Jefferson's preoccupation not only with the building of the house but with the planting and development of supporting orchards

149 Woods on Monticello's slopes. *"The sides of the mountain covered with wood, with scarcely a speck of cultivation, presents a fine contrast to its summit, crowned with a noble pile of buildings"—as Margaret Smith described the site, after her first visit to Monticello.*

and gardens as well, where seedling pears, peaches, nectarines, pomegranates, New York apples, apricots, almonds, and figs were set out on the southeastern slope below the house site, an ideal, protected spot. The location of the first vegetable garden in 1774, on terraces just above the orchard and in view of the upper lawn of the house itself, also took advantage of the southern exposure. The terrace's length of 668 feet and width of 80 feet give some idea of the scale of production required by the Monticello "family." That establishment to be housed, clothed, and fed included forty-two "proper slaves of Thomas Jefferson" according to the earliest census recorded in the Farm Book in 1774. Twenty-nine were assigned to Monticello itself. This was before his slave holdings were tripled by inheritance from the estate of his wife's father John Wayles the same year. At the time of his retirement or shortly after, in 1810, the Monticello rolls listed eighty-six slaves. By the time of the forced sale after Jefferson's death in 1827, fifty-four were assigned to the home plantation in the inventory.

Antonio Giannini wrote in 1786 that Monticello's orchard was in full production as an important element in Jefferson's self-contained Elysium, producing both the amenities as well as the necessities of the good life. Jefferson's grandniece Jane Blair Smith recalled the former president's climbing cherry trees and throwing luscious bunches of fruit into the waiting aprons and hats. "When our childish appetites were sated, the next research was among the fig bushes which grew in rich luxuriance under the terraced wall—such figs." The profusion of fresh fruit on the table impressed more than one visitor. "After tea, fruit as usual was brought, of which he said to partake," Margaret Smith wrote. "The figs were very fine and I ate them with greater pleasure from their having been planted, rear'd and attended by him with peculiar care. . . ."

Even when he was away for long stretches during the years in Europe, Jefferson wrote to Giannini giving him detailed directions in the care of the orchard. "I depend also that you will fill up my apple orchard on the North side of the mountain with the kind of trees I directed, and winding the rows on a level round the hill as was begun before I came away," he wrote from Paris in February of 1786. If fruit trees died, he continued, they were to be replaced imme-

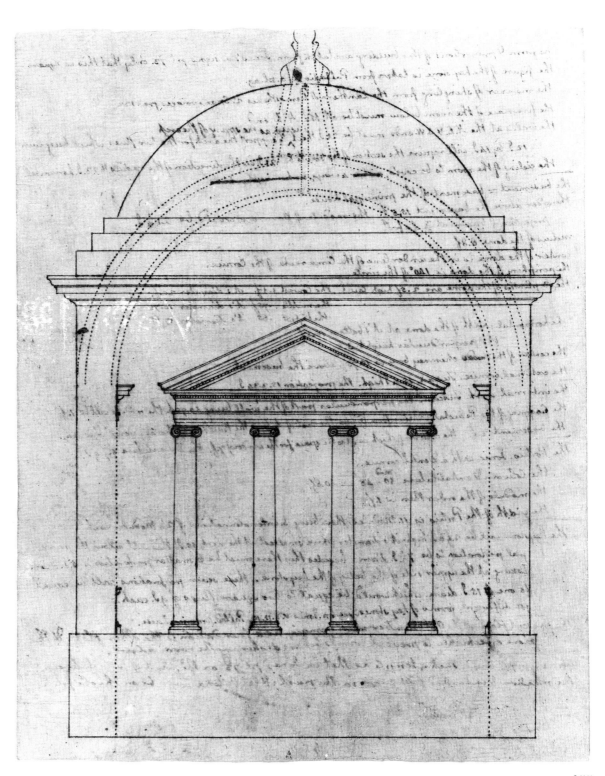

150 Jefferson's drawing for a decorative outchamber at Monticello. *Jefferson consulted the work of Bramante, Palladio, Gibbs, and Kent in developing the design of this garden pavilion. It is similar to garden structures then being built in England, even though Jefferson would not see English gardens until 1786, some ten years after this drawing was made.*

diately with the same variety. Orchard production was, of course, primarily for the feeding of the people who lived at Monticello, but it also provided an organized way to ornament the mountainside and to effect a transition into the wilderness beyond. By 1793, a second orchard was laid out and planted on the north side of the house, while some five hundred peach

151 South terrace, viewed from Monticello's second floor. *"Long terraces, about six feet above the ground, and forming three sides of a square, serve as a prominade in good weather, and cover the offices attached to the building," as George Tucker wrote after his visit. Jefferson originally planned to erect decorative pavilions at the right-angle turns of both terraces, as was indicated on the final plan drawing for the first Monticello, the one with the proposed dependencies, fig. 55. It is interesting to note the similarity between the cistern cover, at the terrace corner, and the dovecote roof in fig. 152.*

trees were set out as boundaries to fields to serve as a tree hedge.

From the beginning, Jefferson envisioned the landscape around Monticello integrated into agricultural and food production as a thriving embodiment of his political ideal of the agrarian state. Through his imaginative planning, beginning with the first work on the buildings—experimenting, learning through travel, and by consulting the published experts—he was able to achieve much of his esthetic goal. "It is the intention of the proprietor," Mrs. Smith reported, "to blend cultivation and forest, in such a manner, as to present that variety most grateful to the eye of taste." However, the economic goal of self-sufficiency at Monticello, to which its creator always aspired, forever eluded its master, as Francis L. Berkeley, Jr., has pointed out in his introduction to Jefferson's Farm Book. The large operating expenses of his plantation required cash crops such as tobacco more than the balanced, diversified kind of farming achieved at Mount Vernon by Washington.

The economic foundation of Monticello was first and always based on the established system of slavery, with all of those violations of and contradictions to Jefferson's political and humanistic ideals that the wretched system implies. Even though Jefferson hated it, never doubted that it would be destroyed, and had worked toward the modification of its legal structure in his youth, it was the prevailing labor system that he had inherited along with his land holdings, a curse from which he was never able to escape. A consolidated roster in 1774, after the settlement of his father-in-law's estate, records 135 "people" assigned to him from the estate. That same year his landholdings included five-thousand acres in Albe-

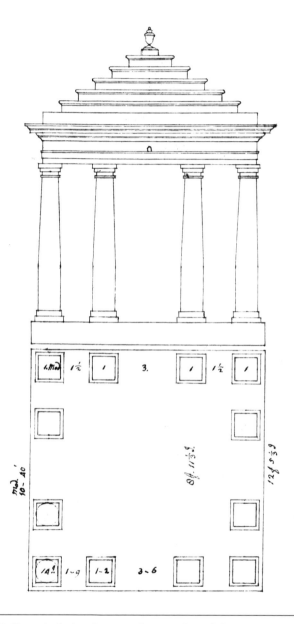

152 Jefferson's design for a garden temple and dovecote. *Inspired by a small pavilion in Gibbs' Book of Architecture, Jefferson got his idea of the stepped roof from antique examples. Always interested in combining the practical with the ornamental, Jefferson designed the top of the building to serve as a dovecote, with access holes provided in the frieze.*

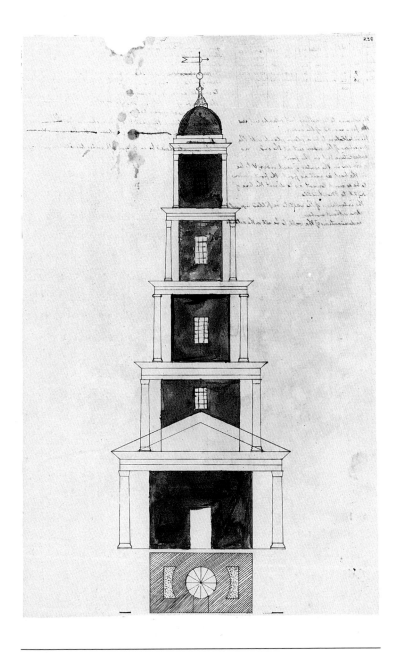

153 Jefferson's design for an observation tower. *The tower was intended for the top of what he named Montalto, the "high mountain" that overlooks Monticello. Jefferson had purchased that promontory dominating the view from Monticello toward the southwest in October, 1777.*

marle County and another five thousand in Bedford, ninety miles to the south. While the center of the operation was the plantation village of Monticello, satellite operations with overseers and slaves were established in other parts of the extensive holdings. Much of the ground was not under cultivation and was heavily forested. The impression of the surrounding countryside one would have had from the house was that of a limitless natural forest, broken here and there with open and well-maintained fields. The European eye of the Duc de la Rochefoucauld-Liancourt in 1796 found the ratio "between the cultivated lands and those which are still covered with forests as ancient as the globe, at present much too great. The eye longs 'to discover' a broad river, a great mass of water—destitute of which, the grandest and most extensive prospect is ever destitute of an embellishment requisite to render it completely beautiful."

Aside from the enormous daily pleasure Jefferson received from the magnificent prospects on all sides of the summit of his mountain—"The grandeur of the objects of nature which surround him, the mountain scenery and elastic atmosphere he enjoys," one visitor wrote, "must have had the effect of producing a corresponding elevation and greatness of soul."— his practical disposition of the grounds, gardens, orchards, and secondary buildings was directed toward an economic self-sufficiency to which these elements were intended to contribute. The placing of structures, along with the walks, roundabout drives, and extensive tree plantings, however, was at all times subordinated to the esthetic consideration for the surrounding views. "The level on which the house stands," Margaret Smith wrote with more sympathy

154 Jefferson's alternate design for an observation tower. *Jefferson's notes indicate that he finally changed his mind on this type of design: "a column will be preferable to anything else. it should be 200f. high & have a hollow of 5f. in the center for stairs to run up on the top of the capital ballustrading."*

for the setting than for the half-completed house itself, "is laid out in an extensive lawn, only broken by lofty weeping willows, poplars, acacias, catalpas and other trees of foreign growth, distributed at such a distance from the house, as neither to obstruct its prospect, nor the surrounding country of which it commands the view."

Jefferson's readings in the classics, with their descriptions of the humanistic villa, powerfully shaped his own vision of the rural existence based on these antique models he was attempting to recreate. The architecture and garden treatises, cast in the humanistic tradition emerging from the Renaissance and continuing through Palladio and on into the classicism of eighteenth-century England, celebrated above all the country villa and villa life that could be understood and adapted to the agrarian existence that Jefferson knew so well and loved. He was rooted in this tradition of the country and the farm, reinforced with the philosophy and imagery of a long line of writers and poets. But the parallels of the actual living conditions of some of the Romans who most eloquently extolled the pleasures of country life to the plantation world of Jefferson, Madison, Monroe, and Washington are even closer. Just as Cicero, Varro, Horace, and the younger Pliny had to spend much of their active life in Rome, away from their beloved estates, Jefferson and the other Founding Fathers from Virginia also had to spend far more time than they wanted to in the urban centers of Williamsburg, Philadelphia, Paris, New York, and Washington. It was often in these cities that Jefferson dreamed of and planned many of the landscape and architectural improvements he eventually would carry out at Monticello. When one reads guests'

155, 156 Jefferson's elevation and plan for a decorative out-chamber (right), and modern perspective elevation (below). While the young lawyer was working in Philadelphia and Williamsburg for the cause of the Revolution, he designed an observatory tower 120 feet high, one of the most remarkable and imaginative structures of his architectural career. The form of the tower is as revolutionary in American architecture as the legislation he was helping to write.

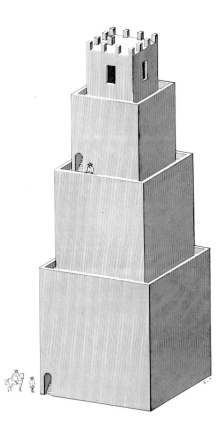

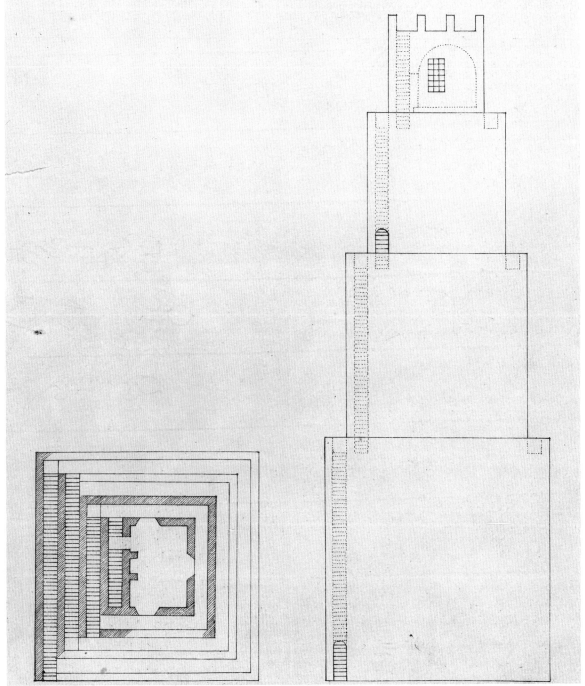

accounts of their visits to Monticello, the picture of Jefferson's life that emerges is, as Karl Lehmann has pointed out, strikingly close to the Roman villa life of the "good *paterfamilias*, who supervised his farms from his luxurious mansions and enjoyed the pleasures of physical exercise and intellectual life on their grounds."

La Rochefoucauld-Liancourt's description of Jefferson's daily routine reads like that of a Roman gentleman of the first century B.C., enjoying the retirement at his country estate outside of Rome:

. . . at present he is employed with activity and perserverence in the management of his farms and buildings; and he orders, directs and pursues in the minutest detail every branch of business relative to them. I found him in the midst of harvest, from which the scorching heat of the sun does not prevent his attendance. His negroes are nourished, clothed, and trained as well as white servants could be. As he cannot expect an assistance from the two small neighboring towns, every article is made on his farm; his negroes are cabinetmakers, carpenters, masons, bricklayers, smiths, etc. The children he employs in a nail factory, which yields already a considerable profit. The young and old negresses spin for the clothing of the rest. He animates them by rewards and distinction; in fine, his superior mind directs the management of his domestic concerns with the same abilities, activity and regularity which he evinced in the conduct of public affairs, and which he is calculated to display in every situation in life.

Nature, which included all of the buildings of an Italian Renaissance estate, was "neither accidental or wild but planned and structured," in the words of Lionello Puppi, the Italian architectural historian, writing of the villa-garden of the sixteenth-century Veneto, and that same ordered environment prevailed at Monticello. It was completely planned and structured by a man to suit his own needs, aspirations, and his inherited rural traditions. It is necessary, therefore, to construct an image of Jefferson's existence, his routines, and above all his outdoor life, energetically lived in an incomparable natural setting, in order to comprehend the close connection that existed between his landscaping ideas and his life as a planter/farmer. Jefferson the farmer, the naturalist, the botanist, and Jefferson the intellectual, the esthete, and the architect is expressed in every detail of the conscious planning between the interior spaces of the house and the enveloping outdoor spaces that served both functions of utility and sensuous pleasure. This is why it is important to consider that large overall design and its integration within the context of the basic economic organization of the place.

The details recorded in his notebooks concerning the layout of the gardens during the first twenty-five years at Monticello remain only details without overall plans or layout of the grounds. Nor do contemporary descriptions by visitors and other documents provide much evidence on the actual state of the gardens and the intermediate spaces between the original house, the outbuildings, and the untamable wilderness beyond.

As we have seen, the position of the house on the crest of a small mountain, with the proposed service quarters suppressed below grade on either side so that unobstructed views could be enjoyed in all directions, is without precedent, although underground service passages are briefly described by Pliny in both of his villas and called cryptoporticus. Very little ornamental planting near the house seems to have

157 *View toward Montalto, or "high mountain"* (facing). *Jefferson had planned to site his projected observation tower—for which he did several designs—on the summit of what he called Montalto, the northern extremity of a long ridge known as Carter's Mountain. He purchased the mountain on October 14, 1777.*

158 *Vegetable garden* (above). *Monticello's vegetable garden, which originally had been laid out by Jefferson in 1774, was regraded and leveled into four terraces in 1809. It stretched along the sunny south slope of the mountain for about 1,000 feet, just below the straight section of the first roundabout that was known as Mulberry Row. It was there that the plantation's slaves lived and worked at the various necessary industries.*

159 *Stone wall and orchard* (right). *This aggressive stone wall was built when the vegetable garden above was terraced level, and it has a monumental Roman quality without precedent in American domestic landscapes. Jefferson placed his orchards and vineyard in the area below this wall.*

160 Isaac Jefferson, daguerreotype by Plumbe (above). *Isaac Jefferson was born at Monticello in 1775 and was the source, in his later years, of many details of Thomas Jefferson's domestic life. He was a blacksmith, nail-maker, and the first manager of the Monticello nailery, which was located on Mulberry Row, to the south of the house.*

161 Jefferson's notes and sketches for barns, c. 1810–14 (facing). *On this page, Jefferson has calculated the number of shingles required to roof the barn and shed at his nearby Tufton farm. He has also made a list of the materials required to build an addition on his barn at Lego, as well as having sketched the plan and front elevation of a brewhouse with a broken pediment incorporating the doorway.*

been carried out initially, and the large, rectangular flower beds that are shown in the plan of 1772 probably were never made.

As early as 1771, a row of mulberry trees was planted along the straight plantation road that ran east and west below the lawn and south of the main house. From the beginning this road seems to have been designated as the location for carrying out those daily domestic routines and plantation services that were basic features of every Virginia plantation of any scale. This plantation "village" eventually would include some nineteen buildings that served a variety of functions related to the life of the plantation. Jefferson's first sketch from about 1774 shows a complex of buildings with some architectural unity, but probably the only structure completed at that time was the stone Weaver's Cottage. Eventually, the buildings of Mulberry Row included the stable, joinery, nailery, and a number of miscellaneous log structures. Placed between the more formally organized grounds immediately around the house above and the vegetable gardens and orchards below, Mulberry Row extended for over a thousand feet by the first decade of the nineteenth century. Inevitably the active, disorderly rustic life of Mulberry Row, with farm implements, stacks of wood and farm produce, raw iron for the nailery, and the noise and confusion of people coming and going, must have been a constant reminder to Jefferson of what it took to support his idealistic existence.

Some of the slave quarters were located on Mulberry Row, and while Margaret Bayard Smith found them better than those on other plantations she had visited, she thought the poor cabins created "a most unpleasant contrast with the palace that rises so near

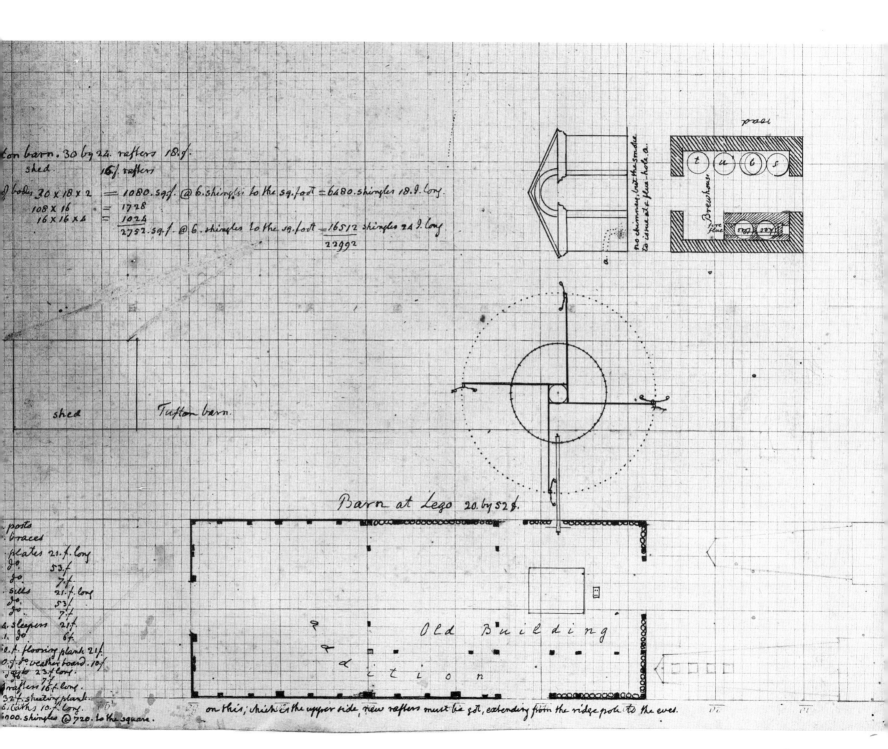

...ton barn. 30 by 24. rafters 18.f.
   shed.   16.f. rafters

of body 30 × 18 × 2 = 1080. sq.f. @ 6. shingles to the sq. foot = 6480. shingles 18.I. long.
        108 × 16 = 1728
         16 × 16 × 4 = 1024
              2752. sq.f. @ 6. shingles to the sq. foot = 16512 shingles 24 I. long
                         22992

no chimney, but the smoke
to issue at a flue-hole. a.

Brewhouse.

t u b s

shed   Tufton barn.

Barn at Lego 20. by 52.f.

posts
braces
plates 21.f. long
do. 53.f.
do.   7.f.
sills 21.f. long
do. 53.f.
do.   7.f.
sleepers 21.f.
do.   6.f.
flooring plank 21.f.
to weather board. 10.f.
do. 23.f. long.
rafters 16.f. long.
32.f. sheeting plank.
laths 10.f. long.
000. shingles @ 720. to the square.

Old Building
dition

on this; which is the upper side, new rafters must be got, extending from the ridge pole to the eves.

them." With the completion of the "Southeastern Offices" beneath the terraces, after 1802, part of the Mulberry Row functions were removed to these new quarters where supporting services were fully integrated into the mansion, a Palladian ideal of domestic organization never before achieved in a Virginia plantation.

The long periods of absentee management of Monticello, which characterized its operations until Jefferson's return at the end of the second term in 1809, left its mark on general upkeep and appearance of the place. An air of neglect must have been quite noticeable in the buildings, grounds, and eroded fields, especially during the years Jefferson spent in Paris (1784-89) and then in New York and Philadelphia as a member of Washington's cabinet until 1794. In 1792 Jefferson described the land as "originally rich" but now "much worried by Indian corn and tobacco."

When Jefferson arrived at Monticello from Philadelphia in January of 1794, he immediately set about to repair the deplorable condition of the estate he had left in the hands of overseers for the previous ten years. Unkempt fields and meadows were cleaned up, roadways were put in order, and it was at this time that some of the unsightly rail fences were replaced by the massive planting of peach tree hedgerows, all adding to the improved appearance of the landscape. Honey locust trees were also used formally to mark the upper roundabouts.

It was at this time also that he began to plan the rebuilding of the house, so it was inevitable that the grounds themselves, especially near the house, would be altered and improved along the lines of gardens that he had studied and admired firsthand during his

162   West Portico, from the south (facing). *"This dwelling, and the whole surrounding scene, is eminently fitted to raise an interest beyond that which such objects ordinarily excite in the mind," a visitor wrote. "Everything moral and physical, conspires to excite and sustain this sentiment." Notice the unusual "lawn" planted on the portico in front of the columns.*

163   Entrance door, West Portico, seen from parlor (above). *"Through the windows at the farther or west end [of the parlor] were seen a lawn of about two acres, skirted with forest trees native and exotic. . . ." The parlor's parquet floor, designed by Jefferson, is one of the earliest of its kind in America.*

stay in Europe. He no longer had to depend solely on "the fine arts in books," his friend Rochefoucauld-Liancourt noted after his visit in 1796. "His travels in Europe have supplied him with models; he has appropriated them to his design." In the matter of gardens, Jefferson certainly had followed his own advice to John Rutledge, Jr., and Thomas Shippen to study the gardens of Europe with care.

After the close of the American Revolution, it once more became possible to visit England to study, especially its great gardens. In 1785, the year before Jefferson would visit the English gardens with John Adams, his friend William Hamilton of Philadelphia had made the requisite tour, and he wrote his secretary from London of the impression the gardens had made on him:

Having observed with attention the nature, variety & extent of the plantations of shrubs, trees, and fruits & consequently admired them, I shall (if God grant me a safe return to my own country,) endeavor to make it smile in the same useful and beautiful manner. . . . The first thing to be set about is a good nursery for trees, shrubs, flowers, and fruits & etc. of every kind. I do desire therefore that seeds in large quantities may be directly sown of the white flowering Locust, the sweet or aromatic Birch, the Chestnut Oak, Horse Chestnuts, Chincpins, Judas trees, Dogwoods, Hallesia, Kalmias, Rhododendron, Magnolias, winterberries, arrow wood, Brooms, annos, shrub, St. John's wort etc. . . . & such others as may occur to you for Beauty or use.

There were several reasons that the picturesque garden and the concept behind it of "scenery's capabilities of being formed into pictures" appealed to experienced gardeners like Hamilton and Jefferson. First of all, in the case of Jefferson, he had been born and raised in an English colony with the closest of cultural ties with the home country. Even if English architecture did not appeal to him, the British way of evolving garden settings out of nature that were at the same time compatible with their sense of open space, their practice of agriculture, and their willingness to relate the environment to the esthetics of landscape painting, was understandable and appealing to someone who loved the natural Virginia countryside. When Jefferson wrote to his granddaughter Ellen Randolph, he listed gardening as "a 7th fine art," having first enumerated painting, sculpture, architecture, music, poetry, oratory, and rhetoric. He recalled the argument of the Scottish philosopher Lord Kames, who insisted that it should be included because it was "allied to landscape painting." Besides, the best designers of gardens were often the landscape painters. Along with Whately's observations, Kames' *Elements of Criticism* helped to shape Jefferson's critical eye regarding the garden, enabling him to take himself out of the view itself as he contemplated its transformation. Other English writers and poets such as Alexander Pope and William Shenstone had influenced Jefferson's appreciation of the new garden philosophy in Virginia just as literature had played an important role in the garden revolution in England earlier in the century. The youthful garden jottings of 1771 with waterfalls, fanciful temples, grottoes, and a park for wild animals came directly out of the English literary tradition with which he had grown up. In fact, the actual gardens he finally saw in England during his brief visit exceeded his romantic inspiration. "The gardening in that country is the article in which it surpasses all the earth," he wrote to his friend John

Page after his return to Paris, "I mean their pleasure gardening. This indeed, went far beyond my ideas."

A third factor that made the English gardens so appealing to Jefferson was the scope with which they reached out and took in the natural wilderness, beyond the bounds of cultivation. This stress on prospect and vista was especially important to Jefferson. Caught up in the dramatic panorama of the Virginia valleys and distant mountain ranges, he had no diffi-

164 Monticello, by William Thornton, watercolor, early 19th century. *This painting was probably done shortly before the extensive roundabout walk and the bordering flower beds were laid out on the west lawn in 1808. The North Pavilion was under construction in 1807, and its incomplete state may have led Thornton astray in his rendering of it.*

culty in "leaping" garden fences and seeing "that all nature was a garden," as Horace Walpole had written earlier of William Kent. By hiding or subordinating walls and fences, and by incorporating the countryside into an uninterrupted landscape plan, a farmer like Jefferson with strong esthetic ideas about the environment and the actual wilderness might in time bring all of the visible landscape and architecture into a balanced, integrated composition.

Having selected a mountaintop for its distant views, Jefferson was to find, however, that this singular feature made his landscape plans for the intermediate space more difficult. "The grounds which I destine to improve in the style of the English gardens are in a form very difficult to be managed," he wrote to William Hamilton, asking the Philadelphia botanist for professional assistance. After describing the steep, timbered slopes that encircled the level lawn around the house, he knew that Hamilton would be "sensible that this disposition of the grounds takes from me the first beauty in gardening, the variety of hill and dale & leaves me as an awkward substitute a few hanging hollows and ridges. . . ." To make it into an acceptable composition, he concluded, "would require much more of the genius of the landscape painter & the gardener than I pretend to."

In the same letter written from Washington in 1806, Jefferson asked Hamilton if he could come to Monticello and work the same wonder there as had been carried out at the Woodlands, Hamilton's own estate outside of Philadelphia. Hamilton had begun to remodel his grounds in the latest English taste and with the nursery plants he shipped home shortly after his return to America in 1789. "You will have an opportunity of indulging on a new field some of the taste which has made the Woodlands the only rival I have known in America to what may be seen in England. Thither we are to go no doubt, for the

first models in the art," the president wrote. He also mentioned that he had tried, with no luck, to secure the services of the English landscape architect George Parkyns, who had spent some time working with Hamilton in Philadelphia. Jefferson had admired in particular a published design of an ornamented farm by Parkyns where a network of inter-connected

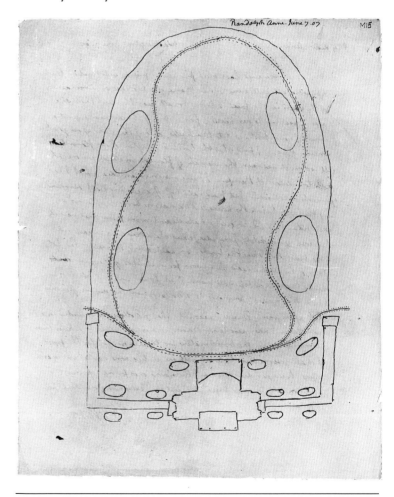

165 Jefferson's sketch of the grounds, showing flower beds, 1807. *This sketch was included in a letter to Jefferson's granddaughter Anne Cary Randolph, who shared his love of gardening. It was dated June 7, 1807.*

encircling walks and drives gave a unity to the various sprawling elements, an idea Jefferson already had played with. Four roundabout roads begun in 1772 completely encircled Monticello's mountain at different levels, a structural order not unlike Parkyns'. Robert Mills in 1803 noted that the uppermost road was lined with mulberry trees, aspen locusts, and lindens planted at twenty-foot intervals. "The hill is generally too steep for direct ascent," Jefferson wrote in 1806, "but we make level walks successively along its side, which in its upper part encircles the hill & intersects these again by others of easy ascent in various parts. They are chiefly still in their native woods which are majestic, and very generally a close undergrowth, which I have not suffered to be touched, knowing how much easier it is to cut away than to fill up." Visitors such as Margaret Smith were taken on drives or walks along these paths to enjoy the spectacular prospects. "There are 4 roads about 15 or 20 feet wide, cut round the mountain from 100 to 200 feet apart," Mrs. Smith noted. "These circuits are connected by a great many roads and paths and when completed will afford a beautiful shady ride or walk of seven miles. The first circuit is not quite a mile around, as it is very near the top. It is in general shady, with openings through the trees for distant views." One of those views was of a conical mountain rising up on the edge of the southern horizon forty miles away. When Lieutenant Francis Hall visited Monticello, his host pointed out that the hill was precisely the dimension of "the greater Egyptian pyramid; so that it accurately represents the appearance of the pyramid at the same distance." The idea of the pyramid decorating his vista was a conceit that appealed to Jefferson's romantic nature.

166 West lawn, showing roundabout walk. *The serpentine walk that encircles the west lawn, fig. 165, and the bordering flower beds were laid out in 1808. The view across the lawn is one of the most commanding in America.*

Even though his "retirement" to Monticello in 1794 had been interrupted by his election to the vice presidency in November of 1796 and the plantation once again was returned to overseers, work proceeded on the remodeling of the house. While the construction moved slowly and intermittently, he wrote with confidence in the spring of 1806 that "this summer will entirely finish the house at Monticello & I am preparing an occasional retreat in Bedford." The house was indeed almost finished that year, but as he had written to Hamilton, "The improvement of my grounds has been reserved for my occupation on my return home." Nowhere is Jefferson's obsession for

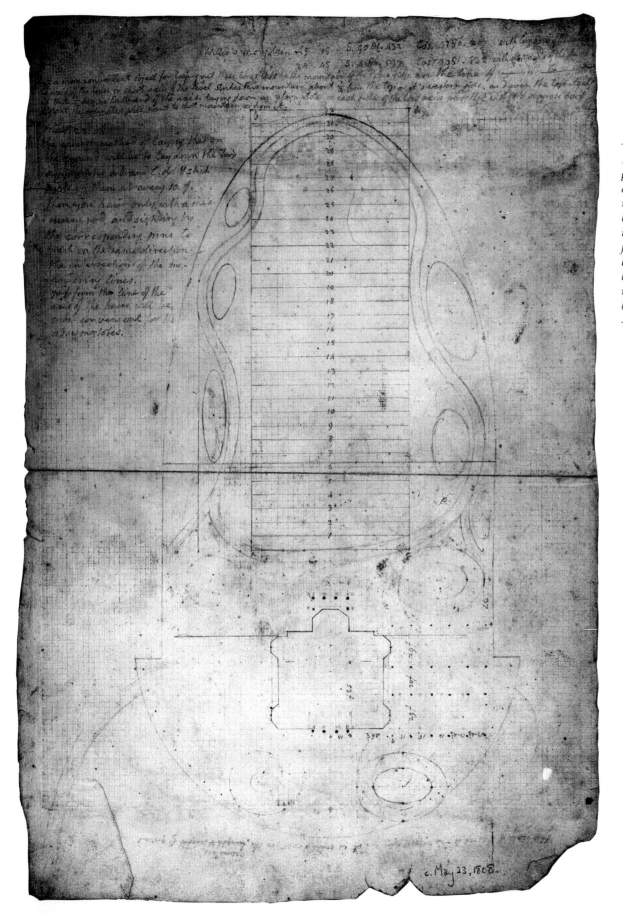

167 Jefferson's drawing of the grounds, 1785–89. *Drawn on coordinate paper that he had discovered while in Paris, which suggests a date between 1785 and 1789, this drawing shows a serpentine walk and oval flower beds similar to those he had laid out in Paris. The relationship of the oval flower beds to the winding walk is close to the design that would be laid out at Monticello in 1807.*

building more clearly shown than in this reference, where plans for a new house at Poplar Forest begin as soon as the last one is completed. From his description, one would think that little had been done to ornament the grounds aside from some leveling, terracing, and cutting away of underbrush. And in fact probably little had been done in the way of landscaping since he had built the first pavilion in 1770. The only project in the Garden Memorandum of 1771 that was carried out and was to become a permanent feature was the deer park, where a herd of deer replaced the "shy" buck-elk and buffalo. The first deer was purchased and installed in 1776 and others were added over the years. Chastellux reported that his host amused "himself by feeding them with Indian corn, of which they are very fond, and which they eat out of his hand. I followed him one evening into a deep valley, where they are accustomed to assemble towards the close of day, and saw them walk, run and bound."

Jefferson's problem with the grounds, he confessed to Hamilton, was to avoid a "satiety" of beautiful views that also could bore for want of variety. Some means had to be found to break up this "rich profusion . . . offering itself at every point of the compass. . . ." Better to present the "mountain distant & near, smooth & shaggy, single & in ridges, a little river hiding itself among the hills so as to skew in lagoons only . . . of shifting scenes as you advance your way" than to have the scenery overwhelm one in unrelieved abundance. Another problem of the open, tidy English style of park, such as the one that Hamilton was able to create and Parkyns espoused, was the age-old problem of maintenance, especially in a mild climate like Virginia's where weeds and everything else grew

168 West lawn and roundabout walk. *Although the flower-bed borders to the serpentine walk were first laid out in 1808, in 1812 Jefferson decided to redo them, planting clumps of single flowers in their own compartments. As he noted, "flower borders. Apr, 8. laid them off into compartments of 10.f. length each."*

abundantly. "I suspect you will find in the grounds you propose to improve on these models," Jefferson wrote to J. P. Reibelt when he returned a set of

173

Parkyns' English designs, "in the highest degree an obstacle which we find considerable even here; that is that the luxuriance of the soil by its constant reproduction of weeds of powerful growth & stature will bid defiance to the keeping your grounds in that clean state which the English gardens require. . . ."

Probably sometime in 1804 Jefferson wrote himself a memorandum called "General ideas for the improvement of Monticello." Both the metaphor of painting—"the canvas at large must be a grove of the largest trees"—and an admiration for English landscape techniques are evident, anticipating in detail the letter he wrote to Hamilton two years later. In the margin of the note, Jefferson drew a sketch to illustrate a thicket of various plants and shrubs planted as a labyrinth and with a temple placed in the center. The temple or decorative structure as a feature in the landscape continued to fascinate him. One of these garden pavilions designed with an Ionic tetrastyle portico and dome is a distinguished piece of draftmanship. Another proposed garden building was a square columnar pavilion equipped with a stepped roof to house pigeons, giving it both a utilitarian and decorative function.

Other ideas that never were carried out called for the complete removal of the buildings along Mulberry Row and the replacement of the paling fence by a ha-ha. He had admired the concealed wall and ditch in England at Stowe, where it allowed the grounds around the house to flow unbroken into the fields beyond through the use of this hidden barrier that kept the livestock at the right esthetic distance without the threat of an unexpected invasion onto well-tended lawns. It was a device suited to the kind of landscape Jefferson had in mind for Monticello. In order to maintain an open appearance around the vast lawn of the house, Jefferson devised his own version of a concealed barrier or cattle guard that functioned as a ha-ha. A visitor in 1823 described it: "Instead of being upright [the fence] lay upon the ground across a ditch, the banks of the ditch raised the rails a foot or two above the ground on either side of the ditch, so that no kind of grazing animals could easily cross it, because their feet would slip between the rails. It had just the appearance of a common post and rail straight fence blown down across a ditch."

Half-way through his second term in 1806 and as his anticipation of retirement to Monticello intensified, the President dispatched cartloads of trees and plants from the nurseries of Washington. Thomas Main, the Georgetown horticulturist and friend of Jefferson, supplied much of this material from his nurseries. "Mr. Jefferson sent home a great many kinds of trees and shrubbery from Washington," his overseer recalled. "I used to send a servant there with a great many fine things from Monticello for his table and he would send back the cart loaded with shrubbery from a nursery near Georgetown . . . and he always sent me directions what to do with it." Jefferson's planting plan for the top of the mountain, dated 1806, survives, and as his overseer Bacon recorded, "the president even with all the political distractions"—the Burr conspiracy took place in 1806 —"knew all about everything in every part of his grounds and gardens. He knew the name of every tree and just where one was dead or missing."

In the spring of 1807 the trial of Aaron Burr opened in Richmond, and in April the president, who had been ill with complicating headaches, was

169 West lawn, showing flower beds bordering the roundabout. *The lawn, "on an elliptical level, formed by art," Mrs. Thornton wrote in 1802, "commands a very grand, uncommon and extensive view." The tall larch tree on the right was planted by Jefferson more than 150 years ago.*

relieved to be back in the country even though he was involved with many executive details related to the trial. It was during this stay that he turned with relief to sketching out the serpentine walks and flowerbeds for the west lawn, a far more congenial task than that of prosecuting one's political enemy. The sketch survives on the back of a letter written to his granddaughter Anne Cary Randolph in June of 1807. The curving walks, with flower borders, are indicated, as are the oval beds, to hold flowers and flowering shrubs. "I find that the limited number of our flower beds will too much restrain the variety of flowers in which we might wish to indulge, & there-

fore I have resumed an idea, which I had formerly entertained, but had not laid by, of a winding walk surrounding the lawn before the house, with a narrow border of flowers on each side. this would give us abundant room for great variety. I enclose you a sketch of my idea, where the dotted lines on each side . . . shew the border on each side of the walk. the hollows of the walk would give room for oval beds of flowering shrubs."

Some time after he had returned home from Paris (and using engraved coordinate paper he had purchased there), Jefferson prepared plans for an even more elaborate scheme he had "formerly entertained" but never carried out. The directions for laying out the plan called for the determination of an axis between the house and a nearby mountain and then to form a coordinate perpendicular to it. A similarly undulating walkway or path surrounding a lawn was part of Jefferson's plan to improve the small urban space of the Hôtel de Langeac, his rented house in Paris, where to the astonishment of his Parisian friends he planted corn to supply his table with roasting ears, an exotic dish unknown in France. "I cultivate in my own garden here Indian corn for the use of my own table, to eat green in our manner. But the species I am able to get here for seed, is hard, with a thick skin and dry," he told Colonel Nicholas Lewis of Albemarle when he wrote to ask his neighbor to send an ear of the "small ripe corn we call Homony Corn as well as the seeds of the common sweet potato, watermelon, canteloupe, and one or two of bacon hams."

Jefferson's taste for the *jardin anglaise* was certainly *à la mode* in Paris, and his little garden essay in the English style on the triangular site of the Hôtel de

175

Langeac, with its miniature berm or mound and exotic American vegetables to provide additional interest, was a most fashionable achievement. English gardens, of course, were all the rage in Paris and the style was pursued by leading members of the nobility. Marie Antoinette's garden at the Petit Trianon and that of her brother-in-law the Comte d'Artois at Bagatelle were only two examples of the "modern style" that had been inspired by the same book sources, such as Whately's *Observations on Modern Gardening*, that Jefferson knew and followed. When the French edition of Whately's book appeared in 1771, Horace Walpole wrote: "They have translated Mr. Whately's book and the Lord knows what barbarism is to be laid at our door." As early as 1771 Catherine the Great also had become fascinated with the English style, and she imported to St. Petersburg an English gardener, John Bush, to transform the earlier formal layouts at Yekaterininky Park, the great baroque palace originally built for the Empress Elizabeth. "I now love to distraction gardens in the English style," she wrote to Voltaire in 1772, "the curving lines, the gentle slopes, the ponds in the form of lakes, the archipelagoes on dry land, and I scorn straight lines and twin allées. I hate fountains which torture water in order to make it follow a course contrary to its nature; statues are relegated to galleries, halls, etc; in a word anglomania rules my plantomania."

Aside from the stylish curves of Monticello's paths, which reflect the new international ideas of garden design, their irregular circulation perhaps has another function. Jefferson's letter to William Hamilton refers to the "advantage of shifting the scenes as you advance on your way," and the winding walk around the west lawn does just that by moving you along to changing vistas, alternating between views of the house and prospects out over the valleys and mountain. Straight walks either parallel or perpendicular to a symmetrical piece of architecture are never the best way to enjoy formal architecture, its differing proportions, scale, the changing relationship of the parts, and the play of light and shadow from different angles. Even though the lawn was level and probably had been conceived as a large flat rectangular space, the graceful free-forms and curves punctuated by rhythmically related intervals of vistas somehow breaks the traditional fixed Renaissance perspective, allowing for the maximum esthetic analysis of the house and grounds.

It was not until the spring of 1808 that the new flower beds and walks were finally laid out by the president himself, no doubt eagerly assisted by his granddaughter Anne Randolph who shared her grandfather's interest in gardening. "The first time I come home I will lay out the projected flower borders around the level so that they shall be ready for the next fall," he wrote from Washington to Anne in February of 1808. "In the spring of the next year I will bring home a full collection of roots & plants. we will then have room enough for every thing." To make room for "every thing" was a big order for Jefferson. The collection and cultivation of plants was almost as absorbing as building, and his interest grew as he eagerly developed new plans for Monticello. Seeds and plants were gathered from near and far; from naturalists William Bartram and Benjamin S. Barton in Philadelphia; from Thomas Main and Dr. William Thornton in Washington; from Philip Mazzei in Italy; from Lafayette's aunt, Madame de

Tessé, and Andre Thouin, director of the Jardin des Plantes in Paris. From Meriwether Lewis, he had received seeds collected on the Lewis and Clark expedition to the Northwest. As Dumas Malone has pointed out in *The Sage Of Monticello*, no small part of his correspondence of a lifetime concerned botanical and horticultural matters. At the age of seventy-one he summed up his delight in the growing of plants: "Botany I rank with the most valuable sciences, whether we consider its subjects as furnishing the principal subsistence of life to man and beast, delicious varieties for our tables, refreshments from our orchards, the adornments of our flower-borders, shade and perfume of our groves, materials for our buildings, or medicaments for our bodies. . . . To a country family it constitutes a great portion of their social entertainment. No country gentleman should be without what amuses every step he takes into his field."

In addition to the flower borders, beds, and walks that were laid out in the spring of 1808, Jefferson instructed Edmund Bacon to work the old vegetable gardens into four levels of 250 feet in length from east to west. These were divided into beds of vegetable "parterres" to make "room enough" for the prodigious planting that Jefferson had in mind.

It was during this great burst of garden activity that it was decided to establish an experimental garden, with Bacon given the following instructions: "1808 Feb. 1 in all the open grounds on both sides of the 3d & 4th. Round-abouts, lay off lots for minor articles of husbandry, and for experimental culture, disposing them into a ferme ornée by interspersing occasionally the attributes of a garden." Just what the Virginia countryman Edmund Bacon understood

by the term "ferme ornée" is not recorded, and it may be the last moment in history when a gentleman could with confidence so instruct his overseer. It is the only time that Jefferson used the word in connection with Monticello, but certainly the landscape of the place was moving in the direction that Jefferson envisioned and Bacon understood the meaning of an ornamented working farm.

As early as 1712 Joseph Addison had proposed a revolutionary gardening idea that was to have far-reaching results. The idea must have appealed to the young Virginian when he read Addison's proposal in *The Spectator*: "Why not a whole Estate," asked Addison, "be thrown into a kind of garden by frequent Plantations. A man might make a pretty Landskip in his own Possessions." It was Addison's revolutionary idea that, as Christopher Hussey the English historian remarked, "gave to the nation its countryside."

The concept of the ornamented farm was further expanded in Whately's *Observations*, with the author's curious mixture of the abstract and the practical that had a special appeal to Jefferson's own approach to gardening, architecture, and other fields of interest. Whately thoroughly discussed the ferme ornée and used the example of Philip Southcote's Woburn Farm in Surrey as the model, which Jefferson visited in 1786. Of the 135 acres at Woburn some thirty-five were "adorned to the highest degree," but these ornamented sections had been "communicated to every part for they disposed along the sides of a walk, which, with its appendages, forms a broad belt round the grazing grounds, and is continued, though on a more contracted scale, through the arable. This walk is properly garden; all within is farm. . . ." Or as

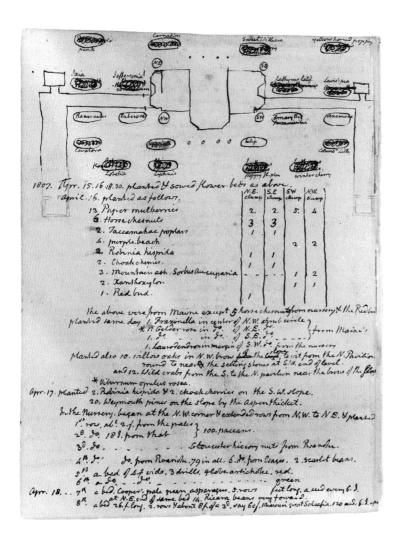

170 *Jefferson's plan for flower beds near the house, 1807. In this draw-ing, Jefferson laid out the round and oval flower beds close to the house, indicating which flowers were to be planted in each bed. Below that he listed all of the trees he put in during the last half of April, 1807. At the bottom, Jefferson noted all of the seeds he had planted in the "Nursery."*

Jefferson recorded his own impression of this min-gling of meadows and fields, vegetables and flowers, "All are intermixed, the pleasure garden being

merely a highly ornamented walk through and round the divisions of the farm and kitchen garden."

Southcote's plan had been adapted by the poet William Shenstone to his own farm The Leasowes, the other celebrated English ferme ornée. "Visited by travelers and copied by gardeners," The Lea-sowes had been called by Whately a perfect picture of Shenstone's mind: "simple, elegant and amiable." Even though it would be difficult to isolate specific comparisons between Shenstone's ornamented farm and Jefferson's, Whately's characterization of The Leasowes applies equally as well to Monticello.

On the 15th of March, 1809, having completed his second term, the former president arrived from Washington at his Virginia plantation. On March 2nd he had written his friend Monsieur Dupont de Nemours: "Within a few days I retire to my family, my books and farms; and having gained the harbour myself, I shall look on my friends still buffeting the storm with anxiety indeed, but not with envy. Never did a prisoner released from his chains, feel such relief as I shall on shaking off the shakles of power. Nature intended me for the tranquil pursuits of sci-ence, by rendering them my supreme delight."

When Margaret Smith arrived for a visit later in the spring she had found, after winding up the "steep and rugged road . . . where nature was left untamed and unadorned by art," that "like the temple of fame, in which he had secured himself a place, his mansion was of most difficult access." The "noble pile of build-ings, crowned with a lofty dome" and surrounded with a "wide and verdant lawn" was impressive. When he complained of the wilderness he had found on his return, Jefferson's guest, with her southern charm told him, "But you have returned and the wilderness

shall blossom like the rose and you, I hope will long sit beneath your own vine and your own fig-tree."

During her tour of the mansion, Jefferson showed her his own private apartments and library, which usually were off-limits to visitors. She was particularly impressed with the greenhouse that was made by glazing the south portico off the library so that Jefferson could closely watch the young plants and

171 Oval flower beds, near south terrace. These beds have been laid out and replanted to correspond to Jefferson's original plan for the house gardens. In the background, one can see the right-angle turn of the south terrace, with its Chinese Chippendale railings adapted by Jefferson.

seedlings he potted there. From the greenhouse, Mrs. Smith and her host walked directly onto the elevated terrace above the service area, where they could look out over the lawn and admire the new oval flower beds and new fish pond, just beyond the southwest pavilion. In rainy or bad weather the terrace served as a kind of promenade where the views could be enjoyed without getting muddy feet.

The same year that Mrs. Smith visited Monticello, George Tucker, who was later to write Jefferson's first biography, referred to the vegetable beds, held in place by a massive stone dry-wall running from east to west above the orchard, as "a large hanging garden." Even though much of the correspondence of this period related to the securing of trees and shrubs for the larger landscape of the grounds beyond the house and lawn itself, flowers were not neglected. The sensuous pleasure of flowers—their color, smell, texture, and variety—had always been an important part of Jefferson's life. In May of 1811, he wrote to his granddaughter Anne Cary Bankhead: "the flowers come forth like the belles of the day, have their short reign of beauty and splendor, and retire like them, to the more interesting office of reproducing their like. The Hyacinths and Tulips are off the stage, the Irises are giving place to the Belladonnas, as these will to the Tuberoses etc; As your Mama has done to you, my dear Anne, as you will do to the sisters of little John, and as I shall soon and cheerfully do to you all in wishing you a long, long goodnight. . . ."

There had been extensive flower beds at Shadwell, and these were methodically numbered and referred to by Jefferson in early entries of the Garden Book. The spring of the year he was introduced to the practice of the law, 1767, he "sowed Carnations, Indian Pink, Marygold, Globe amaranth, Auricula, Double balsam, Tricolor, Dutch violet, Sensitive plant,

Cockscomb, a flower like the Prince's feather, Lathyrus." Roses, lillies, and wild honeysuckles were also set out. Later Monticello was to become a living horticultural encyclopedia as well as a private center of botanic research, and the collecting of flowers, like the cultivation of a great variety of vegetables, trees, and shrubs, was pursued with much the same interest, although their sensuous impact was more intense to Jefferson. Charles Willson Peale saw Jefferson as a dedicated horticultural curator when he wrote, "your garden must be a museum to you. . . ."

Always the perfectionist, he would experiment with different flower combinations in the borders of the winding walk to test the color effect. In 1812, for example, the Garden Book entry that recorded the sowing of bellflower, African marigold, and white poppy was undoubtedly one of these display experiments in color and texture. That same year his Philadelphia nurseryman Bernard McMahon shipped south several collections of flowers that included crown imperials, gladiolas communis, dwarf Persian iris, iris xiphium (which McMahon described as "a new & fine variety"), double ronunculus, cloth of gold crocus, and the seeds "of some very superior Impatience Balsomina." Feathered and double blue hyacinth bulbs arrived in September with more crocus and red, green, and yellow parrot tulips for fall planting.

*172 **South Pavilion.** Built in 1770 as Jefferson's bachelor quarters, the South Pavilion was remodeled in 1808 to match the appearance of the North Pavilion, the last structure at Monticello to be constructed under Jefferson's direction. Several years earlier, the "offices," stables, kitchen, and other domestic functions were established beneath the low terraces that would link the main house with the outchambers. The ornamental fish pond in which the South Pavilion is reflected was put there in 1808.*

The fragrance of plants and flowers was important, and among the "perfumes of our groves" that Jefferson especially enjoyed was the acacia. In 1813 an admirer, Mrs. Judith Lomax, sent along some acacia seed "together with a few of the Flowers, allowing you to be an admirer of the perfume." He so liked the acacia (*Mimosa nilotica*) that he once said that it and the orange "are the only things I ever propose to have in my green house," just off his library and bedroom, where their sweet scent could be enjoyed in privacy. Recalling the particular smell of a potted plant he had once enjoyed in William Hamilton's greenhouse, but having forgotten its name, he wrote to Hamilton, "I cannot suppose you can recollect or conjure in your vast collection what particular plant this might be. I must acquiesce therefore in a privation which my own defect of memory has produced."

As early as 1778, orange trees, "being new shoots from old roots brought from Italy," arrived from nearby Colle, Philip Mazzei's farm, where Jefferson had persuaded the Italian to settle and to begin his vineyard culture and other agricultural experiments. Monticello was to receive a number of European plants and seeds from Mazzei over the next few years in addition to the orange shoots. Italian fruits included the vaga loggia peach, the angelica apricot, the boccon di re plum, and the poppe di venere (or Breast of Venus) peach. The original orange trees

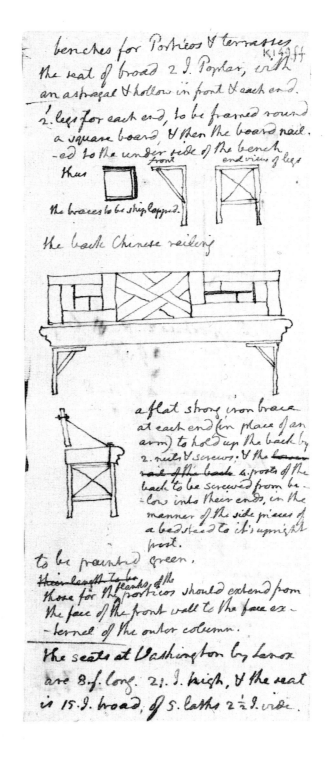

173 Jefferson's drawings for benches, after 1801. Jefferson designed this bench to be used on the terraces and the porticoes. He called for seats of two-inch poplar and noted that the benches should be painted green. "Those for the flanks of the porticoes should extend from the face of the front wall to the face external of the outer column."

probably had arrived in Albemarle County along with other plants and several vignerons, or vineyard workers, whom Mazzei had brought from Tuscany. Ten vignerons had come with Mazzei in 1773 and six more arrived from Lucca in 1774. For his assistance in helping arrange the emigration of these "husbandmen and mechanics" along with "sundry seeds, vine cuttings, plants etc," Mazzei sent back to

the Grand Duke of Tuscany presents of Virginia birds, seeds, and plants. After Mazzei's experiment had foundered in his absence during the Revolution,

174 Terrace bench designed by Jefferson. In his design, fig. 173, Jefferson called for "a flat strong iron brace at each end (in place of an arm) to hold up the back by 2. nuts & screws." He noted on his front elevation drawing of the bench, "the back Chinese railing."

Jefferson hired Antonio Giannini, a vigneron who originally had come to work at Colle.

Jefferson was long fascinated with the viticulture and the production of wine at Monticello. In 1774, his Italian neighbors assisted him in planting thirty vines below a stone garden wall south of the house and just above the orchard. These first grape vines on the south side of the hill, along with the fig trees, would have further heightened the terraced, Italianate appearance of the grounds. In his Garden Book that year he made careful notes of the Italian planting procedures he had learned from his neighbors at Colle. Climate conditions plagued the viticulture

*175 **South terrace, showing railings.** Jefferson used what he called "Chinese railing" extensively at Monticello, to line both terraces and as a parapet around the top of the main roof. He was later to employ the Chinese railing in his designs for the pavilions of the University of Virginia.*

experiment at Monticello but its sponsor did not give up. In 1802, Giannini received instructions from the president to set out thirty vines from Burgundy and Champagne, thirty from Bordeaux, and ten plants from Cape Town, South Africa. In 1807, some twenty varieties of wine and eating grapes were planted on the vineyard "terras."

In spite of difficulties over the years, Jefferson felt

that his particular part of Virginia might in time produce a good if not fine table wine. "The Italian Mazzei who came here to make wine," he wrote in response to one inquiry on the subject, "fixed on these South West mountains, drawing a S.E. aspect, and abundance of lean & meagre spots of stony & red soil without sand, resembling extremely the cote of Burgundy from Chambertin to Montrachet where the famous wines of Burgundy are made. I am inclined to believe he was right in preferring the South Eastern face of this ridge of mountains. . . . Doubtless however, other parts of the state furnish the

176   Plate from **Designs of Chinese Buildings** *by Sir William Chambers (below). Jefferson may well have been inspired by this book, one that he knew as early as 1771, in his designs for the Chinese railing. Chambers called these Chinese designs "toys in architecture," but Jefferson with creative indifference combined the Chinese motif with the classical style.*

*177   **Chinese railing, panel detail** (right). The design of this panel is a near duplicate of the railing above the portico in the Chambers plate.*

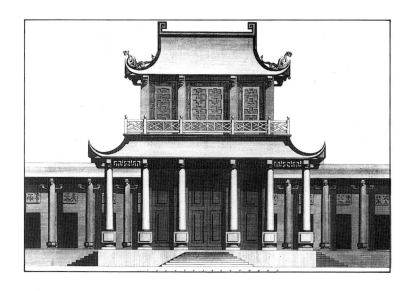

proper soil & climate. Beyond the blue ridge the climate becomes severe, & I should suppose less favorable. this, Sir, is as much as my scanty knowledge of the subject will permit me to say. . . ."

During his stay in France Jefferson had traveled through the wine country of Burgundy, so his comments on the comparison of soils suitable for vineyards were reinforced by his firsthand observation. In Paris he was always anxious to have reports on the farm and garden operations at Monticello and in 1786 wrote Giannini, "How does my vineyard come on? have there been grapes enough to make a trial of wine? if there should be, I should be glad to receive here a few bottles. . . ." No doubt he was anxious to compare his production with the French wines so amply stocked at the Hôtel de Langeac.

In his declining years, four years before he died, he took the time to answer yet one more gardening inquiry. On May 12, 1822, he wrote to Samuel Maverick of South Carolina:

Age, debility and decay of memory have for sometime withdrawn me from attention to matters without doors. the grape you inquire after as having gone from this place is not now recollected by me. as some in my vineyard have died, others have been substituted without noting which, so that at present all are unknown. that as good wines will be made in America as in Europe the Scuppernon of North Carolina furnishes sufficient proof. the vine is congenial to every climate in Europe from Hungary to the Mediterrainean, and will be bound to suceed in the same temperatures here wherever tried by intelligent vignerons. the culture, however is more desirable for domestic use than profitable as an occupation for market. . . .

To Jefferson the endless pleasures of nature, of farming, and of gardening, with all of the contrasting sensations of color, perfumed air, the sounds of song birds, and the sense of touch heightened by contrasting temperatures and the freedom of movement allowed him to celebrate its mysteries to their fullest in their never ending apparition of spring. "I have been in the enjoyment of our delicious spring," he wrote a friend. "The soft general temperature of the season, just above the want of fire, enlivened by the reanimation of birds, flowers, the fields, forests & gardens, has been truely delightful. . . . My peach & cherry trees blossomed on the 9th of March." No Persian caliph dreaming of the Gardens of Paradise could evoke more vividly in simple language the sensuous enchantments of the earthly garden, a vision Margaret Smith conjures up in her splendid descrip-

tion of the president sitting in his White House apartment with a mocking-bird resting on his shoulder.

In the window recesses, where stands for the flowers and plants which it was his delight to attend and among his roses and geraniums was suspended the cage of his favorite mocking-bird, which he cherished with peculiar fondness, not only for its melodious powers, but for its uncommon intelligence and affectionate disposition, of which qualities he gave surprising instances. It was the constant companion of his solitary and studious hours. Whenever he was alone he opened the cage and let the bird fly about the room. After flitting for awhile from one object to another, it would alight on his table and take its food from his lips. Often when he retired to his chamber it would hop up the stairs after him and while he took his siesta, would sit on his couch and pour forth its melodius strains. He loved this bird! How he loved his flowers! He could not live without something to love and his flowers became objects of tender care."

Jefferson more than once claimed that he was an Epicurean—a philosophy he had first encountered in Cicero and later in Horace, who was, next to Homer, his most cherished poet throughout his life. Instead of hypocritically denying and supressing the human sentiment, desire, passion, and sensual enjoyment of all things good in this world, he accepted them as a virtue. Rather than being harmful, they were an essential part of a man's life, one of the tools of his happiness. "I . . . am an Epicurean," he declared in old age. "I consider the genuine (not the imputed) doctrines of Epicurus as containing everything rational in moral philosophy which Greece and Rome have left us." Epicurean philosophy taught how to govern desires and passions by reason and a careful appraisal of consequences, and was not as popularly

178 Cistern top, north terrace. *Adequate water was always a problem in Jefferson's time, since the nearby springs and the wells that were dug never seemed to be reliable. It was, therefore, necessary to collect the rainwater from the roof and the terraces to supplement other sources. A similar structure balanced the layout on the opposite end of the house.*

the mind that was the Epicurean ideal. Even in the arrival of the first peas, his favorite vegetable, to the table at Monticello, the true Epicure's delight can be detected. "Here our first peas were the 29th of May, which shows the inattention here to the cheapest, pleasantest & most wholesome part of comfortable living." It is an expression of an abiding personal philosophy that surfaces again and again throughout the correspondence.

When he thought retirement from public life was imminent in 1793, he wrote James Madison: "The motion of my blood no longer keeps time with the tumult of the world. It leads me to seek happiness in the lap and love of my family, in the society of my neighbors and my books, in the wholesome occupations of my farms and my affairs, in an interest or affection in every bud that opens, in every breath that blows around me, in an entire freedom of rest, of motion, of thought—owing account to myself alone of my hours and actions. . . ." To more than one friend he wrote about the "ardour" stronger than the passion of his youth with which he returned to the form of garden life of Monticello after the conclusion of his term as Secretary of State. "I indulge it because I think it will be more productive of health, profits & the happiness depending on these, and perhaps of some utility to my neighbors. . . ." When reminded of political enemies—"scoundrels"—he had left behind in Philadelphia, he wrote that he preferred "infinitely to contemplate the tranquil growth of my lucerne and potatoes. . . ." "Have you become a farmer?" he wrote to General Henry Knox. "Is it not pleasanter than to be shut up within 4 walls and delving eternally with the pen? I am become the most ardent farmer in the state. . . . If you are half as

understood, an invitation to personal self-indulgence. Since it aimed at bodily ease, which could only be achieved by good and healthy but not extravagant living, Jefferson's robust and active garden life as his years advanced helped to attain that tranquility of

179 **Philip Mazzei,** *by Jacques Louis David. Mazzei was an Italian viticulturist whom Jefferson had persuaded to settle in Virginia before the Revolution, so that he might introduce wine-making to Albemarle County. In 1774, Jefferson planted thirty grape vines to the south of his house site, just above the orchard.*

much delighted with the farm as I am, you bless your stars at your riddance from public cares." To John Adams, "Tranquility becomes daily more and more the object of my life"; to Archibald Stuart, "My philosophy [is] to encourage the tranquilizing passion"; and to Madison he declared that he would not give up his life at Monticello "for the empire of the universe." To Maria Cosway, now working to establish a school for young girls in Lodi, Italy, her former admirer and possible lover spoke more intimately of the quality of Eden that he felt in his idyllic garden retirement. "I am permitted from the innocence

of the scenes around me to learn to practice innocence toward all, hurt to none, help to as many as I am able."

For Jefferson the retirement from public life meant that he could concentrate all of his energy and dreams on Monticello. "I am happy nowhere else and in no other society," he confessed to a fellow Virginian in a letter from Paris in 1787. "All my wishes end, where I hope my days will, at Monticello. Too many scenes of happiness mingle themselves with all the recollections of my native woods and fields to suffer them to be supplanted in my affections by any other." Even though the happy scenes would be replaced by many disappointments and personal tragedies, the remodeling of the house and plans to rehabilitate the neglected and eroded farm seemed to lift him out of his attacks of depression, his "slough of despond." This creative source of rejuvenation and health would serve him repeatedly throughout the remainder of his life and further explains the vital, exuberant language with which he describes its significance to him, and it was the therapy he drew from nature that may have been more important to him than architecture as the years advanced. "My essay in architecture [Monticello] has been so much subordinated to the law of convenience, & affected also by the circumstance of change in the original design," he wrote to Benjamin Latrobe, "that it is liable to some unfavorable & just criticisms. But what nature has done for us is sublime & beautiful and unique. . . ."

The eternal cycles of the garden's yearly rebirth—"a measured and well ordered model of the universe, an experiment in immortality," in the words of the historian Eugenio Battisti—are looked forward to in Jefferson's letter to Peale in which he had declared that if fortune had allowed, he would have chosen the profession of a gardener. "Such a variety of subjects," he continued, "some one always coming to perfection, the failure of one thing repaired by the success of another, and instead of one harvest a continued one through the year. Under a total want of demand except for our family table, I am still devoted to the garden. But though an old man, I am but a young gardener."

In his old age ("with one foot in the grave, and," as he said, "the other uplifted and ready to follow"), if in his reveries he looked toward the distant horizon of the future, it was a future in which, he fervently believed, "The earth belongs to the living, not to the dead," as he wrote to Benjamin Rush. "The will and the power of man expire with his life by nature's law." In this powerful sentiment of each generation's renewal as an expression of new hope and new faith is reflected the practical philosophy and life-long experience of a gardener as much as that of an architect of a republic.

---

180 **Monticello, *watercolor, c. 1820.*** *As Margaret Smith described it, "The level on which the house stands, is laid out in an extensive lawn, only broken by lofty weeping willows, poplars, acacias, catalpas and other trees of foreign growth, distributed at such a distance from the house, as neither to obstruct its prospect, nor that of the surrounding country of which it commands the view."*

THE INTERIOR
LIFE

181   Entrance hall. *The cluttered entrance hall of Monticello was, for most visitors, the nearest thing to a museum they had ever seen. As one visitor wrote, "there is no private gentleman in the world in possession of so complete a scientific, useful and ornamental collection."*

THE SURROUNDINGS BECOME A MUSEUM OF the soul, an archive of experiences . . . the resonance chamber where its strings render their authentic vibration." As one stands in the empty front hall at Monticello and looks at the clock above the door on an early morning before the first visitor arrives, or eats in the candle-lit dining room to honor some modern day architect or artist, the recollection of this passage from Mario Praz's introduction to his history of furnishings takes on new meaning. That a fine interior with its intimate, private associations can also become a kind of mold of the spirit that created it—as Praz suggests—is not to be doubted. No house in America inside or out so completely expresses the complicated, contradictory, even inventive personality of its creator. As in the world of his favorite Roman poet Horace, the delights and rewards of rural living gave meaning to Jefferson's every activity and occupation at Monticello, throughout his long, productive life. The care of plants and trees, the gathering of fruit and vegetables from one's own orchards and gardens, the annual harvesting of crops, the supervision of workers, all of those pursuits, as deep-rooted for the eighteenth-century Virginia planter as for the first-century Roman, provided the fundamental background of domestic life. The prosperity and education of the older aristocracy, to which Jefferson was related, had enabled a few cultivated gentlemen such as the circle Jefferson first knew at the Governor's Palace in Williamsburg to create a private existence where a certain aura of elegance and taste could be seen not only in the private houses themselves but in furniture, silver, and textiles. If, as the century moved on, Virginia planters thought of their

way of life and manners as expressing at least the spirit of the Roman ideal, no one could quite identify its Roman quality when it came to those things associated with everyday living. In fact most of the ornaments and furniture for the better sort of Tide-

182 **Merriwether Lewis,** *by Saint-Memin, crayon on paper.* *The portrait of Lewis was done just before he left with William Clark on their famous expedition to the northwest. Many of the articles gathered on the trip found their way into the collections of their sponsor, President Thomas Jefferson.*

183 Pair of chairs and table, parlor. *Among the numerous pieces of furniture acquired by Jefferson in Paris in the late 18th century, only a few survived the dispersal sales after his death. These simple fauteuils and the table in the parlor are representative of his European purchases.*

water domestic establishment came from England, where the less "profuse" and more "tasteful" style of the brothers Adam, inspired by classical remains, was just beginning to make an impact. But, for the most part the decoration of Southern interiors remained conservative and unchanged over the generations, even though sourcebooks such as Chippendale's *Cabinetmaker's Designs . . . in the Gothic, Chinese and Modern Taste* were known, and, indeed, Jefferson eventually owned a copy of the third edition, published in London in 1755.

Beyond those classic routines of comfortable rural life the young Jefferson grew up with at Shadwell and Tuckahoe, which were not so remote from the quiet country life described in ancient literature, there was little else—and certainly no surviving pictures—to guide in the recreating of a domestic existence based on Roman precedent. To be sure there was an underlying spirit or philosophy that came through from the classical age that was beginning to make an impact on contemporary eighteenth-century writings, especially on architectural treatises that provided a source for Jefferson's own highly critical comments on the provincial standards of Virginia architecture. His concern for "proportion," his love of "light and airy spaciousness," and his preference for "chaste and simple ornamentation" give us a sense of his own esthetic standards for interior decor consistent with his architectural standards. The gentry's furnishings for their houses—and particularly those in Williamsburg—presented an atmosphere of understated good taste and urbanity rather than the "profuse" elegance of the more stylish English drawing rooms of the period.

London factors kept up a steady shipment of chairs, chests, silver, porcelain, and engravings to their Virginia clients. "The chief magnificence of Virginians," Chastellux noted, "consists in furniture, linens, and silver plate, in which they resemble our own [French] forefathers who had no private apartments in their castles, but only a well stored wine cellar and handsome sideboards." Paintings, except for portraits, were scarce. Although there were many portraits in his family, especially on the Randolph side, neither Jefferson's father, mother, or wife seem to have been painted during their lifetimes. Although Jefferson eventually would be recorded in twenty-five life portraits, the first likeness was not done until he went to London in 1786, where he was painted by Mather Brown.

Books, and especially those with illustrations, were the chief instruments to educate and mold Jefferson's own eye and esthetic development. An avid student of history and philosophy, Jefferson was drawn to the new classicism as the perfect symbol for a republic it was hoped would model itself on the political tradition of the ancients. His personal philosophy paralleled his political bias in the belief that man could shape his physical and esthetic environment along rational lines, just as he could construct new political machinery to confirm and support his "pursuit of happiness" and individual freedom.

But in shaping his domestic philosophy, those things that he surrounded himself with—art, architecture, and domestic furnishings—were used to determine and express life as it unfolded. The strict classical ideals and constraints drawn from the examples of antiquity had to be weighed with the American frontiersman's faith in utility. Each creative act, whether it is found in a poem, a novel, the proportions of a room, the color of a curtain, or the curve in the handle of a coffee urn, contributed to the moral organization of one's life and its ultimate value. Even the smallest detail in the profile of a molding, or in the framing of a Trumbull engraving (Jefferson preferred a narrow black frame with its inner edge lined with gold-leaf) added up to the creation of an ordered existence that contained one's image of enlightened history and a continuity with the best that civilization had to offer.

Explaining his inclusion of a few contemporary novels along with Homer, Horace, and Cicero in the recommended reading for a friend, the young moralist wrote: "A little attention to the nature of the human mind evinces that the entertainments of fiction are useful as well as pleasant. That they are pleasant when well written every person feels who reads. But wherein is its utility, asks the reverend sage, big with the notion that nothing can be useful

184 Windsor chair, c. 1800 (reproduction). Jefferson liked the simple "Windsor" chair, and on an order to his business agent, dated July 19, 1800, he sketched the design of the one below, calling it a "stick chair." An inventory of the entrance hall lists 28 "black painted chairs."

but the learned lumber of Greek and Roman reading with which his head is stored? I answer everything is useful which contributes to fix in the principles and practices of virtue. . . . The field of imagination is thus laid open to our use and lessons may be formed to illustrate and carry home to the heart every moral rule of life."

The young lawyer's first bachelor quarters at Monticello—his Adam's House in Paradise—consisting of one plain room and a few sticks of plain furniture, would have been the envy of Jean-Jacques Rousseau, whose hermit's quarters at Ermononville was in fact built about the same time. The fire at Shadwell that had destroyed Jefferson's books and papers also destroyed whatever furniture that belonged to him in that rather homespun household. The inventory of his father's estate listed "a cherry tree desk and book case," another in walnut, a tea table, a number

185   Fauteuil à la Reine, beechwood, upholstered in brown leather, c. 1790 (above). Jefferson may have purchased this chair from James Monroe, who also acquired French furniture during his stay in Paris as minister to France during the period 1794 to 1796, several years after Jefferson had held the same post.

186   Pair of Virginia chairs, walnut, c. 1770 (right). These chairs, made by Peter Scott of Williamsburg and now in the tea room at Monticello, may have been acquired by Jefferson from the estate of his mentor George Wythe. They reflect solid craftsmanship that suited a side of Jefferson's taste.

of chairs, bedsteads, butter pots, "kittles," "sisors," and shoemaker's tools, but there is nothing to suggest that Shadwell was anything more than a modest plantation established on the edge of civilization, where utility ruled over all other considerations. By retiring to a mountaintop without any possessions beyond a library of good books, a table, a chair, and a bedstead, he, too, like his friend Dabney Carr, would "exhibit to the world a new phenomenon in philosophy, the Samian sage in the tub of the cynic,"

187   Clock face above central door, entrance hall (*above*). *The large seven-day calendar clock was made to Jefferson's design by Peter Sprunk of Philadelphia. Cannonball weights power the clock, and the top one on the north wall indicates the day of the week as it passes marks on that wall.*

188   Clock, made by Chantrot of Paris, 1791 (*right*). *Jefferson designed the black marble, ormolu, and brass clock and asked William Short to have it made in Paris. The neoclassical obelisk form appealed to Jefferson, and he once planned chimneys at Monticello in that shape.*

189 Mantel clock, French, late 18th century. Jefferson included many decorative objects, such as this clock, along with sofas, chairs, mirrors, and paintings, in the shipment of household furnishings that William Short packed up for him following his return to the United States after five years in Paris.

servants," made him in the eyes of Jefferson "the happiest man in the universe. He possesses truely the art of extracting comfort from things the most trivial." But "utter neglect of the costly apparatus of life," which Carr had successfully managed, was a condition—however appealing in its simplicity—that was to elude Jefferson throughout his life, if in fact he ever seriously contemplated living such a Spartan existence. The range of his interests, tastes, and curiosity, reflected in the objects that he accumulated around him at Monticello in order to satisfy his relish of sensuous and intellectual enjoyment, made such a style of living out of the question.

When the Marquis de Chastellux wrote that his host had been the first American to consult the fine arts in order to know how to shelter himself from the weather, it is fair to assume that the Frenchman was referring to the general appearance of the first Monticello inside and out, although he gives us few details. Chastellux's comments may have referred only to the architecture, yet his enthusiasm seems to suggest that the furnishings also indicated a mark of cultivation above the average. It is clear from the earliest notes on Monticello that Jefferson intended its basic program to encompass the functions of a museum of art and of natural history as well as to house a comprehensive library, in which he would have an apartment where he could act as both curator and librarian. Family life would be integrated into these first priorities.

In 1771, hardly a year after writing John Page about the happy state their friend Carr had created for himself in his primitive cabin, the young lawyer, who was "given to dreaming with his eyes open" in Dumas Malone's words, composed a list of desiderata

as he wrote to his friend John Page. The rustic life of their mutual friend Carr, who lived in a small house "with a table, a half dozen chairs and one or two

for "Statues, Paintings &" that would have made Monticello one of the first museums of art in the New World if he had been able to carry out his inno-

190 Ariadne, entrance hall. *Baron de Montlezun saw the "natural size marble statue like that of Cleopatre reclining, serpent wound around left arm" when he visited Monticello in 1816. He dutifully noted that "M. Jeff. thinks it represents Ariadne," which, of course, was correct. The classical frieze on the mantel is taken from Desgodetz,* Les Edifices Antique de Rome, 1682.

vative scheme. Jefferson's fashionable interest in classical sculpture placed him in the grand European tradition that began with François I, the king of France who built a collection of both copies and original pieces of sculpture at Fontainebleau, and extended up to Jefferson's own contemporaries in eighteenth-century England who were passionately assembling souvenir galleries as reminders of their tours abroad. There was hardly a great English house of the late eighteenth century that could not boast of a *Venus, Dying Gladiator,* or other classical statuary reproduced in bronze, marble, or plaster. Since Monticello would continue to serve as both a museum of art and of natural history and to house a major library of six thousand volumes, it is worth briefly considering these first ambitious plans without precedent in colonial America even though the original list never materialized into an actual collection.

Beginning with the proposed collection of sculpture, the young curator was ambitious. The list of a score of works, starting with "Venus of Medici. Florence" and followed by "Apollo of Belvedere. Rome," is remarkable for several reasons. At the time the list was jotted into his building notebook, the twenty-eight-year-old squire's esthetic education, as we have seen, had been derived almost entirely from books. "The only help a youth wants is to be directed what books to read, and in what order to read them," he wrote to his cousin Philip Turpin in 1769. For the student in Virginia the vexing problem "is the want of books," a condition Jefferson spent a lifetime and a fortune attempting to overcome. With his Renaissance mind, when he approached the question of sculpture suitable for the Roman-Palladian villa and grounds he was designing, he simply turned to the

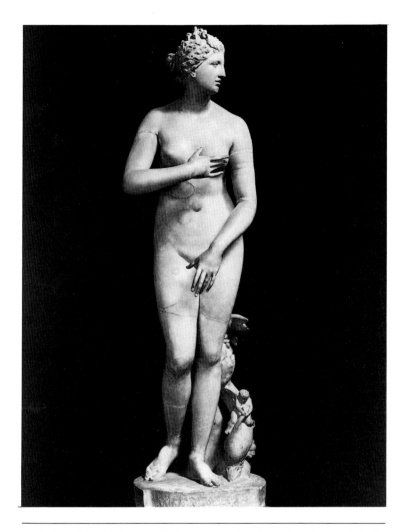

191 **The Medici Venus; Aphrodite Rising from the Sea,** *marble, 1st* *century B.C. A copy of this statue was to be included in Jefferson's proposed collection for Monticello. To the 18th century, this Roman copy of a Greek statue was the most celebrated image of the goddess of love and female beauty.*

judgment of the best European sources then available to him in books and engravings.

In addition to his books, he had an appetite for the visual arts that had been further whetted by his trip north to Annapolis, Philadelphia, and New York

in 1766. In Philadelphia he had been introduced to Dr. John Morgan, the eminent physician and classicist, who had actually made the Grand Tour on the Continent. There Morgan had seen many collections of classical and academic works of sculpture and in

192 **Diana the Huntress, by Jean-Antoine Houdon.** *Jefferson saw the original statue in Houdon's studio in Paris, and he later bought a small plaster version to bring back to America. He remarked that "its nudity may be an objection to some to receive it as a deposit." It has not survived.*

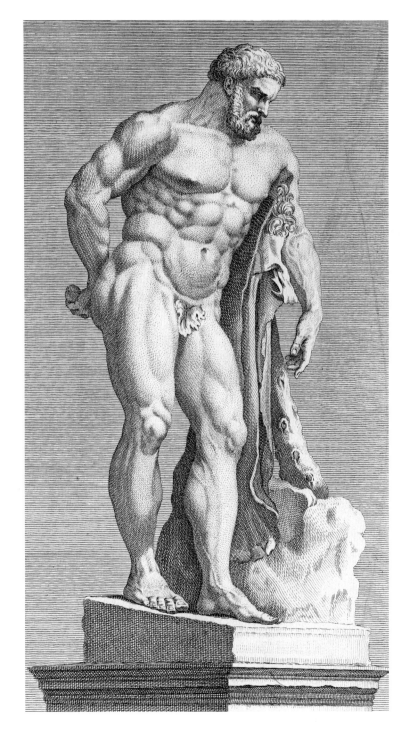

Rome had become an enthusiast of the "perfection" of ancient art. When he returned to Philadelphia, he had managed to turn his house into a small museum of collections of natural curiosities, art works, books, paintings, and sculpture. No doubt, Dr. Morgan's worldly establishment made a lasting impression on the young Virginian at an important and formative moment in his development.

Jefferson also had seen sculpture used in a garden setting on the grounds of Colonel John Tayloe's Mt. Airy, where "four large marble Statues" placed in the "large, well formed beautiful Garden" impressed Philip Fithian, who visited Colonel Tayloe in 1774. Considering the number of pieces of sculpture on Jefferson's list, it is probable that some of the thirteen works were intended to be placed on the grounds. Again, that strange, creative strain of contradiction in Jefferson's personality manifests itself in an unexpected form. In 1771, the same year that he had drawn up his discriminating preference for sculpture of time-honored excellence, and the same year that he was praising the virtues of the simple rustic life in his letters, he had written out the most romantic garden ideas, calling for elegant Gothic temples, statuary, grots, pyramids, and waterfalls arranged in what the English would have called "an artful wilderness." The remarkable thing about Jefferson's

195 **East wall of parlor, during restoration.** *The original niches from the first house were uncovered on either side of the doorway, and Jefferson may have intended these for his copies of antique sculpture. When the Duc de la Rochefoucauld visited the first Monticello, he noted that "the taste and arts of Europe have been consulted in the formation of its plan."*

---

193 **The Apollo Belvedere** *(far left). This famous figure from the Vatican's collection was on Jefferson's list of antique sculptures he wanted copies of.*

---

194 **The Farnese Hercules** *(far right). This engraving of the antique sculpture prompted Jefferson to add it to the list of works he wanted to acquire for Monticello's collection. He was never to visit Rome and Florence to see any of the original pieces or to examine Rome's architecture firsthand.*

---

sculpture gallery, compiled in a province that was, as Hyatt Mayor put it, "sculptureless and all but pictureless," is its touching revelation of a visual hunger and an ambition that far surpassed the meager sources from which it had been compiled. He knew the sculpture only from illustrated volumes such as those of François Perrier, Joseph Spence, and Domenico de Rossi, but he also studied the travel books of Addison and Richardson, favorite companion guides of all English "milordi" and gentlemen making the Grand Tour in search of culture.

Probably most of the sculpture and paintings were planned to be displayed in the large "Parlour" of the original Monticello, and it is possible that Jefferson actually had in mind as a model the Tribunal in

Florence as described by Richardson, where several of the original works on Jefferson's list were installed. The *Venus* and *Apollo* were no doubt intended for the two original niches on either side of the parlor door facing the entry portico, now plastered and covered by mirrors.

Books also must have inspired the would-be connoisseur's first list of paintings entered in the building notebook, though specific sources of inspiration are difficult to identify. The list included "St. Paul preaching at Athens from a cartoon of Ra. Urbin"; "St. Ignatius at prayer"; "Jephtha meeting his daughter by Zocchi"; "The Sacrifice of Iphigenia"; "Selericus giving his wife Stratonice to his son Selericus"; "Diana Venetrix." Six more painting titles were added to the list in 1782, the year that the Marquis de Chastellux visited the still-unfinished villa.

Both the sculpture and paintings were to be good replicas, and later when the Italian Charles Bellini arrived in Albemarle County from Florence with Philip Mazzei, Jefferson consulted him on the price and availability of copies in Italy. In 1782 he noted: "Bellini tells me that historical paintings on canvas 6 f. by 12 f. will cost £15 sterl. if copied by a good hand."

Jefferson's sophisticated blend of republican virtues born of the frontier and a patrician love of style and elegance that comes out of aristocratic European traditions transplanted to eighteenth-century Virginia can be seen both inside and out of Monticello as Jefferson struggled to hold to the best of the past while reaching to embrace a future that had not yet emerged. On the one hand he deeply admired his friend Carr's ability to derive pleasure "from things the most trivial," yet another part of Jefferson re-

quired a background expressing the virtues of classical civilization, a condition the merely practical, everyday rural existence could not provide. Certainly this dichotomy must have been evident in the furnishings of the first Monticello, with its "lofty saloon . . . decorated entirely in the antique style" but its furniture quite plain and straightforward. Some of the furniture doubtlessly was made in the plantation joinery by slave craftsmen following designs prepared

*196 **Parlor, southeast corner** (facing). The musical life of Monticello took place in the parlor, where Martha Jefferson's piano was kept. The large pier mirror is one of a pair Jefferson purchased in Paris, which have been removed only once since Jefferson hung them, during restoration of the parlor.*

*197 **Folding music stand** (above). Jefferson designed this walnut music stand, with five adjustable rests to hold sheet music for as many as a quintet, and it probably was crafted in Monticello's own cabinetry shop. When folded up, it forms a small box suitable for transporting to a musicale.*

by Jefferson. A cabinetmaker was listed along with a gardener, stonecutter, and weaver among the skilled domestic servants he "retained" in 1778.

Several years before Monticello was planned, Jefferson copied out Horace's poem celebrating the self-sufficient, utopian existence of the Roman farm, where everything from food and clothing to tables, chairs, and other household furnishings was produced.

> Happy is he who far from business,
> like the first race of man,
> Can till inherited lands with his teams,
> free from all payment of interest.
> He who avoids the market and
> the proud thresholds of mighty citizens . . .
>
> He may recline now under an old tree
> and, again on soft meadow,
> while the water fall down from the steep banks,
> birds lament in the woods,
> and the springs with murmuring veins,
> suggest soft sleep.

The plantation manufacturing facilities that grew along Mulberry Row were Jefferson's attempt to achieve the Horatian ideal, for "to be independent for the comforts of life we must fabricate them ourselves . . . [and] . . . place the manufacturer by the side of the agriculturists." The joinery located next to the nailery was equipped to make all kinds of articles, including furniture for the plantation, al-

*198 **Mantelpiece, parlor** (facing). Jefferson placed the unlikely Herodiade Bearing the Head of St. John on a Platter above the mantel in the parlor. It was a copy after Guido Renni, and for the most part all of the historical paintings at Monticello were copies.*

*199 **Benjamin Franklin, probably by Jean Valade, oil on canvas, c. 1785.** Jefferson purchased the portrait two years after he arrived in France to succeed Dr. Franklin as the American representative in Paris. Regarding it as a good likeness, Jefferson thought it was by Greuze when he bought it.*

though it is not certain when plantation-made chairs and tables were actually introduced into the main house. In 1809 one visitor was impressed to see both furniture and a carriage being made in the Mulberry Row joinery. Given his blend of Horatian idealism and practicality, it seems likely that household pieces

205

201 Dumbwaiter, dining room mantelpiece. *This dumbwaiter was directly above the wine cellar. "No wine is put on the table until the cloth is removed," Daniel Webster reported after dinner at Monticello, which he found to be "served half in Virginia, half in French style, in good taste and abundance."*

200 Dining room fireplace, looking toward parlor, *with Jefferson's reading chair and candle stand. It was Jefferson's habit in the winter to sit near the fire in the dining room and read after dinner—if there were no guests to entertain. The open door at the side of the mantelpiece indicates the location of one of a pair of dumbwaiters in the dining room that were used to bring up wine from the cellar and to return empty bottles.*

were made and used as needed even though it would be of a quality far removed from the fine craftsmanship that Jefferson knew and admired in Philadelphia, Annapolis, or New York. Chairs, tables, and bureaus were serviceable but unexceptional pieces of furniture, as were the four dozen Windsor or "stick" chairs, painted black, that he ordered from Philadelphia in 1800. Twenty-eight of these chairs were inventoried in the front entrance hall after Jefferson's death.

The name of one cabinetmaker, the slave John Hemings, survives, and several pieces of furniture at Monticello are attributed to him. A member of a talented slave family that had come from Jefferson's wife's family, Hemings himself was born at Monticello in 1776. Edmund Bacon described him as "a first-rate workman—a very extra workman. He could make anything that was wanted in wood-work."

Margaret Smith was impressed by the "pervading elegance and singularity" of the rooms and felt that the owner's eclectic accumulation of artworks and curiosities, from Houdon busts to piles of pre-historic mammoth bones and tusks, "blended with furniture suitable to the dwelling and simple taste of the owner." On her tour of the house she was shown a room (possibly the south piazza) with a carpenter's workbench and "a vast assortment of tools of every kind and description." Making things with his hands

202 Serving table, designed by Jefferson *(far left). Margaret Smith reported that Jefferson used these tables to reduce the intrusion of servants and to encourage "a free and unrestricted flow of conversation."*

203 Pivoting door to dining room *(left). The shelves on the back of this door were a further attempt to reduce the need for servants during meals.*

was apparently a well-established hobby for the retired president. Earlier Mrs. Smith had noticed similar tools handily laid out in the president's office in Washington, so that he could indulge his "favorite amusement" in idle moments—with his pet mocking bird nearby. George Tucker claimed that some pieces of furniture, garden seats, and even his carriage, of which a plan in Jefferson's hand survives, were the joint work of himself and his slave craftsmen.

All of the furniture made from Jefferson's designs is distinguished by simple lines and sparse ornamentation. Often the chief appeal of a piece is in its mechanical ingenuity, as in the case of the walnut folding book or music stand whose fine adjustable rests may be folded down to form a small box. Jefferson's interest in furniture design seems to have developed early, for in 1769 he gives detailed specifications for the construction of a large slant-top desk capable of holding large folios and decorated with a Chinese railing.

Like most well-to-do Virginia plantation owners, Jefferson regularly ordered household articles from England, although probably not in as great a quantity. After his return from France, he also would impose on his former secretary William Short to procure furnishings in Paris, where he had developed a discriminating eye for the latest French design of the Louis XVI period. Recent archeological work at Monticello has unearthed a remarkable array of English and Chinese export porcelain and pottery representing a wide range of design and workmanship. Some of it may have been inherited from Shadwell or the plantation home of Martha Jefferson—The Forest—but much of it had been ordered by Jefferson over the years.

The furnishing of the two houses Jefferson rented in Paris had permitted him to collect a sizable number of articles—paintings, sculpture, prints, furniture, clocks, fabrics—and some would eventually end up at Monticello. He was not alone among his fellow Americans living in Paris in the late eighteenth century in his addiction to French furniture. Whatever lingering Puritan prejudice the Americans brought to the French capital was quickly dissipated by the splendid *fauteuils en cabriolet*, *gueridon* tables, *régulateurs* by Lepine, and *velours d'utrecht*, which appealed even to that upright New Englander John Adams. As Francis Watson has pointed out, Jefferson's architectural training and his early interest in furniture craftsmanship and technique enabled him to appreciate the qualities of Louis XVI furniture far better than any other American living in pre-Revolutionary France. His accounts show that in furnishing the Hôtel de Langeac, at the corner of the rue de Berry and the Champs Elysées, he purchased large quantities of silver tableware, chairs, tables, and lamps. After Jefferson's return to the United States in 1789, William Short was left with the responsibility of packing and dispatching no less than eighty-six cases of possessions from the Paris residence to Philadelphia, where Jefferson was then living. Patsy Jefferson's harpsichord and guitar were packed with clocks, mattresses, books, and busts. In the horticultural department the shipment also included two cork oaks, four melon apricots, one white fig, five larch trees, four cresanne pears, three Italian poplars, and other trees and plants for Monticello's "garden of memory," to recall happy years in the French capital.

Short followed Jefferson's instructions to make a "very exact invoice of contents." Case 18, for example, contained "10 large armchairs new crimson wool coverings"; case 19, "10 blue chairs, six covered with cotton, four with silk." Case 22 was packed with "six chairs of *velours d'utrecht*." In an inventory of Monticello made in 1815, "6 sophas with gold leaf" and "44 chairs gold leaf" are listed and were probably a part of the Paris furniture that was sent to Virginia in 1790, according to Marie Kimball, although some of the gilt pieces came from Philadelphia cabinetmakers. No doubt, these chairs and sofas were of the typical Louis XVI style, with gilt or white painted frames, the seats and backs covered with satin or silk. There were fifty-nine chairs in all listed in the shipping inventory, and Short may have decided to leave some behind since Jefferson's instructions also told him to "use your knowledge of this country" in deciding what might not be suitable for America. Among the "unsuitable" items left behind were "five dumbwaiters," which closely resembled the English "whatnot" table. Though not common in eighteenth-

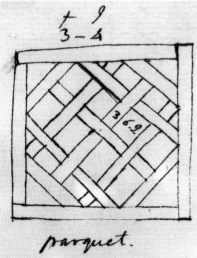

parquet.

century France, where the conventional *gueridon*-type table was set beside each guest's place at a dinner table in order to dispense with servants, Jefferson, who loved uninterrupted conversation, found this "dumbwaiter" an appealing innovation. He later adopted the fashion in the dining room at the White House and again at Poplar Forest as well as Monticello, where three made to his design survive. Again

206, 207 Archeological fragments found at Monticello (left and below). Thousands of shards of pottery, porcelain, and glass have been recovered at Monticello during the excavation of Mulberry Row and the garden area. The pieces shown here are of English manufacture and are typical examples of tableware of the period. Jefferson personally selected the household items, as did other men of taste in the 18th century, including political leaders such as Washington, Monroe, and Gouverneur Morris—judging by their correspondence and accounts.

Margaret Smith provides us with the contemporary detail: "When he had any persons dining with him whom he wished to enjoy a free and unrestricted flow of conversation, the number of persons at table never exceed four, and by each individual was placed a dumbwaiter, containing everything necessary for the progress of the dinner from beginning to end, so as to make the attendance of servants entirely unnecessary, believing as he did, that much of the domestic and even public discord was produced by the mutilated and misconstructed repetition of free conversation at dinner tables by these mute but not inattentive listeners."

Jefferson's aversion to eavesdropping servants was shared by Voltaire, who had installed two hatches in the dining room at Cirey, his chateau retreat, one

208 Tea room, table set with Jefferson family silver, china, and linen (facing). "Our breakfast table was as large as our dinner table; instead of a cloth, a folded napkin lay under each plate; we had tea, coffee, excellent muffins, hot wheat and corn bread, cold ham and butter."

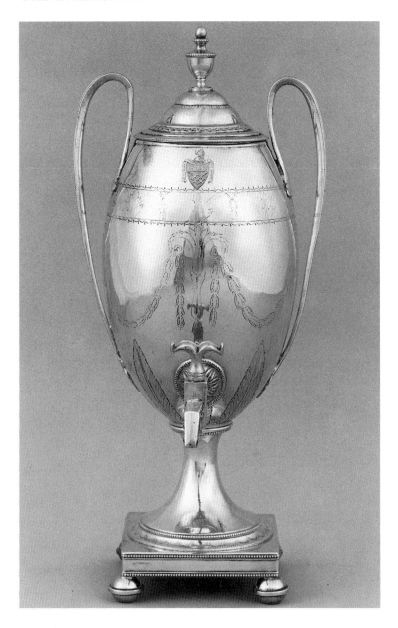

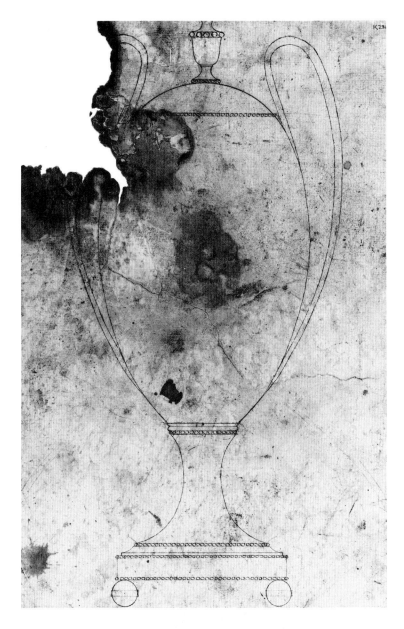

for food and one for dirty dishes, so that he and his guests could serve themselves in order to avoid prying servants. In fact, the highly individual style of life at Voltaire's Cirey, with visitors interspersed with reading, writing, and gardening, often reminds one of the casual intellectual atmosphere in which Jefferson lived and worked at Monticello.

*209, 210 Silver coffee urn, by Leguay, 1789 (left), **and Jefferson's design for it** (right). Jefferson developed his interest in silver design after he went to Paris, where he had this urn made by Jacques-Louis-Auguste Leguay in 1789.*

*211 **Jefferson's designs for goblets** (facing). Jefferson may have drawn these designs for the silversmith Jean-Baptiste-Claude Odiot, who supplied his table.*

The Paris shipping lists also included beds, commodes, chiffoniers, and mirrors as well as decorative objects such as vases of white porcelain, porcelain figures, and a reduced plaster version of Houdon's *Dianne* that Jefferson had purchased after admiring the original in the artist's studio. Short apparently had not thought the stark-naked goddess was unsuitable for chaste republican eyes, and decided to include her in the shipment.

Following Jefferson's return to Virginia, he sent a letter to Short in 1790 asking him to have a clock made in Paris to his design. A sketch in his own hand and detailed specifications were enclosed.

This, Mr. Short may recollect, was the form of the little clock which was stolen from the chimney of my study. The parts a.b.c.d. were parts of a cone, being round and tapering to the top where a gilt head was put on. I would wish one to be made like that as to the pedestal part, but with an obelisk as is represented here a.b.c.d. instead of conical columns as the former had. No gilt head to be on the obelisk, but to be in plain marble cut off obliquely, as is always done in the obelisk. The section of an obelisk,

you know, is square, I mean its iconography.
The clock to have a pendulum vibrating half seconds exactly,
To have a second hand but none for the days of the week, month or moon.
To strike the hour and half hours.
The dial plate to be openwork, or as the French workmen say, *le cadran a jour,*
Of black marble.

There were the usual delays, confusion, and correspondence, but the clock made by Chantrot à Paris finally reached Virginia in 1793 after a brief stay in the Secretary of State's house in Philadelphia. The stylish design with its classical architectural elements had a special appeal for Jefferson and reflected the advanced style of the Empire that would not emerge out of the Directoire for another decade. It was to be placed on a shelf inside the alcove at the foot of his bed at Monticello.

Some of the curtains and draperies of the Hôtel de Langeac that matched the fabrics on chairs and sofas may have been brought back to Virginia. "Six large blue damask curtains, eight medium size of the same, a drapery in two parts . . . six crimson curtains and eight cords with crimson tassels" along with twenty-two bell pulls were included on Short's list. Twenty-five years later eleven pairs of these "foreign curtains" were listed in a memorandum of taxable property at Monticello for Albemarle County. The alcove bed hung with curtains, a fashionable innovation in Parisian houses, appealed to Jefferson and was adapted for the newly renovated bedrooms of Monticello. The alcove beds Jefferson saw in the Column House at the Désert de Retz may have been one of the inspirations. He had first experimented

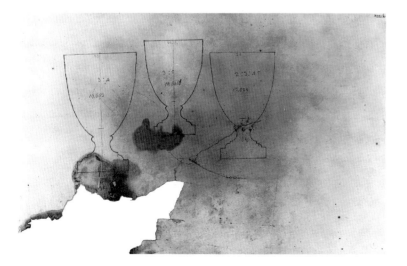

212, 213, 214 **Silver askos made for Jefferson** *(right),* **wooden model for it** *(left center),* **and original Roman bronze** *(bottom left).* Jefferson saw the Roman askos, used for wine or oil, in Nîmes in 1787, had a wooden model made of it, and had it copied in silver in Philadelphia in 1801, the year he began his first term as president.

215 **Silver askos, goblet, and cups designed by Jefferson** *(bottom right).* Jefferson loved good silver and seems to have collected it and had it made throughout his life.

with such an alcove bed arrangement in his Philadelphia house and later used wall beds similar to his own at Monticello to divide the rooms at Poplar Forest.

It is not clear exactly how the different wall decorations and schemes that are mentioned in various accounts and letters were executed. This would include the question of the precise use of the wall paper that Jefferson ordered from the celebrated Manufacture Royal des Sieurs Arthur et Robert after leaving Paris. French wall paper in all of its glory was the rage in Paris in the 1780s and Jefferson ordered quantities of "*rouleaux* of plain sky blue" and "plain pea green paper" along with elaborate borders, but it is likely that most of it was used in the Philadelphia house rather than at Monticello. During twentieth-century restoration, traces of the "lattice or treillage paper" also ordered from Arthur were uncovered at Monticello in the North Octagonal Room.

Entries in the Memorandum Book mention papier-mâché wall ornaments that may have been intended for the ceilings of the first Monticello. In the fall of 1792 when plans to rebuild Monticello were first considered he contemplated the commission of extensive fresco painting on the plastered walls of the house. The specific rooms are not identified but they probably were the entrance hall, the parlor and the dining room. Jefferson had earlier commissioned some wall panels for his rented house in New York from a Mr. Schneider, a fresco painter in New York. Apparently his price of $2 a day was thought to be too high in Albemarle County, where Jefferson had compared the artist's fee with the price of beef— only 2¢ a pound. Like the schemes for Gothic temples, grottoes, and Chinese pavilions, the Monticello

fresco project appears never to have been carried out.

The magnificent parquet floor that was installed in the parlor in 1804 was no doubt inspired by similar floors in Paris and was one of the first parquet floors in America. The geometric design drawn by Jefferson was executed with a center square of cherry and a border of beech. But the most original floor treatment in the house was the front hall. While having his portrait painted by Gilbert Stuart in 1805, he heard from the artist about "the true grass-green floor" that Stuart had tried. He immediately sent his builder John Dinsmore a paint sample Stuart had given him so that he could duplicate it. A green floor cloth was also made to be placed over the painted floor. The floor of the dome room was painted green later, according to a letter Jefferson wrote in 1807.

Even though Jefferson had complained that outfitting his Paris house had taken his entire year's salary, and while he disclaimed any "ambition for splendor," the furnishings must have conveyed a quiet elegance and cosmopolitan refinement. "Mr. Jefferson lives well, keeps a good table and excellent wines which he distributes freely . . ." reported Gouverneur Morris, who knew something about the art of living, in his diary. Something of the Parisian elegance was later added to the Virginia plantation house when the Paris cases were finally unpacked and installed at Monticello. The years in Paris had a profound impact on Jefferson's taste, ranging from Roman antiquities to Louis XVI chairs, and the result of this experience was to be seen inside Monticello in furnishings as well as in the architecture.

Apparently, well-made pieces of French table silver did not, in Jefferson's mind, denote pretensions unacceptable in a minister of the New Republic. Before he left Paris, silversmiths were commissioned to make from his designs a set of two silver goblets and three coffee urns. One of the urns was made as a present for the architect Charles-Louis Clérisseau, who had given Jefferson "assistance about the draughts & model of the capitol and prison" in Richmond, Virginia. Jefferson's drawing for the urn that he actually kept, which later was to grace the dining room at Monticello, has survived and is similar to the fashionable neoclassical models then beginning to appear in Europe. Another remarkable piece of Monticello silver is a Roman askos copied in silver. During his travels in the south of France, he had been captivated by an original Roman bronze askos on display in a cabinet in the Maison Carrée in Nîmes. After gazing on the temple "like a lover at his mistress," he had his *valet de place* in Nîmes make a wooden copy of the Roman artifact to be used as a model for the silver version. He originally had planned to give the Nîmes askos to Clérisseau, but later changed his mind in favor of the coffee urn. The silver askos was finally made in Philadelphia in 1801 and was later used at Monticello.

Music, like architecture and gardening, was to inspire some of Jefferson's most emotional language even if it did not occupy as high a position as these other interests. "Music . . . is the favorite passion of my soul, and fortune has cast my lot in a country [as it had in the case of architecture] where it is in a state of deplorable barbarism." To correct fortune's oversight, serious music became a central part of life at Monticello. Martha Wayles Skelton Jefferson was an accomplished musician and her interest encouraged Jefferson to pursue his own. By the time that he was engaged, he had ordered one of the new "Piano-Fortes" as a wedding present instead of the clavichord he originally requested. "I have since seen a Forte-Piano and am charmed with it," he wrote his London correspondent. "Send me this instrument then instead of the Clavicord; let the case be of fine mahogany, solid not veneered, the compass from Double G to F in alt, a plenty of spare strings; and the workmanship of the whole very handsome and worthy of the acceptance of a lady for whom I intend it." The settlement of his father-in-law's estate records that he paid a William Allegre and a Frederick Victor twelve pounds for two years of "teaching Mrs. J. on the Spinnet."

Two harpsichords were to be added to Monticello's musical instrument collection, one for his daughter Martha ordered from Kirkman in London in 1786 and a second Kirkman purchased in 1798 for his daughter Maria. In 1800, Maria was offered a choice between the newly arrived portable grand piano invented by Isaac Hawkins and the Kirkman instrument. The last musical instrument to enter the Monticello collection was a piano Jefferson ordered for his granddaughter Virginia Randolph Trist in 1826, the year Jefferson died. His financial condition was desperate, and Virginia's brother Jeff, who was now trying to salvage the estate through careful management, opposed the acquisition as "a most foolish extravagant act." Its purchase backed by Jefferson and Virginia's mother, in what became an acrimonious dispute, the new piano finally arrived from Boston at the very moment a public lottery to relieve the Monticello family was being organized.

Jefferson himself played the violin, and there were several at Monticello, as well as a guitar, which had long been a popular instrument in Virginia. Music and dancing were considered essential accomplishments in Virginia, and Jefferson had studied both as a child and later in Williamsburg, where he played violin with Governor Fauquier and "two or three other amateurs in his weekly concerts." When his mind was not on architecture, physics, celestial mechanics, or constitutions it seems that music filled in the gaps with a practice schedule that took as much as three hours a day. Isaac Jefferson reports that his master "played in the arternoons and sometimes arter supper." He also remembered him "always singing when ridin' or walkin'. Had a fine clear voice; sung minnits [minuets] and sich; fiddled in the parlour." Family tradition maintained that only his fiddle was saved from the fire at Shadwell when his books and papers were destroyed.

Francis Alberti, a violinist and harpsichordist from Faenza, was another expatriate friend of Jefferson when he had settled in Albemarle County, where he gave violin lessons to the Monticello family and to others in the neighborhood.

Monticello's musical library was good and had been enlarged with a collection of scores of Haydn, Handel, Pergolesi, Sacchini, Schubert, and Grétry purchased in Paris, where opera and musical concerts became an important part of Jefferson's life. While the first work was going on at Monticello in 1771, the same year that Jefferson settled into his bucolic quarters, he had seen and coveted a splendid imported violin and music library at the house of one of his Randolph kinsmen in Williamsburg. John Randolph had at the same time desired some books he had seen in Jefferson's library, but a trade could not be worked out. Finally they drew up an agreement, or posthumous bargain, giving the survivor the right to buy the other's desired property, depending on the gamble of survival. After a year went by and Jefferson's impatience got the better of him, he persuaded Randolph finally to accept £13 for the violin.

Certainly Jefferson's most ambitious dream for a musical life occurred during the Revolution and is revealed in a letter to an Italian acquaintance in 1778. It called for nothing less than the creation of a private orchestra composed of servants skilled in more practical trades who could earn their keep on the plantation when not making music.

The bounds of an American fortune will not admit the indulgence of a domestic band of musicians, yet I have thought that a passion for music might be reconciled with that economy which we are obliged to observe. I retain among my domestic servants a gardener, a weaver, a cabinet-maker and a stone-cutter, to which I would add a vigneron. In a country where, like [Italy], music is cultivated and practiced by every class of men, I suppose there might be found persons of these trades who could perform on the French horn, clarinet, or hautboy, and bassoon, so that one might have a band of two French horns, two clarinets, two hautboys, and a bassoon without enlarging their domestic expenses. A certainty of employment for half a dozen years, and at the end of that time to find them, if they choose, a conveyance to their own country, might induce them to come here on reasonable urges. . . . sobriety and good nature would be desirable parts of their characters.

The idea joined the list of Jefferson's fantasies that never materialized, although several paroled British and German officers who settled temporarily near Charlottesville in 1779 came to Monticello regularly to perform in neighborhood concerts.

Books were everywhere at Monticello. Isaac recalled that Jefferson would have as many as "twenty of 'em down on the floor at once—read just one, then t'other." Even the small, first version of the house had a library on the second floor that held two thousand volumes. Baron von Closen, who visited Monticello just after the close of the Revolution, was surprised to find that it had survived the brief and unexpected occupation by Tarleton's troops in 1781. When Jefferson's "Great Library" was sold to the Federal government in 1815, about 6,000 volumes were shipped to Washington. Most of these had been shelved in the south study off the bedroom, but the overflow must have spilled into other corners throughout the house.

Special guests usually were shown the library and invited to browse in what was considered the best private collection of books on the continent. Mrs. William Thornton's husband became so engrossed with the illustrated volumes that he "Staid there till it was time to dress for dinner." Sir Augustus John Foster sensed that the library was the President's inner sanctum, but if it "had been thrown open to his guests . . . [it] . . . would have been as agreeable a Place to stay at as any I know." It was here that he saw Jefferson deep in correspondence and sensed that he did not like to be disturbed "by Visitors who in this Part of the world are rather disposed to be indiscreet."

The cluttered entrance hall of the expanded Monticello was, for most visitors, the nearest thing to a museum they had ever seen. Here contemporary portrait busts, paintings, and sculpture after the antique were placed side by side with all kinds of Indian artifacts—bows, arrows, quivers, poisoned lances, peace pipes, wampum belts, moccasins, dresses, and cooking utensils. On the wall hung a large Indian map painted on a buffalo hide of the Missouri River and its tributaries. Beside it was an Indian battle scene also painted on leather. Nearby

216 Marquis de Lafayette, *by Jean-Antoine Houdon, plaster, c. 1785.*
An enthusiast for Houdon's work, Jefferson helped the Virginia legislature carry out its commission of a bust of Lafayette. He arranged to present the marble version to the city of Paris and placed his plaster copy in the tea room.

stood the truncated classical column given to Jefferson by his friend Madame de Tessé as a parting gift when he left Paris. The column, which originally was intended to serve as an "alter" or garden ornament for some secluded grove at Monticello, held the monumental bust of Jefferson by Cerrachi "in the Rome costume" and larger than life. When it was pressed into service as a pedestal in the front hall, its Latin inscriptions paying extravagant tribute to Jefferson were discreetly turned to the wall. The antique world was represented by a marble copy of *Sleeping Ariadne*, or, as she was described by one Monticello guest, Cleopatra "reclining and abandoned to the bites of the asp." *Ariadne*, a gift of Governor James Bowdoin, Jr., of Massachusetts and listed by Jefferson in his catalogue as "Ariadne reclined on the rocks at Naxos," had not been included on the sculpture list of 1771, but he may have first read about it in Richardson, who had "clamber'd up a piece of ancient Wall of Rome: overlooking the Belvedere courtyard at the Vatican in order to see a work of the greatest Greek taste." Copies of the work had been popular as an ornament in English garden grottoes, and Henry Hoare had commissioned one for the grotto at Stourhead. Like Jefferson, he, too, admired the Latin poem the young Virginia squire had copied into his Garden Book for future reference in his own elaborate garden plans, although Hoare had carved Pope's translation rather than the Latin text.

Besides the Cerrachi bust of Jefferson and one of Alexander Hamilton that stood on the opposite side of the entrance, there were plaster versions of Houdon's Voltaire and Turgot. In the parlor beyond were also a marble bust of Napoleon and a plaster version of Alexander I of Russia. One visitor noted

217 George Washington, *by Jean-Antoine Houdon, plaster, c. 1785.*
This bust of Washington is one of four likenesses of Jefferson's friends that he kept on brackets in the tea room. When the Virginia assembly voted to commission a bust of Washington, Jefferson arranged to have Houdon execute it.

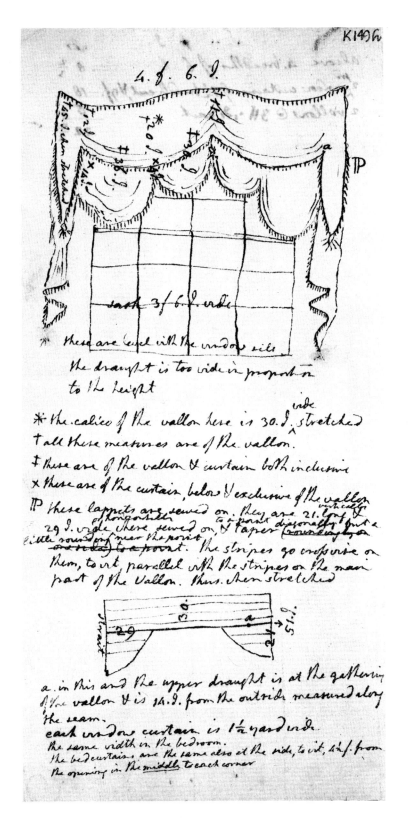

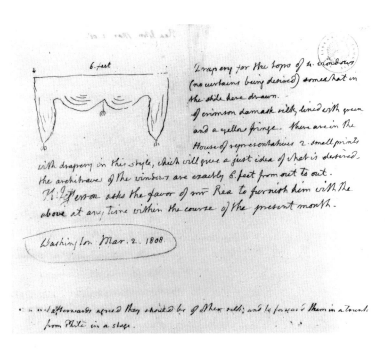

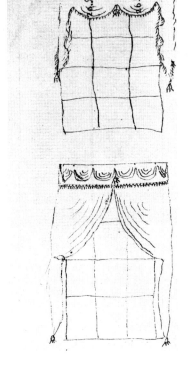

218, 219, 220 Jefferson's curtain designs for Monticello. *The dressing of windows was a detail of interior design that Jefferson never overlooked. In 1808 he ordered new curtains "of crimson damask silk, lined with green and yellow fringe." For his own bedroom, he ordered a counterpane of the same crimson, writing to John Rea in Philadelphia to ask for a "counterpane of the same crimson mantua silk as the draperies. . . ." Jefferson planned to line the silk with furs that he already had, and, to give the elegant silk and fur throw a more democratic quality, he specified that the bolster was not to be hollowed "in the French manner, but plain as is usual with us."*

also a model of the Great Pyramid of Egypt beside the Indian curiosities, but most visitors overlooked it for the mammoth jaw bones (upper and lower), horns of elk, moose, and deer, a head of a mountain ram, minerals, shells, and "petrifactions." The pyramid had been a gift of the French rationalist Comte de Volney. "In short, it is supposed there is no private gentleman in the world in possession of so complete a scientific, useful and ornamental collection," a visitor wrote in a travel guide in 1808. George Ticknor of Boston found the hall odd and amusing. "You enter, by a glass folding-door, into a hall which reminds you of Fielding's 'Man of the Mountain' by the strange furniture of the walls." The curiosities brought back from the "wild and perilous expedition" of Lewis and Clark, and the Indian hide map "in odd union with a fine painting of the Repentance of Saint Peter" were too eccentric for the Bostonian's refined taste.

When Ticknor was a guest at Monticello in 1808, its collections of works of art and curiosities had reached their peak, though the avid resident curator–collector seems always to have been willing to find wall spaces or shelves for one more print, book, medal, or painting. His personal tax inventory of art objects of 1809, just after his retirement from the presidency, gives the location of 115 artworks in the principal rooms alone. Even though Jefferson confessed to little knowledge of art, his Epicurean declaration to Maria Cosway reveals the obvious sensuous pleasure he drew from esthetic experience in nature and in art. "I am but a son of nature, loving what I see and feel, without being able to give a reason, nor caring much whether there be one." Jefferson, in spite of his philistine "I like what I like"

attitude, in fact habitually consulted experts on art matters, feeling his own background limited and inadequate. Young John Trumbull, whom Jefferson had invited to live with him in Paris, served as much as a personal art advisor as he did private secretary. Always the practical American, Jefferson once wrote from Paris what he thought of collecting paintings and sculpture: "Too expensive for the state of wealth among us. It would be useless, therefore, and preposterous, for us to make ourselves connoisseurs in those arts. They are worth seeing but not studying." In spite of these reservations Jefferson bought many works of art, beginning shortly after he had moved into his first Paris house in the cul-de-sac Taitbout in 1784. The Memorandum Book records "Two pictures of heads, 7 livres; d° half lengths viz. an ecce homo and another, 18 livres; two small laughing busts, 21 livres; a Hercules in plaister; five paintings (heads)," purchased within a fortnight after he had occupied the Hôtel de Landron in 1784.

Gradually over the years the walls of Monticello "hung thick" with paintings and prints, many collected during his stay in Europe. The best part of the collections was reserved for the parlor. As he had seen in Paris drawing rooms, and in the biannual Salon exhibitions in the Louvre he never missed, the pictures were hung in tiers, and their catalogue listing was divided into upper, middle, and lower levels in a kind of personal hierarchy. Portraits filled the upper tiers, and the company included Columbus, Vespucci, Locke, and Bacon along with Washington, Adams, Franklin, and Madison. The fine life portrait of Jefferson by Gilbert Stuart was also placed here after it was finally wrested from the painter, who was busy making copies from it in his Washington studio. It was returned to Monticello in 1982, bought in partnership with the National Portrait Gallery.

Ticknor reported seeing over the parlor fireplace, "the Laughing and Weeping Philosophers, dividing the world between them." This work was later replaced with *Herodiade bearing the head of St. John on a platter*, which now hangs there. "There were other pictures and a copy of Raphael's 'Transfiguration,'" Ticknor noted with a patronizing dismissal.

The dining room walls were also fairly covered, mostly with classical and religious subjects. Two engraved landscape views of Niagara Falls after paintings by John Vanderlyn were acquired in 1805 and hung there. A descendent recalled that on either side of the arched opening into the tea room were copies of Raphael's *Holy Family* "which Mr. Jefferson had copied in the Louvre," and Benjamin West's study *Hector and Andromache*, a gift of General Thaddeus Kosciusko. Portraiture by contemporary artists was represented in the collection, for Jefferson had championed, among the moderns, Houdon, Canova, David, Trumbull, Peale, Stuart, and Ceracchi, as well as others. Trumbull, Peale, Houdon, and Stuart were represented in Monticello's collection. Historical and mythological subjects by these artists, however, were not a part of the Monticello collection. Trumbull's great history series, which Jefferson had encouraged when young Trumbull lived with him in Paris, was represented in engravings of the *Battle of Bunker Hill* and *The Death of Montgomery in the Attack on Quebec*. Jefferson had seen both of the original canvases of these works when Trumbull first arrived at the Hôtel de Langeac.

Beyond the dining room to the north was the delightful tea room, a center of family life during Jefferson's time that he called his "most honorable suite." There were Houdon plaster busts of Washington, Franklin, John Paul Jones, and Lafayette, "large as life," as well as smaller busts of Tiberius, Nero, Otho, and Vespasian cast in bronze. More than a dozen miniatures and medals, some bought in Paris, were also displayed in the light and intimate setting furnished with an old sofa and several chairs that once belonged to George Wythe.

By 1815, 120 pictures were listed as taxable property at Monticello, yet the collection was not complete, for gifts and purchases continued to arrive. In 1818 the English sculptor William Coffee visited Monticello, where he executed, as Jefferson wrote to Madison, "the busts in plaster of myself and all the grown members of our family." When he had finished, the Coffee portraits included Jefferson, his daughter Martha Jefferson Randolph, his granddaughters Ellen Wayles Randolph and Cornelia Jefferson Randolph, and his grandson Thomas Jefferson Randolph. One of the last artworks to join the Monticello collections was the gift of a "plaister" replica of the marble bust of John Adams, made for the city of Boston by the French sculptor J. H. Binon. "I place it with pleasure in the line of my cabinet of his predecessors and successors," he wrote the sender, August 5, 1825, less than a year before both former presidents would be dead.

In Monticello's collection of books, works of art, souvenirs, artifacts, and curios had "been assembled more love of liberty, virtue, wisdom and learning than any other private spot in America," one of his adoring granddaughters was to write. The public awareness of the profound identification of the spirit of the man with the place explains the steady flow of visitors through the years who have come to see Monticello and to study it closely for clues to the personality of its builder. Many have left vivid descriptions of their impressions, for they sensed both Jefferson's intensely personal, intimate, emotional involvement in every detail of the house and its projection of the intelligence that also had helped shape the new republic. While he was still alive no other surviving member of that group we call the Founding Fathers attracted such interest, curiosity, and scrutiny. There was something, of course, different in his personality and in the originality of his way of life that set him apart from a Washington, an Adams, or a Madison, and that accounts at least partially for this peculiar attraction.

Because guests and visitors came from all walks of life and parts of the world—from "impertinent gazers" to famous personalities of the day drawn there to see the Sage in situ—the accounts of their visits represent the most sustained body of personal impressions ever devoted to a famous American house. The Marquis de Chastellux was among the first visitors to understand the special relationship between Jefferson's personality and the place he lived when he said that his house like his mind was placed in an elevated position so that he could calmly view the world at a distance. Jefferson no doubt expected many of his guests to record their impressions of the house as well as his conversations, for the house and his presence conveyed to the world an understanding of his philosophy and ideas more clearly than anything else except his correspondence. The entertaining of guests and the writing of letters became his chief occupations in retirement aside from the management of his farm.

The openness with which Jefferson encouraged both friends and strangers to visit him is not without its paradoxes. This is apparent when one considers the inaccessible mountaintop location of the plantation, reached over a difficult and adventurous road that all of his visitors had to climb as part of their pilgrimage to a sacred shrine. Over the years, a number of visitors' accounts say that the sun shone with unusual splendor when they had made the difficult trip and finally reached the summit in front of the house. One pilgrim even seemed to detect an aura or glow around the solitary building itself, to signal his arrival at a special spot.

Another contradiction that surfaces in Jefferson's ambiguous reaction to the constant intrusion of guests was the steady refrain in the correspondence of his devotion to solitude while at the same time even strangers were urged to pay extended visits to Monticello. The house itself expresses this duality in the large amount of space given over to "entertainment rooms" and guest facilities on the one hand, and Jefferson's own private suite of rooms where he regularly retreated with strict orders to family and servants to be left alone. It was, of course, from his study that most invitations to guests to pay a visit whenever they found themselves in the neighborhood flowed out in all directions.

While it has been useful to draw on the letters and journals left by Monticello's guests to describe Monticello at various stages of its history, it is also important to glimpse through these same eyes some picture of the daily life there and the personal animation gained from the presence of Jefferson, always intensely himself on his hill and living in a house that

221 **Cornelia Jefferson Randolph,** *by William Coffee, terra cotta, 1818–19. As a child, Cornelia, Jefferson's granddaughter, lived at Monticello, where the sculptor Coffee enjoyed the hospitality. Planning to return, he wrote that he would "have two glasses of good wine every day after dinner."*

seemed to some odd, uncomfortable, and even whimsical, scarcely habitable by anyone else but its builder. It was the reputation of the idiosyncratic quality of the house as well as the obvious attraction of the man himself that brought in a steady train of "People of wealth, fashion, men in office, professional men, military and civil, foreign ministers, missionaries, Indian agents, tourists, travelers, artists, strangers, friends." Guests were an almost daily fixture of Monticello life and their presence over the years influenced the domestic routines and habits of its residents—who may have complained but never showed to an outsider anything but the most gracious charm and informality. Old neighbors told Henry Randall, Jefferson's biographer, that they recalled how strangers would plant themselves in corridors and consult their watches to know precisely when the great man would move from the study and dining room, in order to get a glimpse. One visitor knocked out a window pane so that he could have a better view, while a party of intruders even entered the lawn while Jefferson was taking his ease on the portico in the late afternoon, "approaching within a dozen yards, and [gazing] at him point-blank until they had looked their fill, as they would have gazed on a lion in a menagerie."

Thus it was not just an obsession for architecture and building that had inspired the retreat at Poplar Forest, in its secluded district far from the confusion and interruptions at Monticello. Monticello's "stationary or every varying guests" (one New England judge with only a letter of introduction stayed for three weeks), the perpetual round of company in the house with all the responsibilities of Virginia hospitality, a condition of old noblesse that Jefferson never gave up even when his straitened financial condition demanded it, seemed to weary him as the years advanced. Once when a stranger advanced onto the portico where Jefferson was sitting after dinner and announced that he was availing himself of "a common privilege" to call on the retired president, Jefferson

222 Martha Jefferson Randolph, *by Thomas Scully, oil on canvas, 1836. *After his wife's death, Jefferson looked to his daughter Martha to play a domestic role in his life that at times was at the expense of her husband and large family. After 1809, she and her husband Thomas Mann Randolph and their eleven children lived at Monticello.*

coldly replied that he did not know to what privilege he referred and declined the honor of the impertinent visit.

The story of strangers noting their watches to anticipate Jefferson's movement has a ring of truth since his routines seemed to have followed a well-established pattern. "An afternoon and evening passed as the two previously," young George Ticknor commented with some boredom on the predictability of Monticello life. Since "everything is done with such regularity . . . one could predict the routines of all the days once you knew how one was filled," he concluded.

A visitor arriving at the front door after the long, rough ride up the mountain road found more often than not the hospitality of an open door. Margaret Smith reported that the entry door was never closed during her stay. A member of the family, usually Mrs. Randolph or her husband, or a passing servant, would greet the visitor in the front hall. If there was a letter of introduction, or if it was an expected friend, Jefferson would be alerted and would soon appear, his tall, bony figure dressed as one guest later recalled, in corduroy small clothes, grey worsted stockings, blue waistcoat, and a rather stiff homespun jacket badly made from the wool of his prized merino sheep. A second flannel waistcoat bound in red velvet was also worn. Daniel Webster on another occasion found the former president's dress "very much neglected, but not slovenly," although his general appearance exuded an "extraordinary degree of health, vivacity and spirit!" Whether or not his dress appeared ill-kempt or negligent in his own house, he conformed to no fashion, wearing whatever he liked and often blending pieces of apparel from different periods of his closet. "Always himself and no one else at second hand," as his kinsman John Randolph remarked of a friend, it is clear that this quality marked Jefferson's personal style in both living and dressing. He once confessed that he lived in a "brick kiln," and there is no doubt that Monticello before its completion in 1809 had an unkempt, disheveled air that Jefferson seemed to enjoy or at least seldom complained of. His daily involvement in every aspect of the work on the house and his active supervision of the farms, gardens, and shops left little time to be concerned with appearances, prompting comments by more than one stylish visitor from Philadelphia, New York, or Europe not prepared for his informal dress, manners, and the disorganized atmosphere that often prevailed.

Amazed to see poplar logs propping up one of the unfinished classical porticoes when he arrived, Sir Augustus Foster was astonished to be greeted in the drawing room by one of Jefferson's sixteen-year-old grandsons, standing barefooted on the polished parquet floor. The fastidious Englishman concluded that it was the president himself and not local custom that had encouraged the Tom Sawyer freedom on the part of young Randolph, who otherwise was neatly dressed. "If he could have ventured it without ridicule," Foster felt that Jefferson would have encouraged "still a greater degree of nakedness, so fond was he of leaving Nature as unconfined as possible in all her works." Foster had indeed detected in the president's conversation a touch of respect for Rousseau's Noble Savage, nourished by a love of personal liberty and unfettered independence complementing his political suspicion of oppressive governments. Men should enjoy nature to the fullest and should be trusted with the formation of their own opinions, even at sixteen and on so innocent a question as to whether or not it was proper to go barefoot into a Virginia parlor. The casual scene seemed to match Jefferson's respect for unpruned nature that pressed in on all sides of the mountain below the orchards and gardens and could be seen through the panes of the French windows of the drawing room looking toward the western mountains.

Guests who stayed overnight were expected to join the family breakfast in the tea room or larger drawing room at nine o'clock (after the second bell had been rung in the front hall), where a folded white napkin was placed beneath each plate instead of a table cloth. Following a breakfast of hot breads, muffins, cold ham, coffee, and tea, Jefferson returned to his apartment to work on correspondence until twelve or one o'clock, while the rest of the family pursued their various occupations and studies. Guests read, walked, or simply sat and admired the scenery. His daughter Mrs. Randolph was in charge of the housekeeping carried out by a large staff, although as a widower Jefferson had learned a great deal and took an interest in the supervision of his domestic arrangements. In Paris he found that he had to maintain a "stile of living" established by Franklin, but with a meager budget that "called for an almost womanly attention to the details of the household" if it were to survive economically.

Daniel Webster said that Jefferson was up and at work on his papers and correspondence before breakfast—as soon as he could see the hands of the clock on the shelf at the foot of his bed alcove. Apparently it was his custom to make his own fire in his room in cold weather and to tend it during the day without a

223 Jefferson's chess set. *This ivory set with its African king may, in fact, have been carved in Africa, as a part of the Portuguese-African industry supplying Europe with carved ivory objects in the 18th century.*

servant disturbing him. When the weather was good, he would spend the middle of the day on horseback, riding as much as twelve or fifteen miles over his plantation. Returning to the house for dinner, which was served at half past three, Jefferson expected his table to be as generous as his own gardens, cellars, and the neighborhood could provide. Though not "lavish" according to plantation standards of the day, "he never would have less than eight covers at dinner if nobody at the table but himself," according to Isaac Jefferson.

Daniel Webster was impressed with the quality and variety of continental wines served at the end of the meal, after the cloth was removed, but Jefferson was widely respected for his knowledge of and taste for wine. "I promised you," he wrote to President Monroe in 1817, "when I should have received and tried the wines I had ordered from France and Italy, to give you a note of the kinds which I should think worthy of your procurement. . . . they are the following: Vin blanc liquoreux d'Hermitage de M. Jourdan à Tains. . . . Vin de Ledanon (in Languedoc), something of the Port character but higher flavored, more delicate, less rough. . . . Vin de Roussillon. The best is that of Perpignan or Rivesalte of the crop of M. Durand. . . . There is still . . . the wine of Florence called Montepulcian. . . . There is a particular very best crop . . . I have imported . . . annually 10 or 12 years." When the New Englander Webster was there, he was also impressed that the menu was "half in Virginia, half in French style." Jefferson had loved the French cuisine he discovered in Paris, and on his return brought with him his maitre d'hotel Adrian Petit, who stayed with him for several years in Philadelphia and Monticello until homesickness overcame him and he returned to France. He was succeeded by another Frenchman, Etienne Lemaire, who served Jefferson during the presidency, and later enriched the menus of Monticello with his recipes. Two Monticello slaves were brought to the White House to learn French cooking and returned to the plantation as cooks when the president retired. Patrick Henry was once heard to grumble that Jefferson "had abjured his native victuals" of Virginia for foreign cooking.

Sometimes Jefferson would retire to his bedroom after dinner to work and then reappear at sunset to walk on the terraces and in the gardens. Tea and coffee were brought into the drawing room at six, followed by fruit and wine, and conversation would continue there until nine. If there were no guests, he would read in his reading chair, often placed in the dining room with its own candle, until finally retiring to bed at ten.

It was his easy, natural, unambitious, and enlightened conversations that his most-favored guests cherished, and the thought of them even now can privately animate one's visit to Monticello like nothing else. "His conversation is the most agreeable kind, and he possesses a stock of information not inferior to that of any other man. In Europe he would hold a distinguished rank among men of letters, and as such he has already appeared there," wrote his friend the Duc de la Rochefoucauld-Liancourt following his stay in Virginia. An earlier French visitor, Chastellux, so relished the conversations on music, politics, poetry, and science that they had continued around a punch bowl until one in the morning.

The women of the household and other women among the guests joined in the Monticello conversa-

224 French chest, Jefferson's bedroom. *European architectural engravings hang on the east wall of Jefferson's bedroom, above a French chest. In Jefferson's day, there probably were a great many more pictures decorating this wall, but they cannot now be identified for replacement. Virtually all of the furnishings in the bedroom belonged to Jefferson, or his family, and among the objects are Jefferson's medicine chest and a brass candelabra mounted with a reflector.*

225 Parlor door, grained mahogany. *The doors throughout the first floor level of Monticello were fashionably grained in mahogany to match the wood used in the window frames and to complement the furniture.*

tions "however high the topic may be." It was a tradition that Jefferson had enjoyed in Paris, where some of his most intimate friends, such as the Countess de Tessé and Madame de Corny, were aristocratic and well-educated ladies who had achieved a remarkable level of intellectual equality. Even though he was expected to lead the conversation at his table, his quiet, amiable, and understated ways did not dominate the talk. "It is not loud, or challenging attention, but usually addressed to the person next to him," one guest reported. "The topics, when not selected to suit the character and feelings of the auditors, were those subjects with which his mind seemed particularly occupied—and these at present seem to be science and letters and especial the University of Virginia. . . . When we were with him his favorites

were Greek and Anglo-Saxon historical recollections, of the times and events of the Revolution and of his residence in France."

Edmund Bacon, his overseer, who had access to him in his private apartment day or night for twelve years, claimed later that only twice did he find him idle; once with a toothache and once with an attack of neuralgia. The reading, writing, studying, gardening, and farming continued, and the modulated conversations never stopped. When the new university was finally organized, students and young professors were regularly invited to Monticello for dinner to help maintain the intellectual tone.

The enlightened table talk, the perfect service, the polished floors, the excellent wines (Daniel Webster was impressed with the bottles of "Ledanon, Muscat, Samian and Blanquette de Limoux"), and above all the warm, gentle, impeccable hospitality of the place seemed to mask the tremors coming from the economic fault on which Monticello and its inhabitants rested. There had been rumors of Jefferson's growing financial problems for some time, aggravated by poor crops, falling agricultural prices, and an unexpected obligation on a note for $20,000 that he had endorsed for a friend. After his son-in-law Thomas Mann Randolph became ill, Jefferson took on the responsibility of all the expenses of the family from Edgehill, adding considerably to his growing financial burdens, even though they had been living much of the time at Monticello since 1809. By the winter of 1825, the situation had become so desperate that Jefferson was compelled to petition the Virginia legislature to allow him to launch a lottery scheme in order to sell large tracts of land that he believed would salvage his beloved Monticello estate itself.

The fact that the lottery ultimately produced very little in the way of relief was due in part to the widespread and unparalleled economic depression that gripped most of the country during the last years of Jefferson's life. A sudden drop in the nation's money supply had in one observer's opinion produced "an entire revolution in fortune" that finally engulfed Monticello in its wake, although popular opinion had blamed Jefferson's financial woes on bad judgment, mismanagement, and personal extravagance in the operation of the establishment.

The depressed Virginia countryside itself in the 1820s was becoming marked by dilapidated fences, decaying homesteads, and worn-out fields on every side, giving an "uninviting aspect to a county perhaps more favored than any other portion of the union." The economic crisis was not something unique to the management and operation of Monticello, although its large population that included 130 slaves and its traditions of open hospitality no doubt complicated Jefferson's appalling financial state. The "hordes" of both friends and strangers continued to climb the mountain to be edified and many would stay to eat and sleep. Martha Jefferson Randolph wrote her daughter Ellen Coolidge in September of 1825 that she had recently entertained a party of thirty-one for dinner, including "11 children and dogs." On another occasion she had had to find places in the house to bed some fifty guests who unexpectedly had arrived to spend the night.

In all of this there was an air of Chekovian drama that hung over Monticello and the Jefferson Family. It was an atmosphere of misplaced hope, an indifference to personal hardship, and a refusal to alter old patterns of life in the face of a new and menacing reality that threatened their very foundation, as when Jefferson insisted that a granddaughter needed a new piano in 1825, at the moment when financial conditions were desperate.

Even though the remodeled and enlarged house of 1809-10 was hardly fifteen years old when its builder died, by the 1820s Monticello struck some visitors as old-fashioned, shabby, and even going to decay. Francis Gray was surprised to see worn leather coverings on many of the chairs, with stuffing coming out in places. Others were shocked by evidence of neglect; "the affects of time left unrepaired." When Lieutenant Hall left Monticello he had the feeling of a traveler departing from the "moldering remains of a Grecian temple," while another guest spoke of Monticello's "solitary grandeur . . . wasting into ruin."

Certainly, Monticello's last great public moment was the visit of General Lafayette in 1824 to see his old friend. As Jefferson and his family waited on the east portico, the general's entourage, accompanied by a local guard of honor, wound up the mountain road. Sabers and military decorations flashed in the sunlight as the procession moved under the shadows of gold and red autumn trees. Appropriately, the two ancient relics of the Revolution met in the Indian Summer twilight of November in front of Monticello's classical facade as in an antique tableau. Shuffling toward each other, the old comrades embraced while the assembled admirers watched in silence. Lafayette spent the night with his friend, and they recalled their former collaborations in Philadelphia and Paris nearly fifty years earlier. The following day they rode together to the University of Virginia, where the general received full honors at dinner in Jefferson's unfinished Rotunda. It was a sign of his physical decline that the former president was unable to stand to give his tribute to the general, asking a friend to read it instead. The two men, like so many other heroes of the Revolution, had ridden "through the storm with heart and hand."

So the clock at the foot of the bed ticked on, measuring out not only Jefferson's life but that of the house itself as he had known it. The two were inseparable. To think of Monticello without the animating spirit of its creator was like attempting to recall the dead to life. Nor could the house be copied or its style translated into an architectural movement, because the personality of Monticello and the associations that gave it its special quality were indivisibly a part of Jefferson's genius.

By the time the white flag was hung on the bush at the corner of the yard to signal members of the family living at nearby Tufton that the end had come, around noon on the 4th of July, 1826, Monticello's fate was sealed. It was too late to warn a "Committee of Safety," as Jefferson had called for in his delirium the night before he died. The precise nature of the alarm—was it public or private?—can only be imagined.

The house "reared on his own model" was Jefferson's true autobiography rather than the short, unfinished, written version he had begun in 1821. Only a few other houses in history, each of which carried such a deep personal imprint of its builder, can be grouped into this special autobiographical genre. Pliny the Younger's villa comes to mind, but we have few details of its actual appearance. Hadrian's Villa at Tivoli, one man's fantastic architectural whim, is another quintessential architectural memoir in stone and set off by an equally autobiographical landscape

contrived to recall his military expeditions to foreign lands. There are the houses of Bess of Hardwick, Hardwick Hall and Hatfield House, perhaps Fouquet's Vaux-le-Vicomte, Horace Walpole's Strawberry Hill, and Philip Johnson's Glass House among the most famous creations in this limited but instructive tradition. A few more probably would qualify, although the work of Jefferson's favorite architect, Palladio, in its purest form is far too abstract and universal to be included in the autobiographical genre.

Jefferson's unwillingness to complete Monticello or to admit that it was ever finished (Isaac Jefferson got it right when he said that he just "stopped building") and its many changes and drastic alterations over the years give it the quality of a living document, an on-going journal of his esthetic and intellectual development. From the first simple one-room pavilion—a beginning point never abandoned but carefully incorporated into the final "draft"—to the domed house of 1809-10, with its recessed offices and covered ways extending two hundred feet from each flank, one can follow Jefferson's evolution as a passionate student of building techniques and of architecture. The various elements of the house not only recorded his profound interest in architectural theory, it also documented his fascination and progress in the study of the history and the personalities of the profession. Beginning with the contemporary architects of Louis XVI's Paris, extending back through the English classicists to the French and Italian Renaissance work of Philibert de l'Orme and, of course, to Palladio and his "bible," reaching into the ancient world through Vitruvius, Monticello's genealogy is evident on every side. Although not as

231

226, 227   Jefferson's cabinet, or study (left)**, and his polygraph** (above). *Jefferson's chaise longue was fitted with candlesticks on the arms for illumination, and its table had a revolving surface. The device on the table, one of three owned by Jefferson, was used to make file copies of his voluminous correspondence. The copy was made automatically by a second pen attached to the device as Jefferson wrote. When he was old, Jefferson was able to continue working at his table, in the half-recumbent position permitted by his chair. Jefferson's telescope still sits on the window sill, and his surveying equipment rests in the doorway out to the south piazza landing.*

didactic as the elevations and ornamentation of the pavilions of the university, where each facade and its order was designed to remind the viewer of a well-known ancient building (the Baths of Diocletian, the Fortuna Virilis in Rome) and with the Rotunda conspicuous as a half-scale version of the Pantheon in red brick, Monticello contained its own personal

233

encyclopedia of the past within its harmonious composition and decoration. Throughout the structure and within the museum hall, the parlor, the dining room, the library, and private apartments, one reads the autobiography of its builder, truly a "house of life."

Not only the building but the objects within and even the grounds were intimate souvenirs of a rich, heroic past. Portraits, paintings, and prints served as daily reminders of the major events of Jefferson's public and private life. His affairs of the Heart—his love of the antique world and its architecture, of music and of gardening—were a part of the experience laminated into the environment. His affairs of the Head were there, too, and catalogued in the vast library, in the scientific instruments, and in his collections of natural history scattered around the front hall. Except for his wife, whose portrait was never painted, his most important friends and colleagues were ever-present, looking down from the walls and pedestals in painting and sculpture.

Outside the house, the gardens and grounds formed another kind of library that he constantly nurtured, drew upon, and savored in his daily rounds. Here were plants, flowers, and trees collected during his travels in Europe or sent to him from remote parts of the world to be cultivated, studied, and documented in his Garden Book, serving as an appendix to the living horticultural autobiography the garden itself represented. Not only were the exploits and discoveries of the Lewis and Clark Expedition's "unknown scenes" celebrated in Monticello's "Indian Hall," but in the gardens were botanical specimens brought back from the Western Country. Wild currants and gooseberries from plants sent back from

the expedition may well have been served with tea in the parlor, giving even the meals at Monticello an unexpected historic dimension.

When old age advanced and Jefferson began to falter, the house and grounds themselves seemed to take on a premature quality of decay like a mirror reflecting his own decline. It was an act of empathy that seemed to grow out of the life-long, almost organic, and fateful relationship between the house and the man. In its advancing state of dilapidation "it harmonizes with . . . its sage," one observer wrote.

The scenes that followed Jefferson's death, in which the family was swiftly overwhelmed by the financial disasters, are sad to contemplate. Though tragic as the total dismantling of the Monticello estate was—the auctions of the slave families, art works, virtu, gifts from friends, and most of the furniture, followed by the sale of the house itself and the plantation in order to pay off the creditors—there was in the final, painful act a drama of classic, even redeeming, proportions, a kind of human grandeur as the survivors stoically departed and descended the mountain with nothing left but an uncertain future and the consolation of their ancestor's own optimistic declaration that he steered his bark "with hope in the head, leaving Fear astern."

They had been freed, moreover, from a long, agonizing, foredoomed attempt to restore a way of life to Monticello that could not have been maintained under the best of circumstances after the death of its creator. Its very reason for existence also had died. Even though Jefferson had desperately tried to save the property for his heirs, there was a Jeffersonian quality and liberation in the defeat. "When we have lived one generation out," he had written to John

Adams, "we should not wish to encroach on another." It would be another hundred years before even an effort would be made to restore the physical quality of the house and grounds to the condition of national and international respect and honor that it and its architect deserve.

228 Rotunda of the University of Virginia. *Jefferson planned to institutionalize at the university he designed the contemplative, intellectual way of life he had invented for himself and tested earlier at Monticello. The center of that life was to be the Rotunda, modeled on the Pantheon, which housed the library. For the dome he proposed a planetarium, and other rooms were to be used for lectures, religious worship, drawing, and music.*

THE
EPILOGUE

$35,000 in part discharge of it. There is, therefore, at this time, the sum of $72,000, remaining unpaid, to pay which, the lands of Mr. Jefferson are now offered for sale.

Valuable Lands for Sale.

The Lands of the Estate of THOMAS JEFFERSON, deceased, lying in the Counties of Campbell and Bedford, will be offered on the premises, if not previously sold privately, on Monday, the 22d of September next.

Likewise, MONTICELLO, in the County of Albemarle, with the Lands of the said estate adjacent thereto, including the Shadwell Mills, will be offered on the premises, if not previously sold privately, on Monday, the 29th of September next. The whole of this property will be devided to suit purchasers. The sale being made for the payment of the testator's debts, the desire to sell is sincere. The terms will be accommodating, and the prices anticipated low. Mrs. Randolph, of Monticello, will join in the conveyance, and will make the titles perfect.

TH. JEFFERSON RANDOLPH, Exec'r.
of THOMAS JEFFERSON, dec'd.

July 12, 1828.

229 *Offer for the sale of Monticello,* Richmond Enquirer, *July 22, 1828.* "The sale being made for the payment of the testator's debts, the desire to sell is sincere. The terms will be accommodating, and the prices anticipated low."

O<small>N</small> J<small>ULY</small> 10, 1976, Her Majesty Elizabeth II drove with her entourage through the gates of Monticello. She had come to pay homage to the man who two hundred years before had drafted the bill of particulars against "poor maniac George" and the colonial policies of Great Britain, setting in motion the cosmic events that were to follow. When this descendant of George III stepped onto the portico of the house, one hundred fifty years had passed since the death of Monticello's architect and builder on July 4, 1826.

For almost a century, a period longer than the Jefferson family's ownership, Monticello had been privately owned by others. Sold by the heirs in 1831, it was not until 1923, with the creation of the Thomas

230, 231   Monticello, west front (above), **and east front** (right), *photographed by William Roads, 1870. "The tooth of time has marred the beauty of the shrine." Monticello's low point in the decade following the Civil War is seen on the east side in the sagging gate, unkempt yard, and broken windows. On the west side, the front steps have crumbled into a ramp, and two buggies are parked in the shelter of the portico.*

Jefferson Memorial Foundation, that public effort to restore the house and to retrieve a substantial part of the original furnishings and artworks could begin. During those long, intervening years, when the house never quite adjusted to any of its new occupants, the question of its survival provided a certain drama in an otherwise uneventful period in Monticello's history.

The public's appreciation of Jefferson's place in American history was ambivalent during most of the nineteenth century, and his career as an architect was often questioned well into the twentieth century. Through most of the nineteenth century, Monticello was in fact his only architectural work whose authorship was not seriously disputed. However, there were even a few historians who believed that young Robert Mills had played a major role in the design of the second phase of Monticello, because Mills happened to have drawn a fine elevation of the house during the three years he studied under Jefferson's tutelage.

When the capitol building in Richmond was being restored, a member of the firm directing its restoration made a reference to Jefferson and his "architect" Claude-Louis Clérrisseau. Glen Brown, who had written a study of the United States Capitol and its architect Dr. William Thornton, concluded that Thornton was the principal designer of the University of Virginia rather than its founder. Other historians thought that Benjamin H. Latrobe had been responsible for the university's more original aspects. Montgomery Schuyler declared that the classical revival in America was, in fact, started by Latrobe.

Nevertheless, when Franklin D. Roosevelt dedicated the Jefferson Memorial in Washington, D.C., on the bicentennial anniversary of Jefferson's birth in 1943, Jefferson's historic image as a national hero finally was placed on an equal footing with George Washington and Abraham Lincoln. The Memorial's design by John Russell Pope brought on a public controversy led by younger architects and critics who

232 Jefferson Lottery ticket, April, 1826. Jefferson's debts had mounted to such an extent that admirers sponsored a lottery for his benefit, just two months before his death. Although the ticket sale was not a success, bringing in no more than $6,000, public sympathy for the former president's plight was stirred.

viewed its classic lines as hopelessly reactionary and its spirit quite out of keeping with Jefferson's liberal political reputation. The vigorous support of Fiske Kimball, who almost singlehandedly had rescued Jefferson's own architectural reputation with the publication of *Thomas Jefferson: Architect*, was a major factor in rescuing Pope's design, allowing the Memorial to be completed along the lines intended by the president who had long been a reverent student and twentieth-century interpreter of Jefferson's political philosophy. The year that Kimball's study of Jefferson's architecture appeared, 1915, marked a key date in the long process to establish Jefferson's credentials as an architect alongside his reputation as a philosopher and politician. Later, Kimball was to play a major role in the restoration of Monticello when in 1924 he was made chairman of the Restoration Committee for the Foundation. His wife Marie, a scholar in her own right, was also to make significant contributions to the study of Jefferson's abiding interest in the decorative arts.

Coming from a country with a tradition of heaping honors, letters, fortunes, and even palaces upon its national heroes, Queen Elizabeth could not have imagined the desolation on a "Monday night" in August of 1829 when Virginia Trist informed her mother Martha Randolph that everything but her grandfather's clothes had been packed for the fami-

233 **Thomas Jefferson, *by P. J. David d'Angers, bronze, 1833.*** *Uriah P. Levy, a great admirer of Jefferson, saw this statue in Paris shortly after it was completed and ordered a cast that he offered to Congress. The gift was ignored, and the statue reposed for years on the White House grounds before being removed to the Capitol. This gesture confirms that Levy's abiding respect for Jefferson antedated his purchase of Monticello.*

234 Uriah Phillips Levy, U.S.N., *American school, oil on canvas, c. 1815.* Painted a number of years before its subject acquired Monticello, this painting shows a proud young lieutenant, who one day would become a commodore, standing before the mast of his ship—a fifth-generation American.

235 Thomas Jefferson Randolph, *after Charles Willson Peale, oil on canvas, 1808* (top). Jefferson's grandson assumed responsibility for the management of his grandfather's estate before he died. He was named trustee and executor in Jefferson's will.

236 Nicholas Philip Trist, *painted by Fanny Maury Burke after John Neagle* (bottom). Young Nicholas came to live at Monticello, where he met and later married Jefferson's granddaughter Virginia Jefferson Randolph.

ly's final departure from Monticello. Martha, now at Edgehill, replied, adding her own melancholy note: "We shall carry all our bedding, some dining tables, your press and Virginia's tall chest of drawers . . . and a great many odds and ends." The last traces of Jefferson's happy society would be gone forever. The parlor that the Queen entered, however, now elegantly restored and furnished, did not reveal to the eye any hint of the derelict setting that Anne Royal found in the winter of 1830, a few months after the Trists had left. "From the snow and our ignorance of the way," she wrote, "we had to quit the carriage at some distance and walk to the house. . . . We knocked at a door which we found open, and receiving no answer, we walked in. . . ." After waiting for a time in the cold, bare hall, the Royal party of 1830 was finally met by "a great coarse boorish woman" who showed them through the desolate house. In the parlor only the splendid parquet floor that has never failed to dazzle visitors was to be found, still glowing with its "ivory smoothness" according to Mrs. Royal. The room itself was stripped of all of its furniture except for the two "massy pier glasses," covered with gauze, that hung on either side of the pedimented entry where they remain to this day.

Jefferson's family had simply inherited a white elephant when he died. The cost of Monticello's upkeep only compounded the larger, catastrophic financial problems of operating the estate itself, and there could be little doubt that Jefferson's debts, which amounted to over one hundred thousand dollars, could not even be discharged with the sale of all of his property. Thomas Jefferson Randolph, who now managed Jefferson's affairs, had advised his grandfather in the spring before he died that the sale of the plantation was the only solution left to the beleaguered family. It was a shock that must have hastened the end when the sick man realized that Monticello itself would have to be included in the proposed lottery sale. Young Randolph was named sole executor of the estate in the will and had been left all of his grandfather's personal possessions, including his vast correspondence, which Gilbert Chinard called "the richest treasure house of information ever left by a single man." Yet it is fair to say that Jefferson's "essay in architecture" is second only to the letters as an autobiographical document in the comprehending of Jefferson's genius.

The hard debts of the estate, including bad notes totaling twenty thousand dollars that Jefferson had endorsed for Wilson Cary Nicholas in 1817, were devastating. Even though Jefferson's plight belatedly had drawn the "liveliest sympathy heightened by surprize," the lottery and later a voluntary subscription plan turned out to be unworkable and inadequate. The hopelessness of the situation was becoming more apparent each day, and with it the growing realization that a sale of the property was the only solution even though the real estate market was depressed, a classic dilemma for land-poor heirs with little cash to meet the demands of creditors. Cornelia Randolph, for one, was not optimistic when she wrote her sister Ellen Coolidge, now living in Boston: "Fortune has persecuted us so relentlessly that even though at last she seems to give us one smile to excite hope, not one of us has spirits to feel it a promise of future good." Her pessimism was well founded, for the rescue efforts of Jefferson's admirers throughout the country were able to produce through subscription only six thousand dollars before he died.

After an agonizing family debate in which Randolph had opposed the sale of his grandfather's slaves, believing such selling to be the most vicious aspect of an unsupportable institution, the stranded family decided that everything would have to go on the auction block—all of the slaves, most of the household furnishings, stocks, grain, and farm equipment. Only the library, which had been left to the University of Virginia, and some of the more important artworks and a few pieces of furniture were to be held out. The paintings and sculpture were later shipped to Boston in hopes that it would prove a more promising market than the farmers of Albemarle County would provide.

Little was recorded at the time of the Monticello sale, and the notice in the Richmond *Enquirer*, January 9, 1827, was brief: "On the fifteenth of January at Monticello . . . the whole of the residue of the personal property of Thomas Jefferson, dec., consisting of 130 valuable negroes, stock crops, etc., household and kitchen furniture. The attention of the public is earnestly invited to this property." The family rescued a few articles of "chamber furniture" and silverware, but all of the French furniture collected in Paris, the furniture made at Monticello, the Indian curiosities, fossils, and maps from the entry hall, the quantity of engravings, and a large collection of mathematical, philosophical, and optical instruments were among the hundreds of items sold.

"We have quitted Monticello," Mary Randolph wrote her sister, "and are doing our best to reconcile ourselves to our change of abode . . . for as yet our hearts refuse to give the title to any other spot on earth than the one we have just given up." Like Chekov's victims, the survivors were dreaming of an end to the futility and frustration that had gradually enveloped their lives and their mode of existence. Left with a "bare castle" and with hardly enough bedding to cover the last surviving guest bed, Virginia Trist passed on further sad details to her sister Ellen. Visitors drawn by both curiosity and respect continued to come as before, but now they assumed a license to take away as souvenirs any of the remaining plants or flowers left in her grandfather's garden. "Mama's choicest flower roots have been carried off, one of her yellow jesmins, fig bushes . . . grape vines and everything and anything that they fancied." The *Virginia Advocate* reported that intruders regarded "the domicile and its contents as though it was an inn . . . to rummage everything from garret to cellar, run their noses into every corner that was open or could be opened, and to intrude upon the privacy of the family. . . ." Nicholas Trist, who was now in charge of the house, followed this story by publishing a legal notice of protest, but apparently this only stimulated further depredations.

In a last desperate attempt to save the house and a few surrounding acres from being sold, Jefferson's old friend General John H. Cocke at Bremo proposed renting the house for a school to be set up by a Presbyterian cleric—Virginia Trist called it "a school for gymnastics"—but this was short lived. There was even speculation on the possibility of turning it into a monastery or convent, if only Monticello had been built in a Catholic country instead of one dominated by Episcopalians, Presbyterians, and Baptists. Had it been located in a Northern state a profitable solution might have been found by converting it to "an asylum for the deaf and dumb or as an academy for female instruction."

Finally in 1831, after fruitlessly advertising the property for sale, an unlikely and adventurous buyer was finally discovered, to the relief of the family who by now were willing to consider anything to rid themselves of the burden. James Barclay, the proposed buyer, was a druggist from Stanton, Virginia, who had developed an interest in silkworm culture, and he planned to establish a center for the production of silk on the 552 acres of hilly ground, for which he paid seventy five hundred dollars.

Barclay found Monticello's cheerless rooms virtually empty, with only ghostly shadows decorating the naked walls where the paintings and prints once hung. Cerrachi's bust of Jefferson and a few Indian relics were all that remained of the museum in the front hall. Scattered around in the bedrooms on the second floor were fragments of chairs and a piano, among "heaps of slain coffee-urns, chinaware and glasses."

Intent on making a go of the silk manufactory, Barclay apparently was unable to spend much on repairs or restoration of the house and grounds, but he at least convinced Virginia Trist of his sincerity when he had "the good feelings to enquire what trees and shrubs were favorites . . . in order to extend his care toward them in particular." Others reported, however, that many of Jefferson's trees were felled by Barclay and replaced by mulberries in order to feed his silkworms.

Even though some silk was actually produced— Barclay showed one visitor twenty pounds of raw silk—the expenses of the place outran the anticipated revenue. In 1832, John H. B. Latrobe claimed he had found Monticello in utter ruin and desolation only a year after the Barclays had taken over. By the fall of 1833, the new owner was ready to give up, and a notice appeared offering "this celebrated seat" for sale, but with little other description since it was too well known to require any, the ad declared. Now it was the Barclays' turn to be gratefully relieved of Jefferson's essay by another unlikely buyer, a forty-two-year-old naval lieutenant who had by chance heard about the Barclays' desire to sell, although the details of how or from whom are not clear.

The *Niles Register* announced in 1834 that Uriah Phillips Levy had acquired Monticello and went on optimistically to say that the naval officer, who recently had inherited a fortune, intended to restore the house to its original condition and then open it to the public once a week. In May of 1836, Levy was able to take possession of his newly acquired 218 acre estate. Uriah Levy and his family would continue to own Monticello for the next ninety crucial years, eight years longer than Jefferson himself owned the property. They would own it in fact until Uriah Levy's nephew Thomas Jefferson Levy would finally sell it, in 1923, to the newly organized Thomas Jefferson Memorial Foundation, marking the beginning of the public phase of its history. Even though the period of the Levy ownership was not without some controversy, criticism of their stewardship and family lawsuits that jeopardized the care of the property, it is fair to say that as a result of their custody Monticello survived reasonably intact through the changing fortunes of the Levy family, the chaos of the Civil War, and the public's indifference to the future of Jefferson's house.

During Uriah Levy's ownership—which was absentee for long periods—there was a good deal of complaint about the physical condition of the estate. Part of the criticism no doubt grew out of the lack of care shown by indifferent caretakers who actually lived in the house. The other part of the problem was the expectations created in the minds of pilgrims by the substantial literary image of Monticello that circulated in articles, books, and memoirs describing the golden years of Jefferson's occupancy. The picture evoked by these idealized accounts of the sage and philosopher of the Revolutionary period, surviving with Roman dignity into a new world he had helped to create, surrounded by an adoring family, his books, paintings, and garden, was a portrait deeply etched in the public's imagination. That the contemporary descriptions of Monticello during Jefferson's lifetime take on a mythological quality and are made to serve universal values extends from the Marquis de

238 ***Monticello, east front, around 1870.*** *This photograph shows the house in advanced deterioration, with weeds growing rampant in the gutters and window panes missing here and there.*

Chastellux's tribute in 1782 to William Wirt's noble eulogy written just after Jefferson's death in 1826.

Jefferson himself painted one of the most compelling word portraits:

I am retired to Monticello, where, in the bosom of my family, and surrounded by my books, I enjoy a repose to which I have been long a stranger. My mornings are devoted to correspondence. From breakfast to dinner, I am in my shops, my garden, or on horseback among my farms; from dinner to dark, I give to society and recreation with my neighbours and friends; and from candle-light to early bed-time, I read. . . . A part of my occupation, and by no means the least pleasing, is the direction of the studies of such young men as ask it. They place themselves in the neighboring village, and have the use of my library and counsel, and make a part of my society. . . . I endeavor to keep their attention fixed on the main objects of all science, the freedom and happiness of man. So that, coming to bear a share in the councils and government of their country, they will keep even in view the sole objects of all legitimate government.

Later, when Jefferson's devoted followers were to find conditions substantially different, with paint peeling, windows broken, and doors carelessly unlocked, their disappointment caused them to reach for words like "ruin," "neglect," and "dilapidation."

In a sense the house had been a victim of the propaganda it had inspired in the emotions of many of its early visitors—of being overcome by both its unique architectural statement and by the particular

241 Monticello, east front, c. 1890. *When this photograph was taken, Jefferson Levy had managed to repair the damage that had resulted from years of neglect. The lattice porches on either side of the south piazza may have been put there by Jefferson, but they have not been restored.*

symbolism that seemed to resonate throughout, recording the sensibilities, aspirations, and personal history of its architect. With Jefferson dead, "patriotism, philosophy, family, fashion—all had fled and vanished with the master spirit who directed them," lamented one Jefferson devotee after braving the freezing winds of December to climb the mountain to visit the shrine. With the wind "piercing every crevice" of the empty rooms, he was shown around by a slatternly caretaker who was now in charge in Levy's absence. On such a day and in the hands of the unlikely hostess, the visitor found the house a tomb, bereft of "its master spirit," with little to recall its golden years.

Uriah Levy, fiery seaman, duelist, passionate defender of religious freedom, and the subject of six unprecedented courts-martial during his naval career, seems an improbable heir to the retiring, scholarly Sage of Monticello and what was left of his humanistic world. Yet Jefferson's political philosphy had a special appeal for Levy, inspiring him to perpetuate Jefferson's memory through the preservation of his house. In particular, Jefferson's views on religious liberty, that religion was "an unquestionable and natural right, to exercise freely [and] according to the dictates of conscience" was a belief that was shared and fought for by Levy throughout his life. Real or imagined slurs against his own faith as a Jew had in fact been involved in virtually all of the confrontations leading to the court-martial proceedings. Even a sympathetic biographer, however, characterized Levy as "a little vain . . . self-righteous . . . domineering and pompous," and the five duels or challenges that he was involved in during his fifteen years of active service in the Navy also speak of excessive pride, or at least a highly developed personal sensitivity. Still, the Navy was not without an undercurrent of prejudice and anti-Semitism that Levy later said had left him "isolated and alone in the very midst of society." That his patriotism as a fifth-generation American could be questioned by a fellow naval officer was to Levy unpardonable. His own elevation from the rank of sailing master to that of lieutenant in a brief four years was a promotion that may also have made him defensive in his new position.

A prickly idealist who wore those ideals on his sleeve, Levy considered Jefferson's profoundly libertarian views on religious and civil liberties to be central to his own patriotic beliefs. "One of the greatest men in history," Levy declared, "he does much to mold our Republic in a form in which a man's religion does not make him ineligible for political or governmental life." It seems entirely plausible, as Levy declared, that his deep veneration of Jefferson was the only motive for his buying Monticello, in answer to the charge that potential financial gain had been his chief motivation.

Levy had first expressed his admiration for Jefferson in a public gesture the year before Monticello came on the market. During an extended leave in Paris in 1833, he had commissioned at his own expense the well-known French sculptor Pierre Jean David d'Angers to make a full-scale statue of the third president. The following year he proudly presented the work to an embarrassed Congress, which did not formally accept the sculpture until forty years later. Neither the Congress nor the country for that matter was yet ready to place the author of the *Declaration of Independence* in the national pantheon of heroes. The statue, pronounced by one viewer as "a most faithful conterfeit of the man," stood in the Capitol rotunda for a short time, until it was transferred to the lawn of the White House, where Andrew

242-245 Monticello, interiors, c. 1890. *Only the strong molding of Jefferson's arched doorways identify the dining room as Monticello's in this photograph taken at the turn of the century (facing, top). In the tea room, the blade of a sawfish reposes on a bracket once graced by the Houdon bust of Lafayette (facing, bottom left). The parlor's 18th-century Parisian mirrors reflect the 19th-century copies of French furniture that Jefferson Levy installed (facing, bottom right). Jefferson's bedroom (above) was fitted out with the most fashionable furnishings of the Belle Epoque and was photographed in the 1890s.*

Jackson was then in residence. Later Levy recalled that it was none other than President Jackson who had been so impressed by the gesture of the gift that he urged Levy to buy Monticello as well, in order to prevent an unscrupulous promoter from taking it over and "exhibiting the tomb of the Apostle of Liberty at a shilling a head." We have only Levy's unsubstantiated word on the matter, but the story does give a symbolic continuity to the history of the house as a political shrine as well as a work of art.

A second cast of the sculpture was given by Levy to the City of New York, where he received a much warmer response than he had in Washington. He was awarded the freedom of the city and given a gold box inscribed with a tribute to Levy's "character, patriotism and public spirit," even though he already had been convicted four times in court-martial proceedings. While Uriah Levy's respect for Jefferson had inspired his purchase of the estate and his opening of it to the public, it is also clear that he intended to make it his part-time country home. His calling cards made shortly after the purchase announced "Captain U. P. Levy, U. S. Navy, of Monticello, Virginia." Because of his naval duties and the fact that he also maintained a house in New York, he actually spent little time at Monticello, where his caretaker Joel Wheeler continued to show the steady stream of pilgrims around. While descriptions differ on the physical condition of the house during Levy's ownership, at least one guest reported it as being "in general appearance, the same as when Jefferson left it." In 1853 Benson J. Lossing thought the house was in good repair and noticed a copy of the Jefferson statue Levy had given Congress earlier.

Aside from the differing impressions that the house made on visitors and the state of its maintenance following Jefferson's death, many visitors dismissed Monticello's design as old-fashioned and impossible by contemporary standards of organization and comfort. The era that it represented and the reminders of the style of life that was lived there seemed as remote to the world of the 1830s and '40s as the hôtel of a Parisian nobleman would have been following the French Revolution. "There is nothing admirable in its interior arrangements," an English Quaker wrote in 1829, and J. H. Latrobe agreed, finding it "too whimsical . . . according to present notions of country houses."

In 1858, Uriah Levy drew up his will, leaving Monticello to the United States government as an agricultural school for orphans of naval warrant officers. If the national government refused the bequest, it was then to go to the State of Virginia for the same purpose. Should this gift also fail, Monticello would then be offered to the Portuguese Hebrew congregations of New York, Philadelphia, and Richmond, who were jointly to operate the farm school to benefit the orphans of these societies. At the age of sixty-one Commodore Levy married his eighteen-year-old niece, and the couple spent the summers of the 1850s at Monticello. Mrs. Levy enjoyed being the mistress of "the dear old house" but she too found the uninvited visitors a problem. "We were overrun with sightseers" who demanded to be shown around, she recalled later in her memoirs.

---

246 Entrance hall, photographed in September, 1912. *Busts of Benjamin Franklin, George Washington, and Thomas Jefferson adorn pedestals in Monticello's entrance hall, but nothing remains of Jefferson's "museum."*

544

In a complicated suit by Levy's heirs following his death in 1862, the will was declared void by the New York Supreme Court. But more suits, among the heirs were filed until finally Levy's nephew Jefferson Levy, a New York Congressman, bought out the interests of other family members as a solution to their attempt to partition the property. However, Jefferson Levy was not able to take possession of the estate until 1879 because of the legal complications. At the beginning of the Civil War the property had in fact been confiscated by the Confederate government and sold as property of "an alien enemy," complicating further the legal issues. Sometime between August, 1861, and February, 1862, possession was taken under the Sequestration Act. Levy died on March 22, 1862, so his agent and lawyer George Carr attempted to block the appropriation. The suit in the District Court of the Confederate States of America for the Eastern District of Virginia finally ordered a sale by public auction "on the premises and for cash in Confederate treasury notes." The sale was finally held in November of 1864, and Benjamin F. Ficklin made the high bid of $80,500. When the Confederacy fell in April, 1865, Monticello reverted to its former owner. *Monticello and its Preservation*, published and probably written by Jefferson Levy even though George Alfred Townsend appears as the author, provides the only account of this period, although most historians consider the facts dubious: "But finally the Commodore's slaves were sold and the dismantling of the furniture began, the losses were amounting to several hundred thousand dollars. Soldiers broke off carved sculpture of many mantels. Other people peddled the bust of Voltaire by Houdon and several similar treasures to rich men in New York. Jonas P. Levy, when he visited the place to save it from confiscation, was held as a hostage. . . ."

According to James Bear, there is nothing to support the charge that Confederate soldiers looted the house or that soldiers were ever on the premises. Except for the hall clock and the pier mirrors in the parlor, there is no evidence that Levy had quantities of Jefferson's furniture at the time of the confiscation.

A young visitor, Miss Sarah Stickler, visited Monticello in the summer of 1864 and has left the following description: "The place was once very pretty, but it has gone to ruin now. It is the property of Commodore Levi I believe. There is a large clock in the hall, you get up to wind it by means of a ladder. The parlour retains but little of its former elegance, the ball room [dome room] is on the second floor, and has a thousand names scratched over its walls. . . . There are some roses in the yard that have turned wild, and those are the only flowers. . . . The family burying ground shows the same want of attention that the house and grounds do. . . ."

During these years, the property had been managed—or mismanaged—by the Wheelers, who, taking advantage of the insecure legal status, had allowed the place to become a shambles. Pigpens were scattered among the weeds and broken fences of the former gardens, loose shutters on the house banged in the wind before broken windows, and bins of grain were installed on the parquet floor of the parlor. The steps of the west portico were allowed to disintegrate, making a convenient earth ramp for Wheeler cows to walk up and rest in the classical shade of the columns, as in a vignette in a seventeenth-century painting of the Roman campagna. One of Jefferson

Levy's first positive acts of restoration was to fire the resisting Wheeler. It was during the Wheeler period that one visitor described the dark rooms as looking like a prison: "We hurried on, and were soon at the mansion, moss covered, dilapidated and criminally neglected. . . . The upper rooms, small and illy ventilated, were originally lighted from the roof, but shingles having been substituted for glass [in the skylights], the rooms are now as dark and gloomy as the cells of a prison."

A congressman who visited Monticello in 1878, a year before Jefferson Levy was able to consolidate

247 East front of Monticello (left). Agnes and Frances Levy, great nieces of Uriah P. Levy, pose in front of their ancestor's house. The pony is held by Levy's great nephew Monroe Mayhoff.

248 West front of Monticello (above). Amelia Mayhoff, niece of Commodore Levy, is shown with her son Monroe seated in her carriage on the lawn in front of Monticello around 1900.

249, 250, 251 Postcard views of Monticello interiors, 1928. *The dining room (top), parlor (bottom left), and entrance hall (bottom right) appear quite bare several years after the house was acquired by the Thomas Jefferson Memorial Foundation in 1923, but part of this was no doubt in reaction to the late Victorian taste that had overtaken the house in the Levy period. Fiske Kimball was in charge of the restoration and the furnishings, working with the best evidence he had at the time of Monticello's original appearance.*

his title, reported in the *Congressional Record* that all was "Desolation and ruin . . . a standing monument to the ingratitude of the great Republic."

By the last decades of the century, Jefferson Levy seems to have managed to put Monticello's exterior into good repair, although he added some un-Jeffersonian dormers on the third floor. Inside, Jefferson's "entertainment rooms" took on the over-stuffed appearance of a Parisian banker's country house during Napoleon III's Second Empire. Elaborate imported chandeliers, mirrors, sideboards, and a spectacularly dedizened bed à la Madame du Barry decorated the hall, parlor, dining room, and Jefferson's bedroom. Uriah Levy's full-length portrait hung in the front hall while nearby was a model of his ship *Vandalia*. The *Vandalia* under Levy's command had been the first ship in the United States Navy to abolish flogging, on Levy's orders. Thus the Levy family had understandably imposed their own "autobiography" onto the older Jeffersonian "text" that still managed to survive beneath.

While there may have been some lingering Albemarle County resentment that Monticello was owned by an outsider, "a son of Abraham" (as one local matron wrote in disgust), Jefferson Levy seems to have been a respectful neighbor during his infrequent visits. He was also generous in accepting the unending trail of visitors that continued to come, the numbers growing from one generation to the next. Levy tried to establish some control by issuing passes and by setting aside certain hours when the grounds would be open, but this was received with little appreciation of the problems visitors posed for the owner.

Shortly after Levy had consolidated his purchases of the interests of the other members of the family, a Jefferson great-granddaughter was impressed and relieved to find the "beloved old place in the hands of a person who appreciates it, & whose wish appears to be, to restore the house to its former condition." By inviting the Virginia Chapter of the Daughters of the American Revolution to hold a gala ball in Monticello, Levy's relations with the local community continued to improve.

Jefferson Levy adored his bachelor's summer retreat and eventually more than doubled the acreage originally owned by his uncle. He also installed a professional superintendent to supervise the work on the house and grounds. The family cemetery, which Jefferson had located in his romantic landscape plans of 1771, where he would bury first his friend Dabney Carr, then his wife and other members of his family, and where he, too, would join them in 1826, had always been a problem. The private plantation road controlled by subsequent owners provided the only access to Jefferson's grave, even though the cemetery itself had been specifically reserved from the sales that followed Jefferson's death. Much of the grumbling voiced by Monticello visitors throughout the nineteenth century seems to have concentrated on the graveyard's shabby state, lacking a fitting marker or even a weeping willow tree to indicate the sacred spot. The original simple obelisk carved to Jefferson's design had been badly damaged by souvenir hunters over the years and may well have been replaced a number of times before the present marker was made in 1883. A granite copy, double the scale of the original, it was enclosed with a heavy iron fence and paid for by an appropriation of Congress.

By the beginning of the twentieth century, because

of improved roads and train service in combination with the indestructible tradition of public accessibility established by Jefferson himself, the hordes visiting Monticello became an avalanche reaching fifty thousand a year. When Theodore Roosevelt visited Charlottesville in 1903, he insisted, to the consternation of the Secret Service, that he would ride a horse up to Monticello rather than use the presidential car. On a single occasion Monticello's owner was asked to play host at lunch to over two hundred fifty members of the St. Louis Jefferson Club, a political organization professing Jeffersonian principles. The project to build a new road up Jefferson's mountain signaled the growing public interest in the creation of a national memorial, even though Monticello would remain in private hands for another two decades.

Realizing the political value in Jefferson's image as the Father of Democracy, William Jennings Bryan— a fervent Jeffersonian—was the first national leader, as Merrill Peterson has pointed out, to lay a claim to Monticello on behalf of the American people. Writing to Jefferson Levy in 1897, he proposed that the property be conveyed to the United States government as a national memorial, thus lifting the Sage of Monticello out of the merely regional association with the South, where his principles were most strongly venerated. Levy replied that there was not enough money in the government's treasury to tempt him to sell. When Amos J. Cummings' article, "A National Humiliation," appeared in the August 24, 1897, issue of the New York *Sun* attacking Levy's ownership, Levy's position hardened further.

Twelve years later, in 1909, Mrs. Martin W. Littleton, wife of a prominent New York Congressman, saw Monticello for the first time as Levy's guest. She immediately fell in love with the place, or rather, with her idea of what it would have been like in Jefferson's day. But when she saw the fashionable contemporary Levy furnishings, as she later wrote, "I did not get the feeling of being in the house of Thomas Jefferson. . . . My heart sank. My dream was spoiled."

After visiting Monticello Maud Littleton had discovered her cause: leading a drive to achieve Bryan's original goal of establishing a public memorial by restoring Monticello to its appearance during Jefferson's lifetime. Remembering Jefferson's moving words, "all my wishes end where I hope my days will end, at Monticello," she produced a patriotic appeal called *One Wish* to launch her Monticello Memorial Association. Even the New England Federalist Senator Henry Lodge was touched and felt that Jefferson's house did indeed embody much of the third president's esthetic autobiography, which had long been forgotten by his fellow Americans who were not aware of "his love of art and architecture in a country where they were hardly known."

Following her efforts in organizing the association, Mrs. Littleton secured the attention of Congress in 1912 with a memorial proposing the purchase of Monticello by a Federal appropriation. Levy replied that he would be prepared to see it whenever the White House itself was put on the market. The proposal, however, did initiate a Congressional hearing in which Mrs. Littleton and her adversary exchanged salvoes. Mrs. Littleton's cause was not advanced when she claimed during the hearings that Levy held the historic shrine for "selfish and sordid purposes." Jefferson's devotion to the rights of private property was upheld when the resolution that would have led to the appropriation of Levy's estate was defeated 141 to 101.

Maud Littleton did not give up, and in 1914 the Senate Lands Committee reported favorably on resolutions to acquire Monticello by purchase or condemnation. When Bryan, now Woodrow Wilson's Secretary of State, again appealed to Levy to allow the government to "commemorate the great Democratic administration of President Wilson which is conducted on Jeffersonian principles," Levy weakened. Three more years of haggling over the price and the conditions of sale led to nothing, and the property actually was offered for private sale by a Washington real estate firm, advertising it as "a dignified country home" in Albemarle County.

The deterioration of Levy's own finances had prompted his effort to secure a higher price than the government was willing to offer. His attempt to offer the property for private sale alerted new citizens groups in Washington, Richmond, and New York to mount last-ditch rescue operations. Finally, these efforts were consolidated into the Thomas Jefferson Memorial Association, which was incorporated under the laws of New York on April 13, 1923, and headed by two New York lawyers, Stuart G. Gibboney and Henry Alan Johnston, both Virginians by birth. Gibboney was elected president and Johnston secretary at the initial meeting held in the Lawyer's Club in New York on April 24th.

As a nonprofit corporation, it was able to organize both broad public support and the backing of a few New York bankers in a successful scheme to "Save Jefferson's old home from the Sheriff." Title was taken by the Foundation with a down payment of

252 Entry gate and gatekeeper's lodge, 1912. *The age of the motorcar brought new waves of visitors to Monticello long before it was to become a national monument, and the Levys found it necessary to restrict entrance.*

one-fifth the price, although not without difficulties. The following year a national drive called "Jefferson Week" was launched across the country. In New York, Charles Evans Hughes declared that "the people of this country look upon Jefferson as they do upon Washington," forgetting to mention that Uriah Levy's statue of the third president failed to be accepted by Congress in 1834 because Washington had not yet been accorded similar memorials. On the one-hundredth anniversary of Jefferson's death in 1926, the one-hundred-fiftieth of the Declaration, Monticello was finally dedicated as a public memorial. The purchase price had been exceeded through the widespread interest generated by thousands of contributors making small donations within the spirit of Jefferson's faith in democratic participation.

As far as the physical restoration of the house and the grounds was concerned, the most important step was taken with the appointment of Fiske Kimball, the distinguished art historian and director of the Philadelphia Museum of Art, as chairman of the restoration committee. A year before, he had written the *Report of the Committee on Preservation of Historic Monuments and Scenic Beauties* for the fifty-sixth annual convention of the American Institute of Architects, taking special note of the urgency to begin work at Monticello. The outbuildings and terraces had slid into advanced states of decay, and there were the inevitable modern accretions, though relatively minor, that had to be removed.

Under Kimball's supervision and research, rotten beams throughout the house were replaced, original furnishings were acquired, and the grounds were restored over the next twenty-five years. In 1940, the Garden Club of Virginia, working with Kimball, Dr. Edwin Betts, and Milton Grigg, began the restoration of the gardens following Jefferson's plan and garden notes. The work begun in 1924 has never stopped, and under the supervision of James A. Bear, Jr., the resident director and a professional staff, including William Bliswanger and Charles L. Granguest, even more extensive physical examination and restoration of the house and grounds have been carried out. The collection of furnishings has been enlarged and refined. The collection of works of art has been enhanced recently by the acquisition of the portrait of Benjamin Franklin probably by Jean Valade and of the superb life portrait by Gilbert Stuart painted at the beginning of the president's second term. Known as the Edgehill Portrait, it had hung in the parlor during the last five years of Jefferson's life and then was given to his daughter Martha Randolph, before passing out of the family in the early part of this century.

When the first restoration of the grounds and gardens was undertaken, Jefferson's manuscripts were consulted but little archeological work preceded the physical restoration. Now a full-scale archeological program has uncovered garden walls, pavilion foundations, orchard planting patterns, walks, terraces, and the foundations of the buildings along Mulberry Row.

Franklin Roosevelt, a close friend of Stuart Gibboney, who earlier had collected the pamphlets produced by Mrs. Littleton and her followers, was deeply interested in Jefferson's political philosophy and his home. From 1934 to 1938, he personally assigned a detail from the Civilian Conservation Corps to clear the woods and to build new roads on the estate. On the 4th of July, 1936, the president gave the Independence Day address from the portico of the east entrance.

As Merrill Peterson has written in his perceptive study, *The Jefferson Image in the American Mind*, "Monticello was Jefferson and Jefferson was democracy, so of course Monticello was sacred to democracy." Certainly this is true in tracing the genealogy of one of our great national icons, but how each generation has attempted to come to terms with the historical image of the man through the contemplation and study of Monticello and what it represents provides a saga of American cultural history that is almost as old as the country itself. This national fascination

253 Design for two dollar bill, as approved on December 29, 1927. The stone lions placed at the sides of the west portico by Jefferson Levy can be seen in this design approved by Andrew W. Mellon, Secretary of the Treasury. They were later removed.

with Jefferson and his house promises to continue as the torrent of visitors, reenacting earlier pilgrimages, continues to move in long lines up the front walk and through the house and gardens.

William Wirt, in his famous *Eulogy upon Adams and Jefferson* written in 1826, said it as well as anyone before or since when he wrote:

The Roman moralist, in that great work which he has left for the government of man in all the offices of life, has descended even to prescribe the kind of habitation in which an honored and distinguished man should dwell. It should not, he says, be small and mean and sordid; nor on the other hand, extended with profuse and wanton extravagance. It should be large enough to receive and accommodate the visitors which such a man never fails to attract, one suited in its ornaments, as well as its dimensions, to the character and fortune of the individual. . . .Can anything be indifferent to us which was a subject of such just admiration to the hundreds and thousands that were continually resorting to it as an object of pious pilgrimage.

In the architecture of Rome, Jefferson detected sym-bolically those simple republican virtues and rationality he hoped to see embodied in the new American experiment of government. He believed that this antique vocabulary could redeem a formless world through its translation into a house that would serve as a public symbol and at the same time express his innermost need for a private existence, uniting within its peculiar composition the life of the mind and the life of the senses. No one has ever come closer to reaching that ideal. As the house of the chief architect of the New Republic, Monticello continues to speak openly of those goals Jefferson held for himself, his family, his government, and his fellow countrymen. As architecture it has attained its own universal value and survives as a monument to a remarkable individual by those special means through which humanity has always attempted to survive. It also serves to simply delight, amaze, and inspire us, the heirs of his bold experiment in the search for happiness, an experiment that, as Learned Hand once wrote, is yet unproved.

254 Parlor, about 1940. *Restoration and furnishings tastes of the late 1930s are reflected in this early color photograph showing elaborate draperies and French furniture. The gilt and marble-top table surviving from the Levy era (see fig. 244) apparently appealed to Fiske Kimball's taste.*

255 Parlor entrance door, West Portico, closed. *"I looked upon him as he walked the top of this mountain, as being elevated above the mass of mankind, as much in character as he was in the local situation."*

GUIDE TO SOURCES

ASIDE FROM THE HOUSE ITSELF, the basic manuscript sources relating to its architectural history must begin with Jefferson's drawings and notebooks for building Monticello, the account books, and his correspondence. The nearest thing to a catalogue raisonné of the drawings is to be found in Fiske Kimball's *Thomas Jefferson, Architect*, 1916, augmented by the more recent *Thomas Jefferson's Architectural Drawings*, a checklist compiled by Frederick D. Nichols. There is a mass of material at the Thomas Jefferson Memorial Foundation on the history of the house and its furnishing down to the present time. This volume's Selected Bibliography covers most of the essential secondary sources. The following guide to each chapter attempts to further acquaint the reader with sources used in this study and to support the text where titles cited are inadequate or left out.

Chapter I The Architect

Kimball, Nichols, Malone, Randall, and William Pierson are relied upon here and in the other chapters. The quote from Price's *Builder's Dictionary* is found in Thomas Waterman's *Mansions of Virginia*, still a major study on Virginia architecture in the colonial period and consulted wherever houses of this period are discussed in the text. In this chapter I begin to attempt to make some autobiographical connection between Jefferson's obsession with Monticello and other biographical material that we know about his life. In the case of Monticello, it is a most significant line of inquiry, and I have greatly benefited from the works of Suzanne Crowhurst Lennard, who almost singlehandedly has identified the subject of architecture as autobiography. Her pioneer research into this aspect of the meaning of architecture has been a stimulating discovery for me and is found in "A House is a Metaphor" and *Explorations in the Meaning of Architecture*.

Chapter II The First Monticello

Aside from the sources already cited, *Jefferson's Garden Book*, edited by Edwin Betts, and Buford Pickens' article, "Mr. Jefferson, Revolutionary Architect," were very useful. Marie Kimball's *Jefferson: The Road to Glory* provides a good background for this period of Jefferson's life. The foreign travelers De Chastellux and La Rochefoucauld-Liancourt each recorded firsthand impressions of Monticello before the end of the 18th century. Chastellux's *Travels in North America* (London, 2nd ed., 1787) and La Rochefoucauld-Liancourt's *Travels Through The United States* (London, 2nd ed., 1800) are cited directly or as quoted in Randall. Jefferson's remarkable letter to Maria Cosway is full of references to Paris architecture and to his obsession with the subject generally. To the "Heart," the "Head's" preoccupation was becoming a bore. Helen Bullock's *My Head and My Heart* is the best book on l'affair Cosway and the background to the letter itself.

Chapter III The Second Monticello

Again the sources are accumulative from those already mentioned, but I must express my debt once again to William Pierson, Jr., for his excellent short account and analysis of Monticello in *American Buildings and Their Architects: The Colonial and Neo-Classical Styles*, pp. 286-316. It is the most sympathetic and perceptive account by a modern scholar.

The view of Monticello and its builder through the eyes of his contemporaries and the subsequent firsthand descriptions after his death, for the most part, have been compiled from many published sources and manuscripts. These have been assembled at Monticello and have been used throughout where appropriate. Among the major accounts, aside from those already cited, are Isaac Weld, *Travels Through the States of North America . . . "During the years 1795, 1796, and 1797. . . ."*; the Papers and Diaries of Mrs. William Thornton, 1793–1806, in the Library of Congress; "Notes on the United States" by Sir Augustus John Foster, mentioned in the Selected Bibliography; Margaret Bayard Smith's *The First Forty Years of Washington Society*. All of Mrs. Smith's quotations are from this volume. Rice's *Thomas Jefferson's Paris* and *The Eye of Thomas Jefferson* give extensive references to French influence on Jefferson's architectural ideas.

Jefferson's *Notes on the State of Virginia*, first published in Paris in 1787 from a manuscript he had begun to work on in 1781 after retiring as governor of Virginia, contains his strongest criticisms of Virginia colonial architecture and in particular the buildings of Williamsburg. Most of his famous quotations on the subject come from the chapter in the *Notes* called "Colleges, Buildings, and Roads."

The quotation from the German prisoner of war near the end of this chapter is from a letter from Jacob Rubsamen, Dec. 1, 1780, *The Papers of Thomas Jefferson*, ed. by Julian P. Boyd. The Rev. Henry C. Thweatt's account of his visit to Monticello was taken from a typescript of his diary in the files of the Thomas Jefferson Memorial Foundation's collections.

Chapter IV The Landscape

Jefferson's own drawings, notes, and correspondence on gardening are extensive. Much of this has been gathered together in Betts's *Garden* and *Farm* Books. A recent study, *Thomas Jefferson, Landscape Architect* by Frederick D. Nichols and Ralph E. Griswold, provides an overall picture of Jefferson's landscape ideas and practice at Monticello and elsewhere. Recent study of the grounds at Monticello by William Beiswanger, historian, and William Kelso, archeologist, and Peter Hatch, head of the garden staff, has both confirmed and modified the understanding of the gardens and grounds. This important work continues with the support of the Thomas Jefferson Memorial Foundation. Mulberry Row has recently been the subject of intensive archeological study, and it is anticipated that Mr. Kelso's final report on the work will contain many new details about the buildings and the work that went on there.

Jane Blair Smith's charming description of the cherries being thrown from the tree by her great-uncle is from a typescript of the manuscript at the University of Virginia.

William Hamilton's landscape contributions are discussed by Eleanor McPeck in *The Eye of Thomas Jefferson* in the section called "The Pleasures of Nature."

Chapter V   *The Interior Life*
The opening quotation of Mario Praz is from the first American edition of his superb *The Illustrated History of Furnishings*. Marie Kimball's books and articles were consulted and amended according to the more recent notes and research on the furnishings of Monticello and particularly those articles designed by Jefferson that were compiled by Charles Granquist for the National Gallery's catalog. The most recent study of Jefferson's painting collection is to be found in "Jefferson Art Collection" by Harold E. Dickson in *Jefferson and the Arts*. Seymour Howard's notes on Jefferson's proposed sculpture collection in *The Eye of Thomas Jefferson* is definitive.

Helen Cripe's work on Jefferson and music remains the last word on the subject. George Ticknor's well-known account of his visit to Monticello is from his *Life, Letters and Journals*, written in 1815 and published in Boston in 1876.

It is difficult to be precise about the physical condition of Monticello during Jefferson's last years, but Samuel Whitcomb's description written in 1824 and found in manuscript in the University of Virginia summarizes several contemporary accounts. "His house is rather old and going to decay; appearances about his yard and hill rather slovenly."

There are numbers of accounts of Lafayette's last visit with Jefferson in 1824, including those of Jane Blair Smith and the *Central Gazette*, Charlottesville, Virginia, November 19, 1824.

The Epilogue
After Jefferson's death and the departure of his family, visitors continued to visit Monticello and many left firsthand descriptions that have been assembled in typescript at Monticello for scholars. The Trist family papers at the Massachusetts Historical Society, the Library of Congress, the North Carolina University, and the Cary family papers at the University of Virginia contain a number of references to the period just before and after Jefferson's death. *A Journey in The United States in the Years 1829 and 1830* by the English traveler Francis Tuckett and published in 1976 describes visiting the deserted house where "there is nothing admirable in its interior arrangements beyond old English solidity." One has to admit that not only the proportions of the public rooms, but Monticello's combination of grandeur and rusticity has a subtle "whiggish" country house quality.

In addition, James Bear, Jr., has worked on this period and made the results available in various research papers, articles, and pamphlets. The Levy family and its long ownership has been the subject of a number of biographical studies and articles cited in the Selected Bibliography.

J. S. Buckingham's description dating from 1836 reported that the cemetery and Jefferson's grave were "a perfect wreck, though little more than ten years have elapsed since his death." See J. S. Buckingham, Esq., *The Slave States of America* (London and Paris, 1842).

Since the changing image of Jefferson in the public's mind is closely related to the image of Monticello as well, students should carefully read Merrill Peterson's *The Jefferson Image in the American Mind*, published in 1962. His bibliography for Chapter VII, "Culture," is an excellent beginning for the study of Monticello's post-Jeffersonian period and the establishment of the Thomas Jefferson Memorial Foundation.

SELECTED BIBLIOGRAPHY

The following works are related to Monticello during and after Jefferson's lifetime.

Adams, William Howard, ed. *The Eye of Thomas Jefferson.* Washington: National Gallery of Art, 1976.

Adams, William Howard, ed. *Jefferson and the Arts: An Extended View.* Charlottesville: University Press of Virginia, 1976.

Bear, James A., Jr. "The Furniture and Furnishings of Monticello." *Antiques*, 102 (July 1972): 113–23.

Bear, James A., Jr. "Thomas Jefferson's Silver." *Antiques*, 74 (Sept. 1958): 233–36.

Bear, James A., Jr., ed. *Jefferson at Monticello.* Charlottesville: University Press of Virginia, 1967.

Bear, James A., Jr. "Thomas Jefferson, Manufacturer." Typescript in The Thomas Jefferson Memorial Foundation Archives.

Beiswanger, William L. "Jefferson's Designs for Garden Structures at Monticello." *Journal of the Society of Architectural Historians*, XXXV, No. 4 (Dec. 1976): 310–12.

Beiswanger, William L. "The South Pavilion: Chronology of Design and Construction." 1972. Unpublished typescript in The Thomas Jefferson Memorial Foundation Archives.

Beiswanger, William L., compiler. "Documents Relating to the First Roundabout and the East Lawn." Unpublished typescript in The Thomas Jefferson Memorial Foundation Archives.

Benisovich, Michael. *"Thomas Jefferson, Amateur d'art à Paris."* Archives de l'art français. (1959).

Berman, Eleanor D. *Thomas Jefferson Among the Arts.* New York: The Philosophical Library, 1947.

Betts, Edwin Morris, ed. *Thomas Jefferson's Farm Book.* Charlottesville: University Press of Virginia, 1976.

Betts, Edwin Morris, ed. *Thomas Jefferson's Garden Book.* Philadelphia: The American Philosophical Society, 1944.

Betts, Edwin Morris, and Bear, James A., Jr., eds. *The Family Letters of Thomas Jefferson.* Columbia: University of Missouri Press, 1961.

Boyd, Julian P. "Thomas Jefferson and the Roman Askos of Nîmes." *Antiques*, 54 (July 1973): 116–24.

Boyd, Julian P., ed. *The Papers of Thomas Jefferson.* Princeton: Princeton University Press, 1950.

Bullock, Helen Duprey. *My Head and My Heart: A Little History of Thomas Jefferson and Maria Cosway.* New York: G. P. Putnam's Sons, 1945.

Bush, Alfred L. *The Life Portraits of Thomas Jefferson.* Charlottesville: The University of Virginia Museum of Fine Arts, 1962.

Chastellux, Marquis de. *Travels in North America in the Years 1780, 1781 and 1782.* Edited by Howard C. Rice, Jr. 2 vols. Chapel Hill: University of North Carolina Press, 1963. (Also quoted in Randall from an earlier translation.)

Clark, Lord, of Saltwood. "Thomas Jefferson and the Italian Renaissance." Typescript in The Thomas Jefferson Memorial Foundation Archives.

Closen, Baron von. "The Journal of Baron von Closen," edited by Evelyn M. Acomb. *William and Mary Quarterly*, 3rd series, X (April 1953).

Cripe, Helen. *Thomas Jefferson and Music.* Charlottesville: University Press of Virginia, 1974.

Dumbauld, Edward. *Thomas Jefferson: American Tourist.* Norman: University of Oklahoma Press, 1945.

Ford, Paul Leicester, ed. *The Writings of Thomas Jefferson.* 10 vols. New York: G. P. Putnam's Sons, 1892–99.

Foster, Sir Augustus John. "Notes on the United States." *William and Mary Quarterly*, 3rd series, VIII, No. 1 (January 1951).

Selected Bibliography

Frary, Ihna Thayer. *Thomas Jefferson, Architect and Builder*. Richmond: Garrett and Massie, 1931.

Gaines, William H., Jr. *Thomas Jefferson Randolph*. Baton Rouge: Louisiana State University Press, 1966.

Golden, Barbara M. "Uriah Phillips Levy: Jewish American." Typescript in The Thomas Jefferson Memorial Foundation Archives.

Guinness, Desmond, and Sadler, Julius T. *Mr. Jefferson, Architect*. New York: Viking Press, 1973.

Hall, Lieut. Francis. *Travels in Canada and The United States in 1816*. Boston: 1818.

Hosmer, Charles B., Jr. "The Levys and the Restoration of Monticello." *American Jewish Historical Quarterly*. LIII, No. 3 (May 1964).

Howard, Seymour. "Thomas Jefferson's Art Gallery for Monticello." *The Art Bulletin*, LIX, No. 4 (Dec. 1977): 583–600.

Jefferson, Thomas. *Notes on the State of Virginia*. London: John Stockdale, 1787. (See also the edition edited by William Peden, Chapel Hill, 1955.)

Kanof, Abram. "Uriah Phillips Levy: The Story of a Pugnacious Commodore." *Publications of the American Jewish Historical Society*, XXXIX (Sept. 1949): 1–66.

Kelso, William M. "Jefferson's Garden: Landscape Archaeology at Monticello." *Archaeology* (July/August 1982): 38–45.

Kimball, Fiske. "Jefferson and the Arts." *Proceedings of the American Philosophical Society*, 87 (July 1943): 238–45.

Kimball, Fiske. "Jefferson and the Public Buildings of Virginia: 1. Williamsburg, 1770–1776." *The Huntington Library Quarterly*, 12 (Feb. 1949): 115–20.

Kimball, Fiske. *Thomas Jefferson, Architect*. Introduction by Frederick D. Nichols. New York: Da Capo Press, 1968.

Kimball, Fiske and Marie. "Jefferson's Curtains at Monticello." *Antiques*, 52 (Oct. 1947): 266–68.

Kimball, Marie. *Jefferson: The Road to Glory*. New York: Coward-McCann, 1943.

Kimball, Marie. *The Scene of Europe*. New York: Coward-McCann, 1950.

Kimball, Marie. "Thomas Jefferson's French Furniture." *Antiques*, 15 (Feb. 1929): 123–28.

Lancaster, Clay. "Jefferson's Architectural Indebtedness to Robert Morris." *Journal of the Society of Architectural Historians*, 10 (1951): 4.

Leighton, Ann. "Thomas Jefferson as a Gardener." *Country Life* (Nov. 5, 1981): 1556–58.

Lennard, Suzanne H. Crowhurst. *Explorations in the Meanings of Architecture*. Woodstock: Gondolier Press, 1980.

Lossing, Benson J. "Monticello." *Harper's New Monthly Magazine*, No. XXXVIII, Vol. VII (July, 1853).

Malone, Dumas. *Jefferson The Virginian*. Boston: Little, Brown & Co., 1951.

Malone, Dumas. *Jefferson and the Rights of Man*. Boston: Little, Brown & Co., 1951.

Malone, Dumas. *Jefferson and the Ordeal of Liberty*. Boston: Little, Brown & Co., 1963.

Malone, Dumas. *Jefferson the President: First Term, 1801–1805*. Boston: Little, Brown & Co., 1970.

Malone, Dumas. *Jefferson the President: Second Term, 1805–1809*. Boston: Little, Brown & Co., 1974.

Malone, Dumas. *The Sage of Monticello*. Boston: Little, Brown & Co., 1981.

Mayor, A. Hyatt. "Jefferson's Enjoyment of the Arts." *Bulletin of The Metropolitan Museum of Art*, 2 (1943): 145.

McPeck, Eleanor, "George Isham Parkyns, Artist and Landscape Architect, 1749–1820." *Quarterly Journal of the Library of Congress*, 30, No. 3 (July 1973): 171–82.

Nichols, Frederick D. *Thomas Jefferson's Architectural Drawings*. 3rd Ed. Boston: The Massachusetts Historical Society and Charlottesville: The Thomas Jefferson Memorial Foundation and the University Press of Virginia, 1961.

Nichols, Frederick D., and Bear, James A., Jr. *Monticello. A Guidebook.* Charlottesville: The Thomas Jefferson Memorial Foundation, 1967.

Nicolay, J. G. "Thomas Jefferson's Home." *The Century Magazine* XXXIV, No. 5 (Sept. 1887): 645–58.

O'Neal, William Banter. *Jefferson's Fine Arts Library.* Charlottesville: University Press of Virginia, 1976.

Peterson, Merrill D. *The Jefferson Image in the American Mind.* New York: Oxford University Press, 1962.

Peterson, Merrill D. *Thomas Jefferson and the New Nation: A Biography.* New York: Oxford University Press, 1970.

Pickens, Buford L. "Mr. Jefferson As Revolutionary Architect." *The Journal of the Society of Architectural Historians,* XXXIV, No. 4 (Dec. 1975).

Pierson, William H., Jr. *American Buildings and Their Architects: The Colonial and Neo-Classical Styles.* New York: Doubleday & Co., 1970.

Randall, Henry S. *The Life of Thomas Jefferson.* 3 vols. New York: Da Capo Press, 1972. Republication of edition first published in New York in 1858.

Randolph, Sarah N. *The Domestic Life of Thomas Jefferson.* 3rd Ed. Charlottesville: The Thomas Jefferson Memorial Foundation, 1947.

Rice, Howard C., Jr. *L'Hôtel de Langeac, Jefferson's Paris Residence, 1785–1789.* Charlottesville: The Thomas Jefferson Memorial Foundation, 1947.

Rice, Howard C., Jr. *Thomas Jefferson's Paris.* Princeton: Princeton University Press, 1976.

Smith, Margaret Bayard. *The First Forty Years of Washington Society.* New York: Charles Scribner & Sons, 1906.

Sowerby, E. Millicent. *Catalogue of the Library of Thomas Jefferson.* Washington: The Library of Congress, 1955. Reissued in 1983 by The Thomas Jefferson Memorial Foundation and the University of Virginia.

Tucker, George. *The Life of Thomas Jefferson.* London: C. Knight & Co., 1837.

Waterman, Thomas Tileston. *The Mansions of Virginia, 1706–1776.* Chapel Hill: The University of North Carolina Press, 1946.

INDEX

(Figures in italics indicate illustrations.)

Picture Credits

American Jewish Historical Society, Waltham, Massachusetts: 234 (Anon./ American School, *Uriah Phillips Levy, 1792–1862*, c. 1815, oil on canvas, 32½ x 27 in.); Archives National, Paris: 89; courtesy of the Author: 8, 18, 22, 32, 38 (photo: O.E. Nelson, New York), 135; Library of the Boston Atheneum, Boston, Massachusetts: 216 (Jean-Antoine Houdon, *Marquis de Lafayette*, c. 1785, plaster, 29 in. high); Langdon Clay, New York: 1, 3, 16, 33–36, 49–51, 56, 57, 59–61, 63–65, 73, 75, 85–87, 90, 94, 95, 97, 101–103, 106, 107, 111, 114, 116, 120, 121, 123, 124, 126–28, 130–32, 134, 136, 138–42, 149, 157–59, 162, 163, 166, 168, 169, 171, 172, 174, 175, 177, 178, 181, 183, 184, 187, 189, 190, 196, 198, 200, 203, 207, 208, 215, 217, 224–27, 255; Devonshire Collection, Chatsworth. Reproduced by permission of the Chatsworth Settlement Trustees, Bakewell, Derbyshire: 77 (William Kent, *Chiswick Villa from the Southeast*, c. 1730, pen and ink with brown wash over pencil on paper, 11½ x 14⅝ in. Photo: Courtauld Institute of Art, London); Joseph Farber, New York: 39; The Frick Collection, New York: 192; Mark Golderman, New York: 21, 31, 72, 96, 113, 122, 129, 133, 137, 151, 228; reprinted from *Great Georgian Houses of America*, 1933: 15; The Historical Society of Pennsylvania, Philadelphia: 170; Kenmore Association, Inc., Fredericksburg, Virginia: 14; Mrs. Richard C. Lewis: 247, 248 (Holsinger Studio); Library of Congress, Washington, D.C.: 193–94 (reprinted from Joseph Spence, 1699–1768, *Polymetis; or, An Enquiry concerning the Agreement between the Works of the Roman Poets and the remains of the Antient Artists.* London: R. Dodsley, 1747, plates 11 and 12), 218; Massachusetts Historical Society, Boston (Photo: University of Virginia Library, Charlottesville): 24, 26, 28, 30, 40, 41–48, 55, 58, 62, 67–71, 81, 83, 84, 88, 99, 105, 109, 110, 115, 117–19, 145, 146, 148, 150, 152–54, 156, 161, 165, 167, 173, 204, 205, 210, 211, 219, 220; Paul Mellon Collection, Upperville, Virginia: 27 (English School, 18th century, possibly Theodore De Bruyn, *The Hermitage*, c. 1770-1776, oil on canvas, 32½ x 51⅜ in.); The Metropolitan Museum of Art, New York, Rogers Fund, 1916: 13 (Parlor from Marmion, home of the Fitzhugh family. View showing painted panel, decorated with urn and flowers. Paneled c. 1735-70; painted 1770–80. Photographed in 1983); Missouri Historical Society, St. Louis: 182 (Charles-Fevret de Saint-Mémin, *Meriwether Lewis*, 1803 or 1807, crayon on paper, 22 x 16 in.); Musée Carnavalet, Paris (Photo: Lauros-Giraudon, Paris): 76 (Anon. *The Construction of the Hôtel de Salm*, c. 1784, oil on canvas, 22¼ x 39¾ in.); Musée des Antiques, Nîmes: 214; Musée du Louvre, Paris: 179 (Cliche des Musées Nationaux); Museum of Fine Arts, Boston, George Nixon Black Fund: 37 and back cover (Jean-Antoine Houdon, *Thomas Jefferson*, c. 1789, saravezza marble, 26⅝ in. high); reprinted from National Gallery of Art, *The Eye of Thomas Jefferson*, edited by W. Howard Adams (1976): 9; National Portrait Gallery, Smithsonian Institution and Monticello, The Thomas Jefferson Memorial Foundation, Inc. Purchase funds provided by the Regents of the Smithsonian Insitition, the Trustees of The Thomas Jefferson Memorial Foundation, Incorporated, and the Enid and Crosby Kemper Foundation: 74 (Gilbert Stuart, *Thomas Jefferson*, 1805, oil on wood panel, 21 x 27 in.); Buford L. Pickens: 155 (reprinted from Buford L. Pickens, "Mr. Jefferson, Revolutionary Architect," *SAH Journal*, Vol. XXXIV, No. 4, Dec. 1975); Private collection (Photo: Allen Studio, Middleburg, Virginia): 164; Private collection (Photo: Greg Heins, Newton Center, Massachusetts): 147 (Anon. American, *View from Monticello*, early 19th century, watercolor on paper, 10¾ x 18½ in.), 180 (Jane Bradick, *View of West Front of Monticello and Garden*, 1825, watercolor on paper, 11 x 18 in.); Private collection (Photo: James H. MacGregor): 188; © Michael Ruetz: 240; Sotheby, Parke-Bernet, Inc., New York, Silver Department: 237; David LeHardy Sweet, Fredericksburg, Virginia: 4, 5, 10, 11, 12, 17, 19, 20; Courtesy of The Thomas Jefferson Memorial Foundation, Incorporated: 52, 53, 66, 91, 92, 93, 195, 199, 201, 202, 213, 221, 222, 223, 229, 232, 235, 236, 238, 242, 243, 246, 249–54; James T. Tkatch, Washington, D.C.: 185, 186, 197, 209, 212; John Troha/Black Star © 1980: 143; U.S. Capitol, Washington D.C.: 233; Galleria degli Uffizi, Florence: 191 (*The Medici Venus; Aphrodite Rising from the Sea*, 1st century B.C.-1st century A.D., marble, 60 ⅔ in. high); University of Virginia Library, Charlottesville, Holsinger Studio Collection: 244, 245; University of Virginia Library, Manuscript Department: 230, 231, 239, 241; University of Virginia, Rare Book Room: 25 (James Gibbs, *A Book of Architecture*. London: 1728, p. 67), 29 (Robert Morris, *Select Architecture*. London: 1755, plate 2), 44 (Morris, *Select Architecture*, plate 37), 54 (*The Architecture of A. Palladio; in four Books. Containing a short Treatise of the Five Orders . . . Revis'd, Design'd, and Publish'd by Giacomo Leoni, A Venetian . . . Translated from the Italian Original* [London: 1742], plate 41, Book II), 78 (Morris, *Select Architecture*, plate 43), 82 (Philibert de l'Orme, *Nouvelles Inventions pour bien Bastir et a petits Fraiz*, 1576, p. 14), 98 (Roland Fréart de Chambray, *Parallele de L'architecture Antique avec la Moderne. Par MM. Errard & de Chambray.* Paris: 1766, plate 2), 100 (Leon Battista Alberti, *L'Architettura di Leon Battista Alberti*, 1565, p. 67.), 104 (Antoine Babuty Desgodetz, *Les Édifices Antiques de Rome, mesurés et dessinés tres-exactement sur les lieux par feu M. Desgodetz, Architect du Roi. Nouvelle édition.* Paris: ches Claude-Antoine Jombert, Fils aîné, de l'Imprimerie de Monsieur, 1779, plate 47), 108 (Desgodetz, *Les Édifices de Rome*, plate 56), 112 (Fréart de Chambray, *Parallele de l'Architecture*, plate 4), 125 (Desgodetz, *Les Édifices de Rome*, plate 44), 176 (Sir William Chambers, *Designs of Chinese Buildings, Furniture, Dresses, Machines, and Utensils*, London: published for the author, 1757, plate II); University of Virginia Library, Thomas Jefferson Papers: 79, 80; University of Virginia Library, Tracy W. McGregor Library: 160 (Isaac Jefferson, daguerreotype by John Plumbe, Jr., taken in Petersburg, Virginia, c. 1845.); Virginia Historical Society, Richmond (Photo: Ronald H. Jennings): 6; White House Collection, Washington, D.C.: 2 (John Trumbull, *Thomas Jefferson*, 1788, miniature in oil on board); The College of William and Mary in Virginia (Photo: Thomas L. Williams, Williamsburg): 7 (John Wollaston, *John Page of Rosewell*, c. 1757, oil on canvas, 50 x 40 in.); Worcester Art Museum, Worcester, Massachusetts: 144 (Charles-Fevret de Saint-Mémin, *Thomas Jefferson*, 1804, crayon on paper, 23 ¹³⁄₁₆ x 17 in.).